Defying Convention

The Convention on the Elimination of All Forms of Discrimination against Women (CEDAW) articulates what has now become a global norm. CEDAW establishes the moral, civic, and political equality of women; women's right to be free from discrimination and violence; and the responsibility of governments to take positive action to achieve these goals. The United States is not among the 187 countries that have ratified the treaty. To explain why the United States has not ratified CEDAW, this book highlights the emergence of the treaty in the context of the Cold War, the deeply partisan nature of women's rights issues in the United States, and basic disagreements about how human rights treaties work.

Lisa Baldez is Professor of Government and Latin American, Latino, and Caribbean Studies at Dartmouth College. She holds a BA from Princeton University and a PhD from the University of California, San Diego. She is the author of *Why Women Protest: Women's Movements in Chile* (Cambridge University Press, 2002) and the coeditor of *Political Women and American Democracy* (Cambridge University Press, 2008). Her articles have appeared in the *American Journal of Political Science*, *Latin American Politics and Society*, *Legislative Studies Quarterly*, and the *Journal of Legal Studies*. She and Karen Beckwith cofounded the journal *Politics & Gender*.

Problems of International Politics

SERIES EDITORS

Keith Darden, *American University*
Ian Shapiro, *Yale University*

The series seeks manuscripts central to the understanding of international politics that will be empirically rich and conceptually innovative. It is interested in works that illuminate the evolving character of nation-states within the international system. It sets out three broad areas for investigation: 1. Identity, security, and conflict; 2. Democracy; and 3. Justice and distribution.

Titles in the Series

Şener Aktürk, *Regimes of Ethnicity and Nationhood in Germany, Russia, and Turkey*

Donald Horowitz, *Constitutional Change and Democracy in Indonesia*

Adria K. Lawrence, *Imperial Rule and the Politics of Nationalism: Anti-Colonial Protest in the French Empire*

Steven Levitsky and Lucan A. Way, *Competitive Authoritarianism: Hybrid Regimes After the Cold War*

Tarek Masoud, *Counting Islam: Religion, Class, and Elections in Egypt*

Shaul Mishal and Ori Goldberg, *Understanding Shiite Leadership: The Art of the Middle Ground in Iran and Lebanon*

Harris Mylonas, *The Politics of Nation-Building: Making Co-Nationals, Refugees, and Minorities*

Defying Convention

U.S. Resistance to the U.N. Treaty on Women's Rights

LISA BALDEZ
Dartmouth College

CAMBRIDGE
UNIVERSITY PRESS

CAMBRIDGE
UNIVERSITY PRESS

32 Avenue of the Americas, New York, NY 10013-2473, USA

Cambridge University Press is part of the University of Cambridge.

It furthers the University's mission by disseminating knowledge in the pursuit of education, learning, and research at the highest international levels of excellence.

www.cambridge.org
Information on this title: www.cambridge.org/9781107416826

© Lisa Baldez 2014

First published 2014

Printed in the United States of America

A catalog record for this publication is available from the British Library.

Library of Congress Cataloging in Publication data
Baldez, Lisa.
Defying convention : U.S. resistance to the U.N. treaty on women's rights / Lisa Baldez.
    pages   cm
Includes bibliographical references and index.
ISBN 978-1-107-07148-3 (hardback) – ISBN 978-1-107-41682-6 (pbk.)
1. Convention on the Elimination of All Forms of Discrimination against Women (1980)   2. Women's rights – International cooperation.   3. Women's rights – United States.   I. Title.
HQ1236.B237   2014
323.3'40973–dc23   2014002489

ISBN 978-1-107-07148-3 Hardback
ISBN 978-1-107-41682-6 Paperback

For John, again, and always

Contents

Acknowledgments

This book is the fruition of years of research, and would not have been possible without the support of countless people who helped me along the way.

First, I would like to thank the students in my Gender and American Politics seminars that played a very special role in the development of this book. I designed the course at the start of the research process and I taught it three times before the book went to press. In 2010, Nina Maja Bergmar, Katie Davis, Kat Eidmann, David Imamura, Gabriel Lopez, Anya Perret, Shannie MacKenzie, and Danielle Sawaya helped me generate a series of insights and research questions that launched me into a productive sabbatical year. In 2012, Damaris Altomerianos, David Becker, Morgan Blackburn, Ally Dutton, Alice Liou, Ariel Murphy, Ellen Perry, Kim Rose, and Ruthie Welch helped me to articulate and clarify my initial ideas. In 2013, Lindsay Brewer, Lulu Chang, Paul Gastello, James Herring, Sam McPherson, Katie Randolph, Jeri Reichel, and Kate Thorstad helped me frame my arguments about CEDAW in a broader context. Every professor should be so lucky to work with such smart and passionate students.

In each of those seminars, we conducted Skype interviews with CEDAW advocates and opponents. I would like to thank all our interviewees for giving us their time and sharing their views: Janet Benshoof, President of the Global Justice Center; Gaynel Curry, Gender and Women's Rights Advisor at the Office of the High Commissioner for

Human Rights; conservative author Christina Hoff Sommers; Harold Koh, Sterling Professor of International Law at Yale Law School and former Legal Adviser to the Department of State; author and former Ambassador Linda Tarr-Whelan; Shari Rendall, Director of House Legislation and Public Policy at Concerned Women for America; and Phyllis Schlafly, founder of the Eagle Forum. Stephanie Farrior, Professor of Law and Director of International and Comparative Law Programs and the Center for Applied Human Rights at Vermont Law School, visited the class in person and gave us an excellent primer on UN human rights treaties.

During this project, I also conducted a series of interviews with key policy makers, who provided important information about the politics surrounding CEDAW. I am particularly grateful to Betty Athanasakos, former delegate to the UN Commission on the Status of Women; Kathy Bonk, Executive Director of the Communications Consortium Media Center; Arvonne Fraser, founder of International Women's Rights Action Watch; Marsha Freeman, Director of the International Women's Rights Action Watch; former congresswoman Constance Morella (R-MD); Eleanor Smeal, President and founder of the Feminist Majority Foundation; and June Zeitlin, Director of the CEDAW Education Project of the Leadership Conference on Civil and Human Rights.

I interviewed many women's rights activists in Malaysia who helped me understand how activists use CEDAW as a policy tool. Thanks to Ivy Josiah, Executive Director of Women's Aid Organisation; Norani Othman, Professor at the Institute of Malaysian and International Studies at the Universiti Kebangsaan Malaysia; Zainah Anwar, former Executive Director of Sisters in Islam and current Director of Musawah, A Global Movement for Equality and Justice in the Muslim Family; and Shanthi Dairam, Director of International Women's Rights Action Watch Asia Pacific and former CEDAW Committee expert. I am grateful to the staff members at Women's Aid Organization, Sisters in Islam, and IWRAW Asia Pacific for their help in setting up these conversations.

Many colleagues provided helpful advice at the early stages of research, including Susanne Zwingel, Jutta Joachim, Billie Heller, Deborah Liebowitz, Janet Walsh, Jane Jaquette, and Jenny Mansbridge. Elisabeth Friedman, Valerie Sperling, Karen Beckwith, and Margaret

Power gave me helpful feedback on the prospectus for the project. Bill Wohlforth very generously read an early draft of the complete manuscript and supplied constructive comments.

I presented drafts to the Second Book Club, and I am grateful for the feedback and encouragement from Leslie Butler, Annelise Orleck, Christopher MacEvitt, Soyica Colbert, Cecilia Gaposchkin, Veronika Fuechtner, and Colleen Boggs. I thank the members of the Upper Valley Women's Network and the New Hampshire Women's Caucus for their enthusiastic reception. I presented parts of the book at the annual meetings of the American Political Science Association, the Midwest Political Science Association, the New England Political Science Association, and the International Political Science Association. Colleagues at University Kebangsaan Malaysia, the University of Southern California, Vanderbilt University, Harvard University, and the University of Connecticut offered outstanding feedback as well. My thanks also to the Feminist Inquiry Seminar, the Department of Government, and the "What's the Big Idea" symposium at Dartmouth College, where I presented chapters.

I am grateful to Dartmouth College for giving me research leave and the resources I needed to write this book. Thanks to Chris Wohlforth for encouraging me to schedule a manuscript review at the Dickey Center for International Understanding at Dartmouth. Thank you to all my colleagues who participated: Mala Htun, Stephanie Farrior, Sonu Bedi, Brian Greenhill, Russ Muirhead, Ben Valentino, Leslie Butler, Annelise Orleck, and John Campbell. The staff at Baker-Berry Library at Dartmouth, the Sophia Smith Collection at Smith College, and the Lamont Library at Harvard University provided indispensable support. The Women and Social Movements collection published by SUNY Binghamton and Alexander Street Press proved invaluable to my research. Thank you to the many Dartmouth students who provided research assistance on this project, especially Kim Rose, Margaret Jessiman, Despoina Sidieri, Damaris Altomerianos, Yang Shanguan, Sanders Davis, Abby Reed, Cathy Lian, Claire Frazer, David Chiang, Becca Heller, Jessie Stefanik, Claire Frazer, and Becca Boswell. Sara Kassir did an excellent job correcting the final proofs. Chelsea Harris and Claire Cravero also pitched in at key moments. The Law and Politics Program at Dartmouth College provided funding for many of my RAs.

Editor Rasna Dhillon helped me see what the book is really about and made incisive suggestions that greatly improved it. Thanks to Lew Bateman, my editor at Cambridge University Press, for his commitment to my work. Shaun Vigil patiently guided the book to publication. I am grateful to Keith Darden and Ian Shapiro for including the book in the Problems of International Politics series. Thanks are also due to two anonymous readers for Cambridge, and to Bindu Vinod and the production staff at Newgen Knowledge Works, who supported this project. I'm grateful to my dear friend Mark Lerner for designing the cover.

The emotional support I received from friends and family has been critical. The Morning Glory group held me aloft during many difficult moments. The Powerbabes kept me fit and laughing. Annual Girls' Weekends with my college friends have sustained me. Karen Beckwith and Christina Wolbrecht shared advice about writing (and shopping). I am grateful to Anne Tergesen and Jimmy Windels for their hospitality when I did research at UN headquarters in New York. Megan Kiely helped me maintain my sense of humor. I am especially grateful to my soul sisters Aurora Matzkin and Mala Htun.

I owe so much to my family. Joe Baldez insisted on reading the first draft and said the two things that are the only things any writer ever wants to hear: "I love it" and "It's really good." Bill and Clare Cumberland resolved a thorny dispute when they came up with the right-hand side of the title. Thanks to my two sons, Joe and Sam Carey, whom I love more than I can say. My husband, John Carey, has supported me lovingly and indefatigably. He read drafts, pushed me, fed me, bought me presents, and reassured me, among many other things. This book is for you, my darling.

I

Introduction

The Convention on the Elimination of All Forms of Discrimination against Women (CEDAW), adopted by the UN General Assembly in 1979, articulates what has now become a global norm. CEDAW establishes the moral, civic, and political equality of women; women's right to be free from discrimination and violence; and the responsibility of governments to take positive action to achieve these goals. The treaty reflects consensus among scores of countries and cultures on a comprehensive framework for the advancement and protection of women's rights. As of 2012, 187 countries have ratified the treaty (United Nations 2013c). Of all the United Nations (UN) treaties, only the Convention on the Rights of the Child (CRC) boasts more signatories (United Nations 2013c). Seven member-states of the UN have yet to ratify CEDAW: Iran, Palau, Somalia, Sudan, South Sudan, Tonga – and the United States. Why hasn't the United States ratified CEDAW? How can we account for opposition from the most powerful actor in the international system given the almost universal global endorsement of this treaty and the crucial role the United States played in drafting it?

On one hand, the reason the United States has not ratified CEDAW is simple: CEDAW has been unable to garner votes from the sixty-seven senators necessary to ratify it. According to the U.S. Constitution, ratification of CEDAW, like all treaties, requires support from the president and the vote of two-thirds of the Senate. This is a high threshold for approval. It is more difficult to ratify treaties in the United States than in almost any other country in the world.

On the other hand, the failure of the United States to ratify CEDAW is not for lack of effort. Few Americans have heard of CEDAW, but advocates of women's rights have worked assiduously to get the Senate to ratify it for the past twenty-five years. The Senate has held hearings on CEDAW ratification five times since 1988. Moreover, the high threshold for treaty ratification in the United States is not an impossible bar to clear. The ratification of four other human rights treaties at the end of the Cold War – the Convention on the Prevention and Punishment of the Crime of Genocide in 1988, the International Covenant on Civil and Political Rights (ICCPR) in 1992, and the International Convention on the Elimination of All Forms of Racial Discrimination (CERD) and the Convention Against Torture and Other Cruel, Inhuman or Degrading Treatment or Punishment (CAT), both in 1994 – has kept the CEDAW ratification debate alive.

To illustrate the complex reasons the United States has not ratified CEDAW, consider the debate that emerged in the context of a Senate hearing on ratification in 2010. The mobilization of women's organizations prior to the hearing and the testimony offered for and against CEDAW during the hearing reveal a couple of arguments:

- CEDAW is a deeply partisan issue: Democrats support ratification and Republicans oppose it. Women's organizations in the United States also disagree about CEDAW.
- Geopolitical factors shape the prospects for U.S. support for ratification.
- The pro and con sides do not agree about how international human rights treaties work or what effect they will have.

As this book will show, these themes complicate the issue of CEDAW ratification and have characterized debates about global women's rights in the United States since the founding of the UN in 1945.

The election of Barack Obama to the presidency in 2008 raised people's expectations about the ratification of CEDAW. President Obama supported CEDAW ratification and explicitly affirmed his support in an interview in the White House on June 1, 2010.[1] Many of

---

[1] Racheal Nakitare, senior producer at Kenya Broadcasting Corporation (KBC-TV), conducted the interview and asked President Obama why the United States has not ratified CEDAW. Obama responded: "Well, keep in mind that if it were simply up to me, it would already have been ratified. I'm a strong supporter of it. It is currently

the people in Obama's first administration were longtime advocates of CEDAW, including Vice President Joseph Biden, Secretary of State Hillary Clinton, and State Department Legal Advisor Harold Koh. On November 10, 2010, Clinton affirmed that "this treaty is a priority of the Obama Administration ... we want to move this treaty forward. We cannot wait any longer to try to put it to a vote" (You Tube 2010). With a Democratic president in office and a Democratic majority in the Senate, ratification seemed guaranteed.

CEDAW advocates leaped into action to mobilize support for ratification. The Leadership Conference on Civil and Human Rights created a CEDAW Task Force that brings together 186 organizations, including most of the leading progressive organizations in the United States – the American Bar Association, the American Civil Liberties Union, Amnesty International, the American Association of University Women, Feminist Majority, Hadassah, the League of Women Voters, the National Organization for Women, the National Association for the Advancement of Colored People (NAACP), the YWCA, and Zonta International, to name just a few. The coalition created a website that prominently features a video clip of President Obama asserting his support for CEDAW (You Tube 2010). The words "equality," "empowerment," "economic development," "ending violence," "education," and "employment" float across the banner of the website. The headline of the website reads, "Support CEDAW. Because Women's Rights are Human Rights," and is accompanied by the following text:

CEDAW ... is a landmark international agreement that affirms principles of fundamental human rights and equality for women around the world. CEDAW strengthens the United States as a global leader in standing up for the rights of women and girls in countries around the world. This international treaty offers countries a practical blueprint to achieve progress for women and girls by calling on each ratifying country to overcome barriers of discrimination. Ratifying the CEDAW treaty would continue America's proud bipartisan tradition of promoting and protecting human rights. (www.cedaw2010.org)

The focus is on how CEDAW has improved women's rights in other countries. Clicking on the sidebar "CEDAW Works" takes you to a

pending in the Senate. We want the Senate to pass it. The Senate has had a busy agenda and it moves slowly as it is, but my hope is that we get it done."

series of video clips of feminist activists from Brazil, Fiji, Gambia, Nigeria, and Senegal speaking about the impact of CEDAW in their countries. A section titled "What's In It for the US" describes issues that American women face:

American women enjoy opportunities and status not available to most of the world's women. But few would dispute that more progress is needed in certain areas, such as ending domestic violence and closing the pay gap. Ratifying CEDAW would not result in any automatic changes to U.S. law. Instead, CEDAW provides a practical blueprint to achieve progress for women and girls and an opportunity for policymakers and advocates to work together on how best to end discrimination and ensure women's full equality. (www.cedaw2010.org)

This broad coalition of organizations that support ratification of CEDAW thus makes two main points. First, CEDAW is not an urgent need for American women. Existing laws and policies in the United States already offer women adequate protection against discrimination and guarantee basic legal equality. Nevertheless, things could be better – and ratification of CEDAW would provide the necessary next step to achieving more progress. Second, ratification of CEDAW would enhance the American position as a global leader on the issue of women's rights by sending a signal of stronger U.S. commitment to women's rights to the international community. CEDAW would further enhance American efforts to strengthen the rights of women in other countries, which is already a central component of U.S. foreign policy.

Obama's election and the increased probability of passing CEDAW also rallied CEDAW opponents. Concerned Women for America, an evangelical Christian women's organization that seeks "to bring Biblical principles into all levels of public policy," revitalized its long-standing campaign against CEDAW (Concerned Women for America 2013). It created an anti-CEDAW website, "Save Mother's Day: A Campaign to Educate America about the Dangers of CEDAW" (www.savemothersday.com), to warn about the dramatic impact that CEDAW would have on daily life: "This treaty would detrimentally intrude on Americans' personal decisions, invite frivolous lawsuits and violate national sovereignty. It could impact every aspect of life and place Americans under the supervision of a U.N. committee of 'gender experts'" (Concerned Women for America 2010). The text on the front page of the site asks "Who Hates Mother's Day?" The answer is CEDAW: "The U.N.'s CEDAW Committee has *already* told other countries to stop the celebration [of Mother's Day]. Why? Because, in their twisted opinion, Mother's Day fosters violence against women" (Concerned Women for America 2010). CWA's focus on Mother's Day derives from a statement that the committee overseeing implementation of CEDAW made to the delegation from Belarus on January 31, 2000. According to the CWA, "The CEDAW Committee criticized Belarus for 'the continuing prevalence of sex-role stereotypes, as also exemplified by the reintroduction of such symbols as a Mother's Day and a Mothers' Award, which [the Committee] sees as encouraging women's traditional roles'" (Wright 2002). CEDAW opponents cite this point about Mother's Day frequently.[2]

The Save Mother's Day website warns that CEDAW is a "hidden weapon" wielded by "radical feminists" who have failed to achieve their goals through the domestic political process. CEDAW would give "radical feminists" free reign to impose their agenda on an unsuspecting American public. From the perspective of opponents, ratification of CEDAW would have a clear and direct effect on domestic public policy. As the website declares, "CEDAW will pressure us to decriminalize prostitution, put infants in government day care, revise our textbooks to reflect non-stereotypical gender roles, criticize the influence of religion on our society, and – unbelievably – to stop celebrating Mother's Day" (Concerned Women for America 2010).

The U.S. Senate did move on the issue of CEDAW ratification, but not as quickly or as decisively as supporters had hoped. On November 18, 2010, the Senate Judiciary Subcommittee on Human Rights and International Affairs held a hearing on CEDAW ratification. The fact that this committee held the hearing, and not the Committee on Foreign Relations, signified that the Senate was unlikely to take action on CEDAW; only the Committee on Foreign Relations has jurisdiction over treaties. Nonetheless, Senator Richard Durbin, a Democrat from Illinois and chair of the Human Rights Subcommittee, used the hearing to make a strong case for CEDAW ratification. The audience for the hearing was so large that its start had to be delayed until a larger

---

[2] What CWA does not mention is that the committee made this statement in the context of concerns about the degree to which government policy "creates further obstacles to women's participation in the labour market" (Committee on the Elimination of Discrimination against Women 2000).

committee room could be procured. It included five witnesses who spoke in favor of U.S. ratification and only one who spoke against. On the "pro" side were Melanne Verveer, ambassador-at-large for the Office of Global Women's Issues in the Department of State; Marcia D. Greenberger, copresident of the National Women's Law Center; Samuel R. Bagenstos, deputy assistant attorney general for the Civil Rights Division of the Department of Justice; Wazma Frogh, leader of an Afghan women's group; and Geena Davis, actress and founder of the Geena Davis Institute on Gender in Media. Steven Groves, a research fellow from the Heritage Foundation, a conservative think tank, was the only witness to speak against CEDAW.

During the hearing, the CEDAW proponents consistently emphasized the foreign policy benefits and negligible domestic costs of ratification. They maintained that CEDAW would have little or no impact at home because American women already enjoy all the rights it guarantees; existing law already protects American women from discrimination. In Senator Durbin's words, "Let's be clear. The United States does not need to ratify CEDAW to protect the rights of American women and girls" (U.S. Senate 2010). Deputy Assistant Attorney General Bagenstos's testimony outlined in impressive detail the degree to which "our existing laws and practices are broadly consistent with the requirements of CEDAW" and how women's rights are protected by the numerous Supreme Court decisions, laws, and programs that enforce those laws (U.S. Senate 2010).

CEDAW proponents maintained that CEDAW would strengthen U.S. foreign policy and bolster U.S. efforts to help women around the world. From this perspective, failure to ratify CEDAW harms our ability to have a positive influence on women's rights elsewhere in the world. Senator Durbin emphasized this point repeatedly in his opening statement during the 2010 hearing:

Why is CEDAW needed? Because the human rights of women and girls are violated at an alarming rate all over the world. So why should the United States ratify CEDAW? Because CEDAW will enhance our ability to advocate for women and girls around the world. Throughout our history, the United States has done more to advance human rights than any other country in the world. But now some are questioning our commitment to women's rights because we have failed to ratify CEDAW. Yesterday I received a letter from retired Justice Sandra Day O'Connor [who] supports ratifying CEDAW and here is what she says: "The Senate's failure to ratify CEDAW gives other countries a retort when U.S. officials raise issues about the treatment of women, and thus our non-ratification may hamper the effectiveness of the United States in achieving increased protection for women worldwide." (U.S. Senate 2010)

Marcia Greenberger's comments echoed Durbin's:

By ratifying CEDAW, almost every other country in the world has affirmed the importance of progress for women and girls and agreed to work to achieve that end. That the U.S. has not done so is deeply unfortunate. It fails to reflect our country's proud tradition of leadership on women's rights. It has denied women and girls around the world U.S. leadership on the implementation of CEDAW, and it has denied women and girls in our own country the benefits of important lessons that could be learned about effective strategies and programs adopted in other countries around the world. Simply put, U.S. ratification of CEDAW will strengthen our longstanding role as a global leader standing up for women's rights and human rights.... Women and girls are crying out for the United States' assistance. (U.S. Senate 2010)

Melanne Verveer also emphasized the costs to U.S. foreign policy:

Some governments use the fact that the U.S. has not ratified the treaty as a pretext for not living up to their own obligations under it. Our failure to ratify also deprives us of a powerful tool to combat discrimination against women around the world, because as a non-party, it makes it more difficult for us to press other parties to live up to their commitments under the treaty. (U.S. Senate 2010)

These statements reflect the view that the United States will reap foreign policy benefits from ratifying CEDAW: the United States will further strengthen its already strong record of support for women's rights in other countries.

In discussing the impact that U.S. ratification would have, CEDAW advocates cited examples of how the treaty has been employed in other countries. Greenberger, for example, reported that "Mexico pointed to CEDAW in creating the Mexican General Law on Women's Access to a Life Free from Violence in 2007, which today has been adopted by all of Mexico's 32 states" (U.S. Senate 2010). She also cited examples of how CEDAW shaped policy in Bangladesh, Colombia, Nepal, Hungary, and Sierra Leone. Verveer explained how the Ugandan women's movement "rel[ied] on both the Women's Treaty and national legislation to pursue land ownership rights and challenge customary land tenure practices" (U.S. Senate 2010). The decision to invite Wazma Frogh to testify further underscores supporters' efforts to highlight the benefits that CEDAW has generated for women in other countries. During her testimony, Frogh reported that Afghan feminists have used CEDAW to promote constitutional reform, draft violence-against-women legislation, and create public education forums during Friday prayers. Frogh took this argument a step further by arguing that U.S. failure to ratify CEDAW harms Afghan women:

> While the U.S. government has many significant domestic measures to address gender inequality, its failure to ratify CEDAW is of huge international significance. Even in Afghanistan, thousands of miles away, conservative elements try to use America's failure to ratify CEDAW to attack women's rights defenders. In all of our efforts, they constantly ask us "Why hasn't the United States ratified CEDAW?" They say that if [the] United States believes in women's rights as a universal right, why haven't they signed on to CEDAW? (U.S. Senate 2010)

The decision to present CEDAW as a treaty that will enhance U.S. foreign women's rights policy but have little effect on domestic women's rights policy reflects a rhetorical strategy that proponents of human rights treaties (not just CEDAW) have deployed since the founding of the UN in 1945. This view portrays the rights guaranteed by UN treaties as redundant to existing domestic policy in the United States. This perspective presents the United States as supporting treaty ratification as a way to consolidate its already dominant position as a global human rights leader. Finally, this view depicts U.S. ratification as a magnanimous gesture of commitment to promoting the rights of people living in other countries. Although the United States has ratified four of the world's core human rights treaties – the Genocide Convention, International Covenant on Civil and Political Rights, Convention Against Torture, and Convention on the Elimination of All Forms of Racial Discrimination – it has attached reservations to those treaties that limit the degree to which their provisions apply to domestic legislation and policy.

Steven Groves, the Bernard and Barbara Lomas Fellow at the Heritage Foundation, was the lone voice speaking against ratification of CEDAW at the 2010 hearing. Groves's testimony did not share the feverish tone of the Save Mothers' Day website; his analysis was more subtle. He began by acknowledging the strong state of women's rights policy in the United States and asserting that the United States has sufficient "avenues of enforcement" to prevent discrimination against women, echoing Bagenstos's testimony. Groves acknowledged that "some of this federal legislation remains controversial and will continue to be debated in Congress and litigated in U.S. courts," but argued that the differences should be adjudicated through the American political process "rather than through the judgment of gender experts sitting on the CEDAW Committee who may possess inadequate specific knowledge or understanding of U.S. laws and practices" (U.S. Senate 2010). The CEDAW Committee is the panel of twenty-three experts that oversees implementation of CEDAW. Despite Groves's sober assessment, his comments nonetheless betrayed the sense that CEDAW would have a dramatic impact on domestic policy and that ratification would entail high costs for the United States: "The CEDAW Committee has for 30 years established a consistent record of promoting gender-related policies that do not comport with existing American legal and cultural norms and has encouraged the national governments of CEDAW members to engage in social engineering on a massive scale" (U.S. Senate 2010).

The 2010 hearing on CEDAW provides a clear overview of some of the most important issues surrounding ratification. The CEDAW question sharply divides women's organizations, with progressive, feminist groups supporting ratification and conservative and evangelical organizations fiercely opposing it. The two sides disagree about the impact that CEDAW would have in the United States. Women's rights organizations focus on the foreign policy benefits, whereas opponents highlight effects on women at home. The former describe CEDAW in somewhat neutral terms as a blueprint for change; the latter portray it as a powerful institution capable of imposing policy on ratifying countries. The partisan nature of the ratification question is evident in the absence of Republican politicians at the hearing. The testimony of the hearing offers some clues about the way in which geopolitical factors shape the prospects for U.S. ratification. Democrats have sought to frame the issue in terms of the U.S. war in Afghanistan in the hopes of building a broader coalition of support among Republicans who supported that war as an effort to liberate Afghan women from the fundamentalist rule of the Taliban. Finally, the rhetoric of conservative women's organizations is silent about the impact of CEDAW on women in foreign countries, language that masks their deep involvement in efforts to change policy toward women in international institutions. These themes appear throughout the history of CEDAW and this book.

In the sections that follow, I discuss the theoretical considerations behind the three questions that motivate the three distinct parts of this book: how women's rights came to constitute a global norm, how that norm is put into practice through CEDAW, and why the United States remains immune to diffusion of that norm.

ESTABLISHING A GLOBAL NORM: THE FEMINIST
EMPOWERMENT THESIS

CEDAW defines what has become a global norm on women's rights. Its power as a norm derives from the large number of countries that have ratified it and participate regularly in the reporting process. How did women's rights come to be a global norm? Existing accounts of the history of global feminism tend to reflect what I call the "feminist empowerment thesis." From this perspective, over the twentieth and twenty-first centuries, women progressed from less to more power. As women gained political experience and a clearer understanding of their status, they began to mobilize collectively on the basis of their shared gender identity and to demand equal rights with ever-greater temerity. This apparent evolution from powerlessness to empowerment focuses on women's agency and reflects feminist ideology. This perspective characterizes many accounts of the status of women's issues within the UN. According to this line of argument, women's issues were not a high priority for the UN and programs had little effect on the actual status of women prior to the 1970s. As historian Judith Zinsser states, "From its founding until 1975 and the declaration of the International Women's Year (IWY), the United Nations did little to advance the cause of women's rights" (Zinsser 2002, 139). Over time, women moved from the margins to the center. By 1985, women "used the United Nations to speak with new assurance and to assert their rights, opportunities and responsibilities as 'equal partners with men,'" demanding equality with greater confidence (Zinsser 2002, 144). Scholar Margaret Galey concurs with this view: "By the 1990s, women's issues had become legitimate subjects on the agendas of governments and international organizations, and women participated in public activity as never before" (Galey 1998).

The UN embraces this progressive view of its own institutional history. *The United Nations and the Advancement of Women 1945–1996*, a history of the status of women's rights in the UN, attributes the inclusion of gender equality in the UN Charter to "the insistence of women delegates and representatives of nongovernmental organizations (NGOs) accredited to the founding conference" (United Nations 1996, 10). A UN history of the Commission on the Status of Women (CSW) affirms that demand for women's rights grew over time in an evolutionary manner: "The need for a legally binding Convention that defined women's rights ... largely grew out of the perception that attempts to implement the Declaration [on Human Rights] had been limited" (United Nations n.d., 8). The website for UN Women, a new entity to oversee women's issues created in 2010, also reflects the view that the UN has evolved toward greater rights for women over time: "Over many decades, the UN has made significant progress in advancing gender equality, including through landmark agreements such as the Beijing Declaration and Platform for Action and the Convention on the Elimination of All Forms of Discrimination against Women (CEDAW)" (UN Women 2013a).

The feminist empowerment perspective rests on two assumptions that I find problematic. First, it lays responsibility for progress at the feet of women themselves and thus underplays the ways in which political context and powerful external forces shape the opportunities for change to occur. My work highlights the domestic and geopolitical situations in which demands for women's rights are made and addressed. Attention to the broader political environment – both domestic and international – provides a more persuasive explanation of the gains and limitations of global efforts to promote women's rights.

Second, the feminist empowerment hypothesis dichotomizes differences between women and men and overlooks differences among women. From this perspective, change occurs when men's inevitable failure or refusal to extend equal rights to women galvanizes women to take action to demand their rights. In the preface to her book on women and the UN, Anne Winslow expresses this view: "Not so long ago human rights activists gave only a passing nod to women's rights ... despite setbacks, the craggy indifference of male counterparts, and the closely knit fabric of male superiority woven over the centuries, women are finally getting things done" (Winslow 1995, viii). This view does not allow us to account for men who champion women's rights and use their political clout to achieve policy success. As scholar Torild Skard asserts, "The UN accounts present a picture of female representatives who simply and straightforwardly ensured the interests of women in a male-dominated organization. But the reality was more complex" (Skard 2008, 42). Skard made this statement in an article about the drafting of the UN Charter – but his assessment remains equally relevant today. As I will show, men are important political actors in the CEDAW story in terms of making policy decisions that constitute opportunities for expansion of women's rights.

A perspective of women's history as necessarily progressive also reifies the category of women and does not allow us to understand that conflicts *among* women are legitimate and important. One of the main reasons the United States has not ratified CEDAW is that reasonable women – and men – disagree about it. Chapter 2 shows that women who support the goals of equal rights for women often disagree about the best way to achieve equality. Chapter 6 focuses on the intense fights between conservative and progressive women over CEDAW that have taken place since the late 1980s. Failure to take these disputes seriously makes it difficult to explain the status of the Convention in the United States.

I develop a different story about the evolution of women's rights as a global norm in Chapters 2 and 3. My account of the origins of CEDAW focuses on two things: disagreements among women – within and across national borders – and the geopolitical context in which demands for women's rights were made. Chapter 2 contends that U.S. political actors limited the power of the UN to address women's rights from the founding of the UN in 1945 until 1970. In the aftermath of World War II, women leaders and women's organizations in Latin America and Europe supported plans for the UN with great enthusiasm, envisioning it as a vehicle for the promotion of peace and protection of women's rights. The promise of the UN to protect and expand women's rights was fulfilled only weakly, however, due to opposition from some American women's groups and the U.S. government. Two factors influenced American views about the status of women's issues within the UN. First, U.S. government officials and many activists within women's groups in the United States feared that creating a separate entity dedicated to women's issues would marginalize women within the UN. Second, they feared that giving the UN power to affect domestic policy on women's rights would strengthen the power of the Soviet Union and Soviet satellite countries within the UN.

The Cold War context helps explain why the U.S. government, with the support of numerous women's organizations, *opposed* the early efforts of the UN to address women's rights. During the Cold War, a state of nonmilitary conflict that would dominate the global landscape from the end of World War II to the collapse of the Soviet Union in 1991, both sides possessed nuclear weapons that could readily annihilate the other if they were to be deployed in a military conflict. The threat of mutually assured destruction kept them from engaging each other directly in a "hot" war. U.S. foreign policy during this era rested on a basic assumption that the United States and the Soviet Union were engaged in a struggle for world dominance. The UN became a battleground for ideological disputes between communism and capitalist democracy. Both of the superpowers claimed superiority on the issue of women's equality. The United States claimed that American women enjoyed full political equality with men, whereas the USSR insisted that women in the communist world enjoyed social and economic equality by virtue of being fully integrated into the labor force. Each side dismissed as insubstantial the type of equality that prevailed in the other, and both sought to impose its ideological worldview on other countries.

The United States fought the Cold War on the domestic front, as well. The government raised fears about communist spies infiltrating the American government and "reds" recruiting members through innocuous-looking "front" organizations. The Red Scare campaign sought to root out communist collaborators from every arena of everyday life. In 1950 and 1954, Wisconsin Senator Joseph R. McCarthy held a series of hearings before the House Un-American Activities Committee to denounce suspected communists. This climate had a direct and chilling effect on American efforts to lead the global community on women's rights.

Despite these obstacles, advocates of women's rights lobbied for the inclusion of specific guarantees of women's rights in the UN Charter and the creation of a standalone Commission on the Status of Women (CSW). Over time, the CSW got the UN General Assembly to approve three conventions that defined three aspects of rights for women within international law: women had the right to vote and to serve in political office, married women had the same citizenship rights as men, and women and men enjoyed equal rights within marriage. The CSW expanded on this set of rights with the Declaration on the Elimination of Discrimination against Women (DEDAW), which affirms agreement with a full complement of rights for women in every arena of society.

In the 1960s, the UN gained forty-four new members, each of which was a brand new nation that recently won independence from a colonial power. These countries, from Africa, Asia, and the Caribbean, brought concerns about poverty and economic growth to the UN. The UN responded by refocusing its attention on development. Developing countries created a shared collective identity as the third world, a coalition distinct from the first world countries of the developed West and the second world countries of communist bloc. As nations forged in the struggle against colonial rule, Third World countries also sought to protect themselves from being taken over as a Soviet satellite or intervened by the United States. During the Cold War, the United States and USSR sought to expand their global power through proxy wars in which they supported third parties. The Americans and Soviets fought proxy wars in Greece (1946–1948), Korea (1950–1953), and Vietnam (1959–1975). The United States engaged in covert operations that resulted in the military coups against Iranian Prime Minister Mohammad Mossadegh in 1953, democratically elected Guatemalan President Jacobo Arbenz in 1954, and democratically elected President Patrice Lumumba in the Republic of the Congo in 1960. The United States supported military governments in Cuba and the Dominican Republic. The Soviets invaded Hungary in 1956, Czechoslovakia in 1968, and Afghanistan in 1979. These conflicts had the unintended consequence of binding the Third World countries together in a defiant alliance. Third World countries came together at the Bandung Conference in Belgrade, Yugoslavia, in September 1961 to create a formal organization to advance their interests, the Non-Aligned Movement (NAM). Twenty-five states attended the 1961 summit, and

NAM has met every three years since then. What the NAM stands for in terms of organizational structure or ideology is loosely defined; what linked the nonaligned countries together was their resistance to being controlled by the two main superpowers. At the 1964 UN Conference on Trade and Development, Third World countries created a formal coalition to advance their economic interests within the UN, the Group of 77, or G-77. The G-77 originally included 77 developing countries (it now includes 125 states).

The rise of the Non-Aligned Movement and a brief period of consensus within the women's movement in the United States reshaped the prospects for women's rights policy within the UN, as I show in Chapter 3. Cold War battles between the United States and the Soviet Union and divisions among advocates of women's rights limited progress on women's issues from the end of World War II. In the 1970s, a window for change opened up as the result of two major shifts, one domestic and the other geopolitical. Within the United States, the emergence of the second-wave feminist movement led to strong bipartisan support for women's rights legislation. Within the UN, developing countries formed a majority bloc that voted down the preferences of the United States and, often, the Soviet Union. U.S. government officials in the administrations of Presidents Richard Nixon (1969–1974), Gerald Ford (1974–1977), and Jimmy Carter (1977–1981) supported women's rights to capitalize on women's electoral support at home, challenge the dominance of the Soviet Union on women's rights, and reassert leadership within the UN. American support for two major initiatives in the UN in the early 1970s – International Women's Year and the drafting of CEDAW – paved the way for significant future advances in global women's rights.

In the mid-1970s, geopolitical considerations drove the United States to shift course and to assume a leading role on women's rights within the UN. The United States led the effort to hold a conference to commemorate International Women's Year in 1975, and it took a leading role in drafting CEDAW. As I show in Chapter 3, it did so in order to assert leadership and reverse a pattern of humiliation and disrespect within the UN, in which developing countries, in conjunction with the communist bloc, consistently criticized the United States. The period of cooperation between Democrats and Republicans on women's issues did not last long. By the end of the 1970s, American celebrations of International Women's Year had triggered an eruption of partisan conflicts over women's rights, struggles that continue to shape electoral politics in the United States today.

TREATY IMPACT: POLICY AND SOCIALIZATION

Part II of this book focuses on the implementation of CEDAW. What impact has CEDAW had in other countries, and what impact would it have in the United States? When it comes to measuring impact, human rights treaties differ from other kinds of treaties in two respects. First, human rights treaties enjoin states to regulate their own behavior in order to comply with international standards. Other kinds of international treaties, by contrast, regulate relationships between states and rely on reciprocal enforcement (i.e., my participation in the treaty is contingent on your compliance with certain actions, and vice versa). Most of the existing research on compliance addresses reciprocal treaties, which constitute the vast majority of interstate treaties. The UN oversees nine human rights treaties, and this book presents a case study of one of them.

Noncompliance is rare among reciprocally enforcing treaties, so rare in fact that the norm of high compliance emerged as a phenomenon worthy of explanation. Abram and Antonia Chayes (1993, 185) have reciprocal treaties in mind when they affirm that "the fundamental norm of international law is *pacta sunt servanda* (treaties are to be obeyed)." For most kinds of treaties, ratification leads directly and unproblematically to compliance. It is unnecessary to define what impact entails because impact follows straightforwardly from the text of the treaty or agreement itself. Impact in this context simply means compliance with the terms of the treaty.

Another perspective maintains that compliance is widespread not because of widespread norms but because countries make rational calculations about which treaties to ratify. According to Downs, Rocke, and Barsoom (1996, 383), "States choose the treaties they make from an infinitely large set of possible treaties" and only ratify those treaties with which they intend to comply. From this perspective, we can expect that treaties will have little impact because the requirements for complying with a treaty are low and can be easily achieved. Measuring treaty impact is unproblematic (1) where a treaty is sufficiently specific and enforced by other parties, (2) where countries write their preferences into a treaty via the drafting process (Chayes and Chayes 1993), or (3) where "treaties require states to make only modest departures from what they would have done in the absence of an agreement," which some argue holds true in most cases (Downs et al. 1996, 380).

Assessing the impact of human rights treaties is a different exercise because the norm of compliance is less widely obeyed. In fact, known rights violators are often the first to ratify human rights treaties (Hafner-Burton and Tsutsui 2005). Countries diverge widely in terms of the degree to which they comply with human rights treaties, so there is more variation to be explained than with reciprocal interstate treaties. Recent increases in the visibility and significance of human rights treaties have raised the level of attention to questions about impact.

A growing body of research on the impact of CEDAW centers on two questions. First, to what degree does ratification of CEDAW lead countries to adopt laws and policies that they otherwise would not adopt? The question of how CEDAW affects policy outcomes has been addressed almost exclusively by qualitative research in which experts familiar with the treaty or a particular region evaluate the weight of the Convention as opposed to other factors in prompting countries to adopt new policies. Second, what effect does CEDAW have on the lives of individual women? Is the quality of women's lives better in those countries that have ratified CEDAW than those that have not? These questions have been addressed mostly by quantitative studies that examine the substantive impact of treaties on women's lives, either in terms of level of rights or quality of life.

In qualitative studies, experts familiar with CEDAW evaluate its impact using a case study approach (Avdeyeva 2007; Byrnes and Freeman 2012; Heyns and Viljoen 2002; McPhedran et al. 2000). Andrew Byrnes and Marsha Freeman, both of whom have worked with CEDAW for many years, defend a qualitative approach to assessing treaty impact on the grounds that "identification of specific changes resulting from the CEDAW Convention requires a close examination of the reporting and review processes in the context of individual States" (Byrnes and Freeman 2012, 2). This approach looks for two kinds of evidence of CEDAW's impact: policy change that has a close temporal connection to the reporting process, and policies or laws that reference CEDAW explicitly.

The main limitation of the qualitative approach to assessing treaty impact is the challenge of establishing a direct causal link between ratification of CEDAW and the adoption of specific policies. It is difficult to discern the precise impact that CEDAW has had on policy as opposed to the many other factors that shape women's rights policy such as domestic mobilization, lobbying, partisan support, or electoral commitments. CEDAW might be one of many factors that has led to the establishment of formal laws, policies, programs, and initiatives geared at improving women's rights, as well as informal changes in cultural norms and practices. Finally, endogeneity problems dog qualitative approaches; it is difficult to know whether policy changes resulted from CEDAW, or if ratification of the treaty itself reflects the impact of other factors.

Even where policymakers cite CEDAW explicitly in the text of legislation or justify the adoption of a certain policy as an effort to comply with CEDAW, other factors may have also contributed to the change. The Brazilian government, for example, indicated in one of its CEDAW reports that it had adopted certain laws in order to comply with CEDAW, but Brazilian women's rights activists later reported that those reforms "were not directly prompted by CEDAW" (Heyns and Viljoen 2002, 102). A case study of CEDAW compliance in Colombia reported that the overlap between domestic legislation and CEDAW "tends to be more the result of fortunate coincidence than of the conscious effort on the part of an enlightened Congress or government to transform domestic law in accordance with the provision of a given treaty" (Heyns and Viljoen 2002, 171). Hanna Beate Schöpp-Schilling, a longtime CEDAW Committee member, acknowledged this even as she affirmed the treaty's importance:

While there is no doubt that the Committee's work has contributed to a worldwide awareness of women's human rights and an increase in their factual enjoyment of these, it is sometimes difficult to identify the Committee as the decisive influence. Many other factors – such as the UN world conferences or national developments apart from the CEDAW review process, and, more lately, the communication and inquiry procedures – also have been significant. (Schöpp-Schilling 2007, 259)

Thus, although qualitative research presumes to examine the impact of the Convention on policy, problems of inference limit the degree to which one can make definitive claims.

Questions about the potential impact of CEDAW in the United States raise particular methodological problems. The United States enjoys a unique status in the international arena. To what extent can we draw inferences about the possible impact of CEDAW on the United States on the basis of experiences of other countries? The hegemonic power of the United States makes it difficult to make comparisons with other countries when it comes to the impact of ratifying CEDAW. No other country could be considered comparable to the United States when performing a controlled comparison (a "most like" pairing). The US is sui generis in this regard; there are no countries that could serve as analogous cases from which to draw inferences about how CEDAW ratification might affect the United States. Even if we were to consider countries that are "most like" the United States in terms of key variables such as level of development and status of women's rights prior to ratification, the amount of time that has lapsed since other countries similar to the United States ratified CEDAW would mitigate the value of comparison. Finland, for example, might be a good case to examine relative to the United States for some reasons – a similar level of development, support for women's rights, the fact that international treaties are not self-executing, and a lag between signing and ratification – but Finland ratified CEDAW decades ago, in 1986. The world has changed with regard to women's issues in those twenty-five years.

A growing body of quantitative literature finds that CEDAW exerts positive influence on the de facto status of women. Quantitative studies address the methodological limitations of qualitative work by relying on statistical analysis to isolate the effect of the treaty versus other factors (Cho 2010; den Boer 2008; Englehart and Miller 2012; Gray, Kittilson, and Sandholtz 2006; Simmons 2010). Quantitative research can also endogenize treaty ratification by testing the variables often attributed to a country's decision to ratify (Simmons 2009, 2010). Furthermore, measuring CEDAW as a time-lagged variable provides evidence for the dynamic nature of the reporting process over time.[3] Simmons (2010), for example, finds that CEDAW has a positive impact on women's educational attainment, access to family planning, and employment opportunities. Englehart and Miller (2012) find that CEDAW exerts a stronger effect on rights than do other treaties.

---

[3] I thank Neil Englehart for this observation.

One conclusion that almost all studies reach, regardless of methodology, is that CEDAW's effectiveness ultimately hinges on domestic political factors. Qualitative and quantitative studies alike consistently point to domestic factors as the mechanisms by which human rights treaties achieve an effect. Simmons (2010), for example, attributes the improvements that human rights treaties have on the quality of people's lives to the way in which treaties reshape the domestic policy environment. The effectiveness of CEDAW stems from the extent to which it changes the priorities of domestic elites, strengthens the prospects for filing legal claims against discrimination, and fosters mobilization that generates support for the goals articulated by the treaty. These factors depend in turn on the nature of the domestic regime. Simmons finds that the value and effectiveness of human rights treaties are greatest in transitional or partially democratic regimes. In transitional democracies, for example, ratification of CEDAW is associated with a 6 percent increase in the ratio of girls to boys in primary and secondary education. The effect is much lower in stable democracies and stable autocracies.

The literature on socialization captures the way in which human rights policies empower domestic actors. This approach maintains that compliance emerges as the result of repeated engagement with a treaty over time. Domestic political actors come to internalize the norms of international agreements, prompting convergence on policy preferences and agreement among those initially supportive of a treaty and those resistant to it. As the public becomes more aware of a treaty, it will expect the government to comply with it and will demand greater compliance. As Harold Koh (1997, 2655) writes, "It is through this transnational legal process, this repeated cycle of interaction, and internationalization, that international law acquires its 'stickiness,' that nation-states acquire their identity, and that nations come to 'obey' international law out of perceived self-interest."

Existing literature on the socialization of international norms misses two things about how human rights treaties work. First, treaties themselves evolve over time. Most of this literature presumes that treaties are static. Existing research obscures the ongoing politics that shape the drafting, implementation, and impact of treaties. Human rights treaties develop over time in part because their provisions can be quite vague. In order to get countries to agree to global principles of human rights, UN committees often had to phrase those principles in general terms. Social science approaches have not explained how human rights treaties do – or do not – come to be significant or powerful over time. Research that measures treaties as discrete events masks the degree to which they change as the result of continuous negotiation and engagement. In Chapter 4, I argue that CEDAW has grown stronger over time as UN officials, Committee experts, government officials, women's rights organizations, and academics around the world have engaged with it. Second, the meetings at which governments present their progress before human rights treaty bodies are an important venue in which socialization takes place. Few accounts of treaty impact devote sufficient attention to the interactions that occur between treaty body officials, government representatives, and members of NGOs during the presentation of periodic reports. If the socialization approach is valid, we should expect to see evidence of increased commitment to comply over time, as countries submit in subsequent reports.

The Convention itself has evolved a great deal since it was first drafted in the 1970s. Through the interpretive mechanisms available to them, the experts on the CEDAW Committee have kept pace with changes in global understandings of what constitutes discrimination against women. The text of the Convention has not changed since 1979, but the Committee experts continuously revise their understandings of the articles of the treaty in ways that reflect the evolution of women's rights. The institutional autonomy of the Committee has allowed it to develop an extremely progressive understanding of women's rights, one that outpaces the status of women or women's rights in any UN member country. I support this claim by providing a historical analysis of the evolution of the work of the Committee in Chapter 4. The chapter begins with a basic overview of the text of CEDAW. Then, I examine the General Recommendations that the Committee has written to clarify and articulate its interpretation of the Convention. Subsequently, I show how greater involvement by NGOs has made CEDAW more visible and more relevant to activism at the domestic level. Finally, I document a series of institutional changes that have helped the Committee to operate more effectively and efficiently. Chapter 4 shows that CEDAW cannot be viewed as a static document.

Chapter 5 focuses on the reporting sessions that the CEDAW Committee holds with government officials and nongovernmental organizations to assess compliance with the Convention. My analysis of the impact of CEDAW rests on the CEDAW Committee. The impact of CEDAW on the countries that have ratified it is best understood as a process, rather than as a set of specific policy outcomes. Ratification of CEDAW commits countries to participating in a periodic reporting process by which countries prepare reports on their compliance with the Convention. The CEDAW Committee reviews and assesses their progress. The Committee lacks the power to require countries to comply with its suggestions, but the process provides international accountability for women's rights policy and reshapes the contours of the policy-making process by bringing the CEDAW committee into the domestic policy arena. I argue that much of the work of socialization – the translation of international norms into concrete impact at the domestic level – takes place at these sessions themselves. In examining the work that occurs during the reporting sessions, I suggest that American social conservatives' worst fears will not be realized if the United States ratifies CEDAW. The CEDAW Committee, the body that oversees implementation of the treaty, has extremely limited power over the governments that ratify it and cannot impose its agenda on anyone.

TREATY RATIFICATION: INSTITUTIONS, NORMS AND COST-BENEFIT ANALYSIS

Part III turns to the question of U.S. ratification. Why, despite repeated consideration over the past thirty years, has the United States not ratified CEDAW? Many people think the United States does not ratify any international human rights treaties. Legal scholar Catherine Powell (2002, 422) aptly summarizes this perspective: "Despite the United States' key role in establishing the UN, current U.S. policy in the fields of human rights and public international law more generally could be described with two words: isolationism and unilateralism." U.S. history in the twentieth and twenty-first centuries provides ample empirical support for this claim. The United States' failure to ratify the Kyoto Protocol and Law of the Sea Treaty come to mind as prominent recent examples. In a few cases, the United States has withdrawn from treaties it had previously ratified. The United States signed and ratified the Anti-Ballistic Missile Treaty and the Biological and Toxic Weapons Convention in 1972, but then withdrew from them in December 2001. The United States signed the Rome Statute that created the International Criminal Court in 2000, but President George W. Bush "unsigned" it in 2006. The United States has neither signed nor ratified the Convention on the Rights of the Child.[4] The United States is one of just two UN member countries that have failed to ratify the CRC – along with Somalia.

CEDAW is one of nine "core international human rights instruments" overseen by the UN Office of the High Commissioner for Human Rights, which in turn is overseen by the UN Secretariat. The nine treaties, listed along with their acronyms and the year the General Assembly passed them, are:

- International Convention on the Elimination of All Forms of Racial Discrimination (CERD), 1966
- International Covenant on Civil and Political Rights (ICCPR), 1966
- International Covenant on Economic, Social and Cultural Rights (ICESCR), 1966
- Convention on the Elimination of All Forms of Discrimination against Women (CEDAW), 1979
- Convention against Torture and Other Cruel, Inhuman or Degrading Treatment or Punishment (CAT), 1984
- Convention on the Rights of the Child (CRC), 1989
- International Convention on the Protection of the Rights of All Migrant Workers and Members of Their Families (CMW), 1990
- International Convention for the Protection of All Persons from Enforced Disappearance (CED), 2006
- Convention on the Rights of Persons with Disabilities (CRPD), 2006 (Office of the United Nations High Commissioner for Human Rights n.d.)[5]

---

[4] The United States has signed two of the optional protocols to the CRC: the Optional Protocol to the Convention on the Rights of the Child on the Involvement of Children in Armed Conflict and the Optional Protocol to the Convention on the Rights of the Child on the Sale of Children, Child Prostitution, and Child Pornography. For more information see United Nations 2013b.

[5] Seven of the nine treaties have been discussed within the U.S. Senate: CERD, ICCPR, ICESR, CEDAW, CAT, CRPD, and CRC. Why there has been no action on the CED or the CMW is an interesting question, but one beyond the scope of this study.

A treaty body or committee made up of independent experts adminis-ters each of those nine treaties. A tenth treaty, the Convention on the Prevention and Punishment of the Crime of Genocide, was adopted in 1948. I treat the Genocide Convention as a human rights treaty because it has been considered that way in the United States, even though it is structured differently from the others and does not fall within the jurisdiction of the Office of the High Commissioner for Human Rights.

The American record on human rights treaties may not be exemplary, but the United States does ratify some of them. The United States has ratified four human rights treaties: the Genocide Convention, ICCPR, CAT, and CERD. If we were to expand the pool to include other UN treaties as well as those under the jurisdiction of the International Labor Organization and the Organization of American States, the U.S. record is more impressive (Melish 2009). Whether one regards U.S. accession to human rights treaties as a glass half full or a glass half empty, this variation warrants explanation. Why does the United States ratify some treaties but not others?

The literature on treaty ratification aims to identify the conditions under which countries will ratify human rights treaties, but almost all approaches fall short when it comes to explaining U.S. behavior with regard to CEDAW. In this section, I discuss three competing hypotheses drawn from cross-national studies of treaty ratification that highlight institutional rules, norms, and cost-benefit analysis, respectively. The institutional barriers to ratification in the United States are high but not insurmountable, yet the research highlighting institutional rules cannot account for why the United States ratifies some treaties and not others. Norms-based approaches predict that countries are more likely to ratify and implement a treaty if they already share the norms that the treaty reflects. Cost-benefit approaches explain state action as the reflection of rational calculation of costs and benefits – a state will ratify a treaty if the costs for complying with it are low. Each of these perspectives would predict that the United States would have ratified CEDAW already. At the end of this section, I introduce a new perspec-tive that explains variation in treaty ratification in terms of conflicts at the domestic level.

Institutional design significantly shapes the prospects for treaty rati-fication (Simmons 2010). Article II of the U.S. Constitution stipulates that international treaties require both presidential approval and a two-thirds vote or a supermajority in the Senate. This is a high threshold and relatively rare: "Only five other countries in the world – Algeria, Burundi, Iraq, Micronesia, and the Philippines" have the same requirements for treaty ratification (Hathaway 2008, 1236). Nonetheless, high institutional barriers have not constrained these other countries to the same degree that they have the United States: Algeria, Burundi, and the Philippines have ratified all nine human rights treaties (see Table 1.1). In the United States, the process generally works like this: the president signs a treaty, signaling an intention to ratify. The president then transmits the treaty to the Senate for its advice and consent. Treaties begin their legislative journey in the Senate Committee on Foreign Relations, which holds a public hearing to discuss ratification and then votes on whether to send the treaty for a vote on a resolution of ratification on the Senate floor.[6] The two-thirds threshold is difficult to meet for any legislation, but has proven particularly problematic in the history of treaties in the United States. The Senate's refusal to ratify the Treaty of Versailles in 1919 prompted a move to amend the Constitution to remove the supermajority requirement, but this effort failed. Even when the Democrats have controlled the Senate, they have been well short of a supermajority.

A second approach predicts that countries will ratify a treaty when they already share the norms espoused by that treaty. From this perspective, countries ratify treaties either because it is the morally right thing to do or because they already share the norms that a particular treaty promotes. Jay Goodliffe and Darren Hawkins (2006, 369), for example, find that global and regional norms strongly influence ratification and that "states that already respect individual liberties like free speech are more likely to both sign and ratify" the Convention against Torture earlier than other states. Having a state religion reduces the odds of ratification; countries in which Islam is the state religion are half as likely to ratify CEDAW (Simmons 2010). We would expect countries in which most people support women's rights to ratify CEDAW. Indeed, by 1990, all but four countries in Western Europe

---

[6] "The Senate does not ratify treaties – the Senate approves or rejects a resolution of ratification. If the resolution passes, then ratification takes place when the instruments of ratification are formally exchanged between the United States and the foreign power(s)" (Senate n.d.).

TABLE 1.1 *Countries That Require a Two-Thirds Vote to Ratify Treaties*

	Genocide	CERD	ICESR	ICCPR	CAT	CEDAW	CRC	CED	CMW
Algeria	+	+	+	+	+	+	+	-	+
Burundi	+	+	+	+	+	+	+	-	-
Iraq	+	+	+	+	-	+	+	+	-
Micronesia	-	-	-	-	-	+	+	-	-
Philippines	+	+	+	+	+	+	+	-	+
U.S.	+	+	-	+	+	-	-	-	-

Source: University of Minnesota Human Rights Library 2008.

had ratified CEDAW, in addition to Russia and Japan.[7] According to the norms-based approach, the United States should have ratified CEDAW long ago.

We might also expect the United States to ratify CEDAW because doing so is consistent with American values. The United States ranks among the top ten countries in the world in terms of support for gender equality, with approval from close to 80 percent of the population (Inglehart and Norris 2003, 33). A belief in equality of all kinds is central to American culture, and many Americans believe the United States to be a world leader in terms of promoting women's rights. From a norms perspective, U.S. failure to ratify CEDAW offends American values. Many Americans find it shocking to see the United States grouped with some of the world's worst offenders on women's rights (such as Iran and Somalia, two other countries that have not yet ratified CEDAW). From a norms-based perspective, the United States is the only "real" outlier among the seven countries that have not ratified CEDAW – the only advanced industrial democracy that has failed to do so.

Another variation of the norms-based approach emphasizes regional diffusion: states are more likely to commit to a treaty if they are located in a region in which other states have already ratified (Goodliffe and Hawkins 2006; Hathaway 2007). Simmons (2010, 110) confirms that regional effects "surface in practically every measure of [treaty] commitment – from ratification to reservation making to the acceptance of [optional protocols]." The United States remains immune to regional diffusion in this case: by the time the U.S. Senate first considered CEDAW in 1990, every other country in North and South America had already ratified it. CEDAW ratifiers surround the United States, but U.S. ratification seems as unlikely now as it did twenty years ago.

Emilie Hafner-Burton and Kiyotera Tsutsui (2005) offer a slightly different norms-based account: countries may ratify in order to signal their support for the norms expressed in a treaty, whether or not they actually espouse those norms and, in some cases, to mask the fact that they do not. This becomes more likely as more countries ratify.

---

[7] The Netherlands ratified in 1991, Liechtenstein in 1995, and Andorra and Switzerland in 1997.

The U.S. case challenges this view, as well; arguments highlighting the United States' pariah status have had little effect thus far. The legitimacy of CEDAW has grown over time, but the United States remains unmoved.

A third body of research maintains that countries accrue material benefits for ratifying treaties or face costs for failing to do so. The cost-benefit approach predicts that ratification will occur when the costs of meeting the requirements of a treaty are low. A cost-benefit perspective makes intuitive sense for the thousands of treaties that imply reciprocal benefits for signatory countries. A cost-benefit approach also makes sense where more powerful countries can coerce less powerful countries to commit. The relevance of the cost-benefit logic to human rights treaties is less clear. On the one hand, it seems irrational for any country to ratify a treaty that imposes constraints on government action but does not require other states to provide reciprocal benefits. Unlike trade agreements that regulate interstate relations, human rights treaties hold domestic governments accountable for "purely internal activities" (Moravcsik 2000, 218). Nonetheless, scholars have generated considerable leverage by applying a cost-benefit rationale to human rights treaties. As legal scholar Oona Hathaway (2003, 1835) asserts, "Countries considering signing or ratifying a treaty consider not only the cost of complying with the treaty but also the probability that the costs of complying will actually be realized." The more changes a treaty requires, the less likely it will be ratified.

A cost-benefit analysis gives us better traction in explaining why the United States has not yet ratified CEDAW, but the U.S. case exposes some limitations in the way that scholars have measured the costs of treaty compliance. Cross-national studies that explain treaty commitment in terms of the costs of compliance rely, not surprisingly, on the nation-state as the unit of analysis. Scholars have argued that costs differ in terms of national wealth, age of regime, democratic stability, and legal system, for example (Goodliffe and Hawkins 2006; Hathaway 2007).

As I will show, analysis of the U.S. case suggests that ratification of a treaty is decided on the basis of debates over anticipated compliance costs that occur *within* a particular country. Andrew Moravcsik (2000) and James Vreeland (2008) begin to get at this point. The take-home message of Moravcsik's study has been interpreted as the "lock-in" hypothesis: new regimes commit to treaties to lock in their preferences against potential challengers at the domestic level. My account emphasizes a slightly different aspect of Moravcsik's study – the domestic conflicts that lie at the base of the decision to ratify. Moravcsik argues that leaders in newly democratic regimes ratify treaties in order to strengthen their position against possible challenges from retired tyrants, the authoritarians still loyal to the old order who used to be in power. Vreeland (2008) also illustrates the importance of factors at the subnational level. He asks why dictatorships that practice torture are more likely to ratify the UN Convention against Torture than dictatorships that do not practice torture. He argues that multiparty ("open") dictatorships are more likely to sign CAT as a concession to coalition partners, whereas single-party ("closed") dictatorships have no incentive to share power and individuals have little incentive to challenge the regime. Andrew Cortell and James Davis (1996, 452) also show that domestic actors appeal to international norms to "further their own interests in the domestic political arena." In each of these accounts, treaty ratification hinges on domestic political disputes.

Given the institutional rules governing treaty ratification, under what conditions should we expect the United States to be most likely to ratify a treaty? The need for a supermajority magnifies the power of opposition where it exists. In the US, the Democratic Party generally supports human rights treaties and the Republican Party opposes them. The most propitious conditions for treaty ratification should exist when Democrats control both the presidency and the senate. Republican control of the presidency and the senate provide the least favorable conditions for ratification of human rights treaties. Table 1.2 provides partial support for these hypotheses. CEDAW's best chances for approval were (are) during the Carter administration, President Bill Clinton's first term in office, and the Obama administration. President Carter did transmit CEDAW to the Senate before he left office, but the Senate took no action on it. The Senate held a hearing on CEDAW during both Clinton's and Obama's terms, but did not vote on it (yet). The bottom line here is that institutional factors are insufficient to explain why the United States has thus far failed to ratify CEDAW.

Chapter 6 examines the history of efforts to ratify CEDAW in the United States. It begins with President Carter's transmission of

TABLE 1.2 *Conditions for Action on Human Rights Treaties*

Congress	Years	President	Party of President	Senate Majority	CEDAW Action	Other Treaties
96	1979–1980	Carter	D	D	Carter transmits CEDAW to Senate	
97	1981–1982	Reagan	R	R		
98	1983–1984	Reagan	R	R		Genocide Convention approved
99	1985–1986	Reagan	R	R		
100	1987–1988	Reagan	R	D	CEDAW hearing	
101	1989–1990	GHW Bush	R	D	CEDAW hearing	
102	1991–1992	GHW Bush	R	D		ICCPR approved
103	1993–1994	Clinton	D	D	CEDAW hearing	CAT and CERD approved
104	1995–1996	Clinton	D	R		
105	1997–1998	Clinton	D	R		
106	1999–2000	Clinton	D	R		
107	2001–2002	GW Bush	R	D*	CEDAW hearing	
108	2003–2004	GW Bush	R	R		
109	2005–2006	GW Bush	R	R		
110	2007–2008	GW Bush	R	50/50		
111	2009–2010	Obama	D	D	CEDAW hearing	
112	2011–2012	Obama	D	D		CRPD rejected

*Partisan control of the 107th Senate switched back and forth twice in 2001. From January 3 to January 20, each party had fifty senators, but the Democrats held the deciding vote with Al Gore as vice president. From January 20 to June 6, 2001, the deciding vote went to Vice President Richard Cheney. Effective June 6, Senator Jim Jeffords of Vermont switched his party status from Republican to Independent, putting the majority back into Democratic hands (U.S. Senate n.d.).

the treaty to the Senate in 1980 and addresses each of five hearings dedicated specifically to CEDAW, in 1988, 1990, 1994, 2002, and 2010. What the chapter reveals is a gradual but decisive movement of Republicans away from support for ratification. Republican leaders made the drafting of CEDAW possible in the late 1970s. Moderate Republicans voted in support of CEDAW in the mid-1990s. But by 2002, party lines had hardened and no Republicans supported it. Supporters of CEDAW in Congress and civil society have responded to this defection by shifting the focus of the debate toward the impact that CEDAW would have on women in other countries, and away from CEDAW's ostensible effect in the United States, but to no avail. This strategy facilitated the ratification of other human rights treaties, but not CEDAW. Analysis of congressional hearings reveals that, despite rhetoric that warns of dire domestic consequences, social conservatives care deeply about the international impact that U.S. ratification of CEDAW would have. Their concerns reflect the fact that CEDAW has become a powerful institution in terms of setting the agenda for women's issues worldwide.

While Chapter 6 highlights increasing divisions between the two parties over CEDAW ratification, Chapter 7 identifies two points that advocates and opponents share in common and then challenges each in turn. Both the pro and con sides of the CEDAW debate agree that women in the United States already have all the rights that CEDAW guarantees. Furthermore, they concur that the "private jurisdiction" clause of CEDAW, which obligates states to protect women from private discrimination, is at odds with the U.S. legal system. I examine these assumptions in light of the issue of domestic violence to suggest that American women do not, in fact, enjoy sufficient legal protection from this form of private discrimination. I evaluate three possible remedies to the limitations of U.S. domestic violence law: appeal to international human rights standards, the passage of an Equal Rights Amendment to the U.S. Constitution, and CEDAW. I conclude that, of these three, CEDAW provides women with the most comprehensive protection from the harms of domestic violence. Chapter 7 thus departs from the historical analysis that guides most of the book to develop a legal theoretical perspective on CEDAW. Chapter 8 concludes by summarizing the arguments and highlighting the implications of my arguments for future research and for current efforts to ratify CEDAW.

2

A Scaffolding for Global Women's Rights, 1945–1970

The first sentence of the Charter of the United Nations, written in 1945, vows to put an end to war. The second sentence establishes gender equality. As the Charter reads:

We the peoples of the United Nations determined

- To save succeeding generations from the scourge of war, which twice in our lifetime has brought untold sorrow to mankind, and
- To reaffirm faith in fundamental human rights, in the dignity and worth of the human person, in the equal rights of men and women and of nations large and small. (United Nations 1945)

It is extraordinary to read an explicit affirmation of gender equality, so prominently placed, in a document of profound global importance, drafted at a moment in time not generally associated with strong support for feminism. The statement stands out for suggesting that "the equal rights of men and women" is a "fundamental human right," an idea whose meaning took the world many decades to acknowledge fully. The clear guarantee of gender equality promised in the UN Charter provided an unprecedented opportunity for the women of the world to claim a new status as equals in the postwar era. It set the United Nations on a path toward becoming an institution of primary importance to advancing the status of women into the future. Nonetheless, many decades passed before the commitment implied in the UN Charter became a global norm.

During the UN's first twenty-five years, advocates of gender equality accomplished many things. The explicit inclusion of gender equality in the UN Charter counts as their first success. The UN then created the CSW as an independent entity within the Economic and Social Council in 1946. In the 1950s and 1960s, the CSW got the UN General Assembly to approve a series of international treaties on specific areas of women's rights: the Convention on the Political Rights of Women (1952); Convention on the Nationality of Married Women (1957); and Convention on Consent to Marriage, Minimum Age for Marriage and Registration of Marriages (1962). In 1967, the General Assembly adopted the Declaration on the Elimination of Discrimination against Women, a comprehensive statement affirming the political, civil, social, and economic rights of women. Although the international community heralded these four documents as unprecedented achievements, these agreements did not require signatory nations to take concrete action, so they did not have a significant impact on the status of women in UN member nations.

The women who supported the formation of the CSW and who led it during its first few years espoused an ambitious agenda, but the CSW achieved far less than its initial supporters had hoped. The Commission issued statements and drafted treaties that urged, recommended, suggested, and invited – but did not require – countries to expand legal rights for women. It approved proposals that centered on civil and political rights and rejected those that sought to strengthen social and economic rights. At many points, the CSW considered policies that could actually promote women's rights in member countries, but in the end, its efforts resulted in nominal affirmations of support for improving the status of women that had little practical effect. Disagreement about whether women's issues should be treated separately or mainstreamed proved a significant obstacle to progress within the Commission. Efforts to set standards on specific areas of rights unique to women met with ample resistance. The fact that so few countries ratified them made them weaker. As historian Laura Reanda affirms,

The Commission was created as an instrument of negotiation among governments, not as an agent of change ... it was not given powers to review governmental performance, to investigate specific situations, nor to develop recourse procedures in case of violations. It was, in fact, barred even from addressing itself directly to governments, having to couch its recommendations in general terms and to forward them through its parent bodies. (Reanda 1992, 301)

The actions of the CSW may have been groundbreaking at the time, but can only be seen as timid in comparison to the UN's later efforts to promote women's rights starting in the 1970s.

Two factors explain why the UN commitment to women's issues was initially so weak. First, women's organizations vehemently disagreed about the best strategy to pursue equality between men and women. One sector argued for a separatist approach that addressed women's rights as a discreet set of concerns. Another sector believed that equality could be achieved only by incorporating women's concerns into the broader rubric of human rights, that is, by mainstreaming them. They feared that segregating women's issues would marginalize them. These disagreements penetrated deeply into the activist community; they divided women not only within the United States, but across international lines, as well.

A second factor that explains the limited success of the CSW in its first few decades of life is the geopolitical context in which these conflicts played out. The United States intentionally sought to prevent the CSW from having any concrete impact on the domestic policies of UN member nations and thus to prevent the Soviet Union from using the UN to expand its power. The United States feared that the Soviet Union would use the UN to enforce its agenda on UN member countries. These concerns had a domestic aspect as well. More pointedly, some within the United States, primarily southern politicians, feared that African Americans would use the UN to denounce human rights violations in the United States, which would in turn further strengthen the Soviets' hand within the UN. The United States consistently supported measures that would keep agencies within the UN weak and ineffectual. The U.S. government pursued its goals by instructing its delegates on the CSW to challenge the Soviet bloc on its claims about the status of women and oppose any proposals that required governments to take action to improve the status of women. As long as tensions between the two superpowers dominated the international arena, the CSW was hamstrung.

The rapid expansion of UN members in the 1960s disrupted the balance of power between the United States and the USSR. In the 1960s, newly independent nations joined the UN and came to form a majority within the General Assembly. The power of the Third World countries proved particularly strong within the Economic and Social Council (ECOSOC), the entity that oversees the CSW. The Commission's scope of action increased as a result. The prospects for the CSW to generate effective policy grew as the dominance of the US-Soviet conflict within the UN eroded.

This chapter focuses on three phases in the history of UN policies toward women. First, I describe women's efforts to influence the drafting of the UN Charter at the Dumbarton Oaks Conference and the Conference on International Organization in 1945. This section also explains how women in foreign delegations and U.S. women's groups led a successful effort, despite strenuous opposition from the United States government, to create a stand-alone CSW in 1946. The second section examines the international conventions that the CSW drafted in the 1950s and 1960s. The third and final section of this chapter describes the drafting of the Declaration on the Elimination of Discrimination against Women.

The evidence on which this chapter relies comes from two sets of primary sources: transcripts of CSW sessions and media coverage. The UN keeps summary records of all CSW sessions, which are condensed versions of the statements made during a meeting, recorded by a third party. The summary records allow us to follow debates among members of the Commission. The *New York Times* amply covered the workings of the CSW in the 1950s and 1960s. It reported on conflicts among members and published editorials heralding CSW accomplishments. This chapter also relies on the private papers of Dorothy Kenyon, a lawyer who was the first American delegate appointed to the CSW. Although Kenyon eventually ended up serving on the Commission, she initially participated in efforts to oppose creation of the Commission and kept careful records of these meetings as well as her activities on the Commission. Her records are archived in the Sophia Smith Collection at Smith College.

WOMEN DEMAND A SEAT AT THE TABLE: DUMBARTON OAKS, 1945

The UN grew out of World War II, which pitted the Allied forces against the German-led Axis powers. In 1942, the Allied nations formalized their relationship by signing the Declaration by United Nations. The leaders of the "Great Powers" in this coalition, the United States, the United Kingdom, the Soviet Union, and China, met in 1944 to map out plans to establish the United Nations as a formal organization. This three-month series of meetings is known as the Dumbarton Oaks Conference, named for the mansion in Washington, DC, where they met. The following year, from April to June 1945, representatives from the Allied nations drafted the Charter of the United Nations at the Conference on International Organization in San Francisco.

Not all American women's organizations supported the creation of the UN (Rymph 2006), but those that did greeted the plans for it with high hopes. Some viewed the UN as a guarantee for international peace and believed that women's participation in it would curb men's amply demonstrated propensity for war. Others envisioned the UN as a venue for translating women's wartime employment into careers in international service. Still others saw the UN as the institutional embodiment of the Atlantic Charter, the broad declaration of rights made by Franklin D. Roosevelt and Winston Churchill in 1941, and hoped it would be a vehicle for expanding the rights of women around the globe. Women expected to be included in the plans for the new organization *as a matter of course*, in recognition for their massive participation in the war effort. Their hopes mirrored the overall climate of postwar optimism in the United States and anticipation that the UN would usher in an era of lasting international cooperation. Women were not alone in their enthusiasm for the new organization; many people eagerly waited for the UN to get to work and had high expectations for what it could accomplish.

Tempering this enthusiasm was the knowledge that any treaty creating the UN would require Senate approval. In 1919, the Senate had voted down the Treaty of Versailles despite intense lobbying by President Woodrow Wilson. The Treaty of Versailles was the agreement that ended World War I and created the League of Nations, the precursor to the UN. It was the first time in history that the United States had rejected a peace treaty. The "Wilsonian debacle," as some called it, remained prominent on people's minds as plans to create the UN got underway (Robins 1971). Under the helm of John Sloan Dickey, the Department of State coordinated a massive campaign to publicize the upcoming Dumbarton Oaks Conference in order to generate public support for the UN and thus ensure that the Senate would ratify the Charter. The State Department distributed hundreds of thousands of copies of the Dumbarton Oaks proposals to civic organizations, libraries, schools, churches, and other organizations, and urged state governors to declare April 16–22, 1945, as "Dumbarton Oaks Week" (Robins 1971).

The State Department's efforts to mobilize public support for the UN Charter generated expectations that the new organization would include institutional measures to guarantee the protection of human rights, but the initial plans for the UN focused almost exclusively on security concerns. During the Dumbarton Oaks Conference, which took place from August 21 to October 7, 1944, growing fears about Soviet aggression made the United States reluctant to delegate any real power to the UN or give the organization any jurisdiction over domestic issues. The Dumbarton Oaks document mentioned human rights only briefly and women's rights not at all. These omissions, "despite the Atlantic Charter, despite Nazi atrocities, and despite Japanese brutality" incited women and African Americans to mobilize to demand that rights be put on the agenda and that they be appointed as delegates to the San Francisco conference where the United Nations would be formed (Anderson 2009, 8). Republican Congresswoman Clare Boothe Luce's complaints about the absence of women "began early and attracted international attention" (Lauren 1998, 334). Strenuous opposition and awareness of the need to court public support ultimately forced the Great Powers to put social and economic rights on the agenda. The State Department invited forty-two NGOs, including five women's groups, to participate as non-voting representatives at the conference.

Latin American governments also reacted with outrage to the Dumbarton Oaks Proposal. They had been excluded from the conference despite a promise from the United States "that as allies in the Western Hemisphere they would be fully consulted on any plans on a postwar organization" (Lauren 1998, 175). In response, forty Latin American countries organized a conference of their own. The Inter-American Conference on Problems of War and Peace took place at Chapultepec Castle in Mexico City from February 21 to March 8, 1945, prior to the Charter conference in San Francisco. The Chapultepec meetings highlighted the human rights issues that had been omitted from Dumbarton Oaks (Lauren 1998).

Several of the delegates who attended the Chapultepec Conference were women. Minerva Bernardino, a leader in the feminist movement of the Dominican Republic, for example, had extensive diplomatic experience thanks to her years of service on the Inter-American Commission on Women (IACW) (DuBois and Derby 2009). By the time of the founding of the UN, Bernardino had already demonstrated considerable political skill in strengthening the IACW and maneuvering her way to the presidency of the organization. Bertha Lutz and Amalia Castillo de Ledon were leaders of the women's suffrage movement in Brazil and Mexico, respectively. Mobilizing support for women's rights had catapulted these women to political power in their own countries. At the Chapultepec Conference, they successfully lobbied to get official recognition for the IACW. Bernardino, Lutz, and Castillo de Ledon had thus risen to prominence nationally and regionally by supporting women's rights. Their victories at the Chapultepec Conference reinforced their beliefs in the wisdom of creating separate institutions to promote women's rights within international institutions. They traveled to the San Francisco conference flush with these victories.

THE CONFERENCE ON INTERNATIONAL ORGANIZATION IN SAN FRANCISCO

Smaller countries constituted a majority at the San Francisco conference and with twenty out of fifty votes, Latin American countries were a majority among the smaller countries. Latin America thus wielded some influence over the negotiations (Lauren 1998, 193). Pressure from Latin American nations was another factor in prompting the United States to support the inclusion of human rights provisions in the UN Charter and the creation of a human rights commission.

Although Latin American countries were well represented, women were a minority. Overall, the number of women who attended the conference was "pitifully small" relative to women's expectations and the efforts they had expended to demand representation (Laville 2008). Six of the official delegates were women and an additional fifteen women served in advisory roles, making up about 3 percent of the total (Skard 2008). President Harry S. Truman appointed one woman to the American delegation: Virginia Gildersleeve, then dean of Barnard College. Gildersleeve had worked to promote women's participation in international affairs and get women appointed to wartime jobs. She helped found the International Federation of University Women, a group that worked to achieve world peace by building networks of educated women around the world. During the war, she also helped establish the Navy's Women's Reserve (Snider 2007).

Gildersleeve supported equality for women, but believed that the best way to achieve it was through integration rather than separatism. She insisted that women should not be given special or separate treatment. In her autobiography, *Many a Good Crusade*, Gildersleeve relates a telling anecdote. She describes two women arriving at the San Francisco Conference and being asked by reporters "how it felt to be women delegates." The women responded by insisting, "We are *not* 'women delegates.' We are delegates of our country and ministers of our government" (Gildersleeve 1954, 349). Gildersleeve acknowledges that "I myself knew I had been appointed partly because I was a woman, an appointment urged by a committee representing women's organizations," but she distanced herself from the "militant feminists" who fought for separating women's rights out from human rights (Ibid., 352).[1]

Women were of two minds with regard to the inclusion of women's interests in the United Nations. One faction included Virginia Gildersleeve and her advisers, Dorothy Kenyon and Mary

---

[1] Gildersleeve uses the term "feminist" disparagingly to describe women who supported organizing separately from men. Gildersleeve snidely refers to Bertha Lutz, the generously proportionated delegate from Brazil, as "Lutzwaffe" and reports that "British and American men were bored and irritated by the repeated and lengthy feminist speeches" (Gildersleeve 1954, 352).

Anderson, who headed the Women's Bureau at the Department of Labor from 1920 to 1944. They opposed incorporating women's rights in the UN Charter and did not want the UN to separate women's issues from human rights. The delegates from England and Canada shared this view (Skard 2008). A second faction included the delegates from Europe, Asia, and Latin America. Bertha Lutz led the charge to incorporate women's rights into the Charter (Skard 2008). They were joined by five women's groups from the United States that had official consultative status at the San Francisco conference – the American Association of University Women, General Federation of Women's Clubs, National Federation of Business and Professional Women's Clubs, National League of Women Voters, and Women's Action Committee for Victory and Lasting Peace. These five organizations formed a coalition to press for the incorporation of women's concerns in the UN Charter.[2] The coalition focused its efforts on "the preamble, the working principles of the Organisation, participation in the organs of the United Nations and establishment of commissions under the Economic and Social Council" (Skard 2008, 39). Jessie Street, the Australian delegate, "distributed copies of telegrams from 1200 traders [businesses] and women's groups in Australia urging the conference to support equality of status for women and men" (Skard 2008, 47). Other organizations, such as the National Women's Party, the main advocate for an equal rights amendment in the United States also weighed in. The separatist faction persuaded the U.S. delegation to support the equality provision in the UN Charter, despite Gildersleeve's opposition. This faction also supported an amendment that would guarantee equal positions for men and women within the UN itself, a proposal that became Article 8 of the UN Charter: "The United Nations shall place no restrictions on the eligibility of men and women to participate in any capacity and under conditions of equality in its principal and subsidiary organs" (Skard 2008, 51). If it had been up to the American delegation, the UN

---

[2] Interestingly, this delegation included Equal Rights Amendment (ERA) proponents and opponents: the AAUW and the League of Women Voters opposed the ERA, whereas the GFWC and the BPW supported it, suggesting that the division between separatists and mainstreamers was limited to a small group of individuals. The AAUW and the National League of Women Voters both switched positions on the ERA in 1971 and 1972, respectively. I was unable to find out what position the Women's Action Committee held on the ERA.

Charter would not contain a sex equality provision in the preamble and would not guarantee equal employment opportunities for men and women within the UN itself. Foreign delegations proposed these initiatives and, together with a range of U.S. women's organizations, succeeded in getting them passed.

Gildersleeve's skepticism about separatist approaches to women's rights dovetailed with her male colleagues on the U.S. delegation who did not want the UN to address human rights at all. They worried that "international human rights law would develop in ways antithetical to U.S. conceptions of rights and that it would be used by the Soviet bloc in its ideological campaign against the United States" (Bradley 2010, 20). Southern Democrats fiercely opposed all human rights initiatives because they feared African Americans would use the UN to challenge racial discrimination in the United States. "A major part of the clout [Americans] were able to exert [on the UN Charter] came from Texas Senator Tom Connally, who chaired the Senate Foreign Relations Committee, and who had also been instrumental in scuttling three anti-lynching bills in Congress" (Anderson 2009, 8). To address these concerns, John Foster Dulles, an adviser to the U.S. delegation, inserted the "domestic jurisdiction" clause into the Charter, which essentially precluded the UN from having any substantive effect in the United States. His proposal became Article 2 (7) of the Charter: "Nothing contained in the present Charter shall authorize the United Nations to intervene in matters which are essentially within the domestic jurisdiction of any state or shall require the Members to submit such matters to settlement under the present Charter" (United Nations 1945). This clause sharply limited the effect that the UN could have on the domestic politics of UN member nations. The U.S. and Soviet delegations supported Dulles's proposal enthusiastically (Anderson 2003).

CREATION OF THE COMMISSION ON THE STATUS OF WOMEN

Delegates to the San Francisco Conference agreed that the UN would house five principal organs: the General Assembly, the Security Council, the International Court of Justice, the Secretariat, and the

Economic and Social Council.[3] The General Assembly is the legislative body of the UN, where representatives from each of the member states deliberate and vote on issues relevant to the UN Charter.[4] The Security Council, which is made up of five permanent and ten elected UN member states, is charged with maintaining international peace and security. The International Court of Justice adjudicates disputes among UN member countries. The Secretariat oversees the day-to-day operations of the UN.

The ECOSOC is the fifth of the main organs of the UN. Its mission is to generate reports and draft conventions on matters related to economics, culture, education, and health. During the San Francisco conference, advocates of women's rights proposed that a commission on the status of women be created within ECOSOC. Again, Brazilian delegate Bertha Lutz took the initiative by presenting a proposal that outlined an ambitious set of powers. It proposed that the new entity would have the power to conduct and commission research, mobilize support, provide training, and serve as a central "clearinghouse" for information on women. It directed members of the Commission to live near UN headquarters so they could mobilize quickly to address key issues as they arose. It called for the "drafting of an all-encompassing 'woman's charter' which, in their view, should be the primary goal of the new organ" (Reanda 1992, 266). Delegations from thirty-five of the fifty states present supported Lutz's proposal to create a stand-alone commission for women. "The Europeans and Latin American women argued that women needed a dedicated office at the UN because women's societal roles were different from men's and some of their interests were gender specific. This 'separatist' view ultimately prevailed" (Garner 2010, 142).

The U.S. delegation supported the general principle of gender equality and "any move designed to eliminate such discrimination and limitations as may still exist," but Gildersleeve opposed the proposal to create a CSW, "contending that women should be regarded as human beings as men were and that the Commission on Human

---

[3] A sixth organ, the Trusteeship Council, established to promote national independence, was disbanded in 1994. An organizational chart can be found at United Nations 2013a.

[4] The General Assembly meets from September to December each year, and each country has one vote. A plethora of subsidiary organs, including boards, commissions, committees, councils, panels, and working groups perform the work of generating and evaluating proposals for consideration by the General Assembly.

Rights would adequately care for their interests" (Gildersleeve 1954, 352). Gildersleeve feared that a separate commission would marginalize women's issues: "I am anxious that nothing should be done to isolate women, but I hope we shall rather insist on their being regarded as 'people,' as we have long tried to do in this country" (quoted in Laville 2008, 45). State Department officials in the Truman administration vigorously opposed having a CSW at all, let alone one with the power to compel states to take action.

Women in foreign delegations feared that U.S. opposition would derail their efforts to include equality measures in the UN Charter (Laville 2008). American women were well aware of their pariah status on the CSW question. The U.S. delegates to the San Francisco conference viewed a separate commission as something that women in other countries wanted. The Americans wanted to cooperate, but argued that a separate commission would not serve the interests of American women. In response to the call for creation of the CSW, Dorothy Kenyon recalled, "Leaders from other nations asked our help to achieve more for women everywhere and are critical of what they term our 'complacency'" (Dorothy Kenyon, September 19, 1945).

The conference delegates agreed to create a subcommission on the status of women. Efforts to raise its status to a full commission continued in the period leading up to the first meeting of the UN in 1946. American women's organizations and the State Department expended considerable energy on the question of the Commission. Under the leadership of Mary Anderson, women's organizations lobbied the State Department to oppose the creation of a separate commission. They expressed their views in a conference on the UN and Special Interests of Women held in Washington, DC, on September 19, 1945. Anderson sent a letter to all who participated in the Washington conference, urging them to endorse a set of recommendations. As Anderson's letter states,

While those present sympathized with the objectives sought by [the Brazilian] proposal, they believed that better work could be achieved by the selection of qualified persons regardless of sex. The [Washington] Conference agreed that in general the special interests of women would appropriately be considered by various organs and specialized agencies of the United Nations organization, but that initiative may be lacking on many problems where the traditional position of women limits their influence. The proposed consultative committee to the Economic and Social Council would have the responsibility of reviewing progress in relation to women and making necessary recommendations. It was recognized that the chief objection to this problem is likely to be the fear of precedent. This objection is based on the error of classifying women as a minority group, when instead their interests are both universal and of universal concern. (Dorothy Kenyon, September 12, 1945)

This statement betrays a view that women needed powerful allies – men – to promote women's concerns because they would be powerless on their own ("the traditional position of women limits their influence"). Anderson and her supporters believed that the Commission on Human Rights could and would address women's issues and obviated the need for a separate commission. They trusted that the main organs of the UN would address any concerns that women had. They did not want women to be treated or viewed as a minority group because minority groups lack power.

CSW opponents followed up by requesting a meeting with Undersecretary of State Dean Acheson to discuss plans for the proposed subcommission. On October 12, 1945, they met with Alger Hiss, then director of the Office of Special Political Affairs of the State Department, the division most directly responsible for the issue of women's interests in the UN.[5] The meeting included Dorothy Kenyon and Mary Anderson, Frieda Miller, and Rachel Conrad Mason from the Women's Bureau. Hiss expressed gratitude that American women's organizations had come forward to express their concerns, as he "had feared there would be no spontaneous effort to offset the Brazilian Declaration which he regarded as difficult." U.S. delegates argued that a separate CSW, comprised solely of women, would violate Article 8 of the UN Charter, which calls for equality between men and women on UN bodies:

[Hiss] was much interested in our suggestion that a consultative committee on women's interests need not be composed wholly of women. He agreed with our theory and thought it probable that article 8 of the charter would

---

[5] In 1950, Hiss would be convicted of perjury for statements relating to allegations that he was a Soviet spy. If Hiss did in fact perform espionage for the Soviet Union, as more recent sources suggest he did, it would be worth looking into his role as advisor on women's issues.

preclude discrimination against men as well as women. He thought, however, that the nature of the subject would make it unlikely that men would qualify and that it therefore would become a women's committee with all the dangers usually associated with a special approach to the women's problem. (Dorothy Kenyon, September 19, 1945)

By "dangers," Kenyon meant an equal rights approach to women's issues. Kenyon and her allies in the Women's Bureau wanted to limit the influence of American and foreign organizations that promoted the equal rights of women as separate from those of men (Dorothy Kenyon, March 29, 1946).

Department of State officials met with leaders of national women's organizations again in 1946 prior to the first meeting of the UN. Kenyon spoke on behalf of the women's organizations: "The group recommends that the program of the Sub-commission be one of fact-finding, dissemination of information, and formulation of standards." They explicitly opposed "a program of direct activity" for the subcommission: "Such a position, in the view of the group, would be exceedingly unfortunate. An educational, rather than a protagonistic approach, should be the goal." This group also advocated that "arrangements for according a consultative status" to NGOs "should proceed slowly" (Dorothy Kenyon, March 29, 1946). Ironically, this coalition of women's organizations sought to restrict NGO involvement with the CSW, at least initially:

The war and its aftermath have created a state of uncertainty regarding voluntary international organizations in this field [of women's issues].... Time for careful consideration of this general question, perhaps two years, would be desirable, both to ascertain major patterns in voluntary organizations and to protect the Economic and Social Council from being overwhelmed with a multitude of organizations. (Dorothy Kenyon, March 29, 1946)

Kenyon's aim was to limit the participation of organizations that opposed her views. In contrast to Brazilian delegate Bertha Lutz's ambitious vision for the CSW, Kenyon recommended that the organization's scope be limited to information gathering.

When the UN met for its first session in London in February 1946, support for women's rights was high. Eleanor Roosevelt and the other female delegates presented "An Open Letter to the Women of the World," a manifesto that framed women's demands for participation in the UN in terms of women's efforts during WWII, echoing claims for citizenship rights by African Americans justified in terms of soldiering. The letter acknowledged the various ways women participated in the war, on the side of the Allies as well as the Axis powers. The letter calls upon women "not to permit themselves to be misled by anti-democratic movements now or in the future," a specific reference to women's participation in the fascist movements that had precipitated the war (Roosevelt et al., February 12, 1946). Eleanor Roosevelt initially opposed the proposal for a separate women's commission, but eventually consented after a private conversation with Danish delegate Bodil Bergtrup (Skard 2008).

Australian delegate Jessie Street reintroduced the issue of the CSW. As a result of these efforts, the ECOSOC created a Sub-Commission on the Status of Women, under the Commission on Human Rights. A few months later Alice Paul introduced a proposal that would elevate the Sub-Commission to a full Commission. The ECOSOC acceded to this demand on June 21, 1946. The CSW finally established in 1946 had a far narrower mandate than its proponents initially envisioned and far less power than the Human Rights Commission, which was charged with setting standards and protecting minorities from discrimination. The CSW was granted the power to gather information, but the practice of requesting reports from member countries was not established until years later. Until then, it was decided that CSW "members themselves were best qualified to speak on the situation of women in their own countries" (Reanda 1992, 274).

THE WORK OF THE COMMISSION ON THE STATUS OF WOMEN, 1946–1970

Women who lived in occupied countries during the war held particularly high expectations about what the UN could accomplish and were anxious for the UN to get to work. They envisioned the UN, and the CSW, as a powerful institution that could effect real change. A representative from Uruguay proposed setting a deadline for granting political rights to women and recommended that countries that failed to comply "be expelled from the United Nations." Bernardino wanted members of the CSW to be selected on the basis of their independent expertise rather than as representatives of governments (*New York Times*, October 17, 1946). The General Assembly unanimously passed a resolution that "recommends that all Member States, which have not already done so, adopt measures necessary to fulfill the purposes and aims of the Charter in this respect by granting to women the same political rights as men" (UN General Assembly 1946). Prior to the CSW's first meeting, UN Secretary General Trygve Lie made a public statement, asking UN member countries to heed "the Assembly's recommendation that all nations that have not already done so, 'adopt measures necessary' to extend political privileges equally to men and women" (*New York Times*, January 16, 1947).

Prior to the CSW's first meeting, U.S. government officials set up an informal working group to articulate policy goals for the CSW. The group held its first meeting in Washington, DC, on Wednesday, November 27, 1946. It included seven officials from the State Department, two women from the Women's Bureau, a man from the Department of Justice, a woman from the Federal Security Agency, and Dorothy Kenyon, the U.S. delegate to the Commission. They sought to shape the agenda of the CSW by holding informal conversations with the staff in the UN Secretariat and by circulating proposals to CSW members prior to meetings. Anticipating that the majority of CSW members would prefer proposals that required concrete action, Kenyon proposed a compromise that involved "bring[ing] forth an active proposal to help women get the vote," an issue relevant to many other countries but moot in the United States. Kenyon and Frieda Miller, the director of the Women's Bureau, prepared four reports for consideration by the working group, written with the aim of directing the Commission agenda toward (1) studying the legal status of women; (2) training women for participation in citizenship and political affairs; (3) organizing exchange programs for women leaders; and (4) planning an international conference. They sought to focus the new commission on these issues rather than on proposals for substantive change in the status of women (Dorothy Kenyon, November 27, 1946).

American women were not the only ones who felt that a separate CSW marginalized women from mainstream human rights and thus constituted a form of discrimination. In his memoirs, John Humphrey, one of the drafters of the Universal Declaration of Human Rights, recalls the animosity that Canadian women expressed toward the CSW during a speech he delivered to the women's branch of the Canadian Institute of International Affairs in 1947. In his remarks, he suggested that his audience might want to hear about the Commission's work:

I was not a little embarrassed when, in the discussion that followed my talk, I was criticized for having dared to talk to them on that subject; the unanimous opinion of the women present was that it had been a mistake to set up a separate commission. I thought so too, because I felt very strongly that the status of women is a human rights question and that women are entitled to the same rights as men. (Humphrey 1984, 19)

These remarks provide a taste of the divisions over strategy that existing among advocates of women's issues. Those who supported the creation of the CSW believed that women's issues needed to addressed separately, while advocates of equal rights fervently believed that separating women's rights out from men's would doom the prospects for achieving equality.

The effort to create an international organization dedicated to the preservation of peace existed somewhat uncomfortably alongside growing mistrust between the United States and Soviet Union, the world's two dominant powers after the war. Taking the long view, cooperation between the United States and Soviet Union during and just after the war represented a brief cessation of tensions between them. By 1947, struggles between them had resurfaced and the Cold War began. The first meeting of the CSW took place that year, on February 25, at the UN's temporary headquarters, a remodeled airplane factory at Lake Success, about twenty-five miles east of Manhattan on Long Island. The meeting was open to the public, with 250 seats available to the general public and 250 seats reserved for members of "educational groups and accredited voluntary organizations" (*New York Times*, February 8, 1947).[6] On the first day of the meeting, the delegates immediately became embroiled in debate about the central mission of the CSW: whether to promote rights specific to women, or to focus on

---

[6] Poor weather kept attendance low, however. The women's commission was the only one of the six economic and social commissions that met despite a snowstorm that hit Long Island, prompting Kenyon to make what she herself called a "wholly inappropriate remark." The *New York Times* reported that Kenyon "wanted the record to show that 'on the day of the great tempest the Security Council decided to stay at home but the Commission on the Status of Women decided to meet as usual'" (*New York Times*, February 27, 1947).

equal rights between men and women. The representative from India, Mrs. Hamid Ali, criticized the focus on equal rights as inappropriate in the developing world. She maintained that equal rights are insufficient in "countries where men enjoy negligible rights. The idea is rather to guarantee real rights" for women (*New York Times*, February 12, 1947). This view dovetailed, unintentionally, with the U.S. insistence that women's rights should not be considered apart from men's rights. Dorothy Kenyon concurred with Mrs. Ali: "What we want, [Kenyon] added, is that women shall receive human rights and privileges in a free world," not equal rights with men (Ibid.)

During this first session, the delegates initially voted to extend consultative status to all the international organizations that had requested it. In a subsequent vote, the delegates voted to rescind consultative status for one of those organizations, the Women's International Democratic Federation (WIDF), a peace organization that had been founded in 1945, on the grounds that it was a Communist front. The *New York Times* reported that U.S. delegate Dorothy Kenyon "hotly condemned as 'utter folly'" the proposal to give consultative status to the organization (February 20, 1947). Delegates from the Soviet Union, White Russia, and Australia supported the WIDF. At the end of a "long and sometimes heated argument," the Commission voted to forward all future requests for consultative status to the Economic and Social Council. Thus, in response to a political disagreement, the delegates voted to reduce the CSW's power by giving away the authority to grant consultative status.

Many criticized the CSW's inaugural efforts as unimpressive. The *New York Times* reported that "the chief accomplishment of this session was a resolution calling on the Economic and Social Council to urge each member of the United Nations to fill out a questionnaire on the political rights of women and a request to the Secretariat to act as a clearing house for information on this subject." These actions prompted the British delegate Mary Sutherland to criticize the Commission's work as "disappointing" (*New York Times* February 25, 1947). Sutherland's British counterpart to the Economic and Social Council condemned the CSW as "superfluous" (*New York Times*, March 20, 1947). At a meeting of the International Council of Women in Philadelphia later that year, a Swedish delegate criticized the Commission for being sluggish: "I cannot understand ... that year-long investigations should be necessary to state, for example, that women must have the same right to vote as men," stated M. Stael Von Holstein (*New York Times*, September 9, 1947, p. 41). These reports suggest that the Truman administration had succeeded in its effort to keep the CSW weak. Cold War divisions would continue to hamper the work of the CSW for several decades.

Regardless of American efforts to impede the work of the CSW, it made many contributions in its first few decades. CSW delegates advised the Commission on Human Rights on women's issues, persuaded the drafters of the Universal Declaration of Human Rights to use female pronouns as well as male, conducted studies on the status of women, and worked in conjunction with other UN agencies to raise awareness of women's issues. The Commission's most enduring contribution to the global architecture of women's rights was the drafting of two international conventions on women's rights: The Convention on the Political Rights of Women, approved by the General Assembly on December 20, 1952, and the Convention on the Nationality of Married Women, approved on January 29, 1957. The agreements were the first to address women's rights in international law.[7]

Delegates proposed both of these conventions during the CSW's third session, held in Beirut, Lebanon, in 1949. The issue of nationality was an important topic in the wake of World War II, which had displaced millions of people as refugees. Janet Robb stated the problem concisely in a report she wrote for the American Association of University Women: "In unsettled times it is no trivial matter to find oneself stateless" (Robb, October 20, 1951). The status of women refugees was doubly problematic because laws in many countries required a woman to assume the nationality of her husband upon marriage. At that time, seventeen countries required women to accept their husband's nationality and forty countries permitted women to choose which nationality they preferred. The Universal Declaration of Human Rights established that all people have the right "to a nationality" and that all people of age have the right "to marry and found a family," but did not address the status of married women. Would a woman lose her citizenship status if she married a noncitizen? What happens to a woman if her husband changes his citizenship status? Dorothy Kenyon

---

[7] The CSW drafted a third convention, the Convention on Consent to Marriage, Minimum Age for Marriage, and Registration of Marriages, that is beyond the scope of this research.

proposed that the CSW draft a convention to address these questions. She had first encountered the issue when she wrote a report on the issue for the League of Nations in 1938. Her main concern was that "no distinction be made on the basis of sex and that neither marriage nor its dissolution should affect the nationality of either party" (quoted in Robb, October 20, 1961).

The nationality question provoked particular tensions between the U.S. and Soviet delegates. When Kenyon presented the idea for proposal for a convention, she made a public statement about the status of Russians married to U.S. citizens who were not permitted leave Russia. Soviet delegate Elizavieta A. Popova responded by launching into "a long and bitter attack" on racial discrimination in the United States, noting that "fifteen states of the United States prohibited mixed marriages between Negroes and whites, that five prohibited marriages with Malays and five with Indians" (*New York Times*, March 26, 1949). Popova demanded to know "where the principle of women's freedom of choice existed in the United States," freedom of choice over nationality being a key principle in the proposed convention (Ibid.) Popova and Kenyon blamed each other for obstructing the work of the Commission. Popova complained, "This is not a matter for the CSW. Our problem is discrimination against women. Why was this problem brought to our attention at all?" (*New York Times*, March 26, 1949). Kenyon, in response, "pleaded that the commission be permitted to get on with its work" (*New York Times*, March 26, 1949, p. 5).

Mexican delegate Amalia Castillo de Ledon also introduced a proposal to draft a convention on the political rights of women during the 1949 session. Dorothy Kenyon initially opposed the proposal, claiming that the CSW already had a full agenda and had already agreed to draft a convention on the nationality of married women. Kenyon's stance drew public ire within the United States. It prompted none other than Katharine Hepburn, the actress, to write a letter to the editor of the *New York Times*. Hepburn, along with Florence L. C. Kitchelt and Alma Lutz, leaders of the National Women's Party and advocates of the ERA, accused Kenyon of opposing women's equality: "Miss Kenyon seldom speaks without belittling the word 'equality'" (*New York Times*, March 31, 1949). Kenyon defended her position in a letter of her own in which she said she had voted in favor of the CPRW, but considered it to be a futile effort because eight of the twelve countries that did not yet allow women the right to vote were not even members of the UN (*New York Times*, April 15, 1949). A month later, in May 1949, the 300 delegates representing 24 organizations of the New Jersey Federation of Business and Professional Women's Clubs voted to issue a complaint to the State Department about Kenyon's actions. They opposed Kenyon on the grounds that she "has shown opposition to equal rights for women" (*New York Times*, May 24, 1949). Zelia Rubhausen, a UN observer and member of the League of Women Voters, wrote a letter to the editor defending Kenyon:

I was shocked to read ... of the charge ... that she did not support women's rights ... she is a champion of women's rights, as the record clearly shows. Not only did she vote for but she initiated resolutions asking for greater participation of women in the UN Secretariat, equal pay for equal work, married women's property rights and political equality for women in voting. (*New York Times*, May 28, 1949)

The *New York Times* published an editorial calling for Kenyon to be reappointed to the CSW (December 12, 1949), but President Truman appointed Mrs. Olive Remington Goldman, a Democratic Party leader from Illinois, for the next term instead (*New York Times*, January 11, 1950).

Despite Kenyon's spirited defense of the United States against the Soviet Union, she was the very first victim of Senator Joseph R. McCarthy's redbaiting attacks. McCarthy charged that Kenyon had been affiliated with at least twenty-eight Communist-front organizations. She was the first witness he called to testify before the Senate Committee on Foreign Relations in March 1950. Numerous organizations and newspapers rushed to defend Kenyon. In an editorial titled "A Poor Beginning," the *New York Times* condemned McCarthy's decision to call Kenyon to the stand as a "feeble start." Kenyon mounted a fearless response to McCarthy, calling him "an unmitigated liar." She remarked that "Senator McCarthy comes from Wisconsin, sometimes called the state of great winds ... He is a wonderful example" (*New York Times*, March 9, 1950). She affirmed that her record on the CSW demonstrated her antipathy for the Soviet Union: "Just ask Mme. [Elizavieta A.] Popova, the Soviet delegate on the commission, whether she thinks I am pro-Communist," she said. "She and I battled for years on that commission and I told her repeatedly that the equality she claims exists in Russia is nothing better than the equality of slavery" (*New York Times*, March 9, 1950).

As the CSW began to draft the two treaties, groups within the United States moved against human rights treaties altogether. When Seattle-based lawyer Frank Holman became president of the American Bar Association in 1948, he used his new position to raise concerns that treaties such as the Genocide Convention would trump the U.S. Constitution, thus potentially subjecting the United States to standards imposed by the Soviet Union and other countries. Conservative Republicans latched onto fears about treaty law in the context of growing concerns about the spread of communism. Republican Senator John W. Bricker embarked on a series of efforts to pass a constitutional amendment prohibiting the United States from ratifying human rights treaties. On July 17, 1951, Senator Bricker introduced a bill that would have required the president to denounce all human rights treaties and to pull the United States out of the drafting process for them. On September 14, 1951, Senator Bricker introduced a constitutional amendment to this effect, but the bill died in committee. On February 7, 1952, Bricker introduced another constitutional amendment; this bill got fifty-two co-sponsors – including all but one Republican senator. The Senate Judiciary Committee held hearings on the proposal and voted the bill out of committee, but the Senate adjourned without taking a floor vote. Bricker introduced a third bill on January 7, 1953, with sixty-two co-sponsors. Bricker's actions put newly elected President Dwight Eisenhower into a difficult situation: Eisenhower opposed the amendment on the grounds that it would limit executive power to sign treaties, but he did not want to come out against a bill that so many of his co-partisans supported immediately upon taking office, which he did just a few weeks later. Eisenhower responded by affirming his opposition to human rights treaties and denouncing Bricker's proposal. The Senate voted fifty-two for and forty against the third Bricker measure, well shy of the two-thirds vote required for a constitutional amendment. To maintain unity within his party, President Eisenhower made a public vow not to ratify any human rights treaties.[8] Ratification of human rights treaties remained off the agenda until President John F. Kennedy took office in 1961.

[8] The persistence of the legal arguments that Senator Bricker and the American Bar Association first made in the 1950s has led some to attribute causal power to the senator that extends far beyond his death, leading some scholars to blame low rates of treaty ratification to the "ghost of Senator Bricker" (Henkin 1995).

In the context of "Brickeritis," we should expect to see the U.S. delegates to the CSW take actions to obstruct efforts to draft the conventions on married women and political rights, which is exactly what happened. When the CSW completed a revised draft of the Convention on the Nationality of Married Women, some members of the CSW recommended that it be sent to governments for their comments. The Belgian delegate proposed that it be sent to the International Law Committee instead. John Humphrey recalled this incident in his memoirs,

I suspected that the Americans, who with the Belgians moved a resolution to that end (and who didn't want this or any other convention on human rights) thought that this would be a good way to bury it. But the women, who wanted to retain some control over the text and to have the convention adopted quickly, were able to defeat the stratagem; and, although the draft was sent to the law commission for information, it was also sent to governments for their comments, which were studied by the commission at its next session. (Humphrey 1984, 193)

The Americans were not the only ones responsible for slowing down the process of drafting the treaty. Humphrey characterized the politicization of women's issues as "typical." When the General Assembly debated the Convention on the Nationality of Married Women, "The most hotly debated issue related, not to the substance of the instrument itself, on which there was general agreement, but to a Byelorussian amendment, the purpose of which was to open it for signature by 'any state,' and not merely the restricted category devised to ostracize mainland China" (Humphrey 1984, 229). The General Assembly passed the Convention on the Nationality of Married Women and it entered into force on August 11, 1958. The convention essentially gives women full control and decision-making power over their own nationality, and requires "specially privileged nationalization procedures" for wives of nationals. Seventy-four countries have ratified it since then – the most recent being Montenegro, on October 23, 2006.

Similar issues emerged with the Convention on the Political Rights of Women (CPRW). Concerns with equal opportunities *and* equal outcomes motivated the drafting of the CPRW. In 1950, the UN Secretary General drew attention to the fact that equal rights for women were not always put into practice. Nonetheless, the Convention provides only for equality of opportunities. In 1952, at its sixth session, the CSW approved a draft convention on women's political rights. Delegates from the Soviet Union, Poland, and Byelorussia abstained from the final vote in opposition to the Commission's failure to prohibit "discrimination against women on the grounds of 'race, color, nationality, birth, property status, language or religion'" (*New York Times*, March 28, 1952). The other commission delegates hailed the Convention as an "important milestone" (*New York Times*, March 28, 1952). Nonetheless, at the time the Commission passed the resolution, women had already won the right to vote in fifty-six countries of the UN, with only twenty remaining in which women did not yet enjoy that right. During consideration by the General Assembly, the Soviet delegate again proposed an amendment that would add the text "without discrimination on the grounds of race, colour, national or social origins, property status, language or religion." He proposed that Article 2 be amended by adding the words "state and public" before the word "bodies," and by adding the words "both central and local" after that. The Soviet delegate also proposed inserting an article that would require states parties to the Convention to take "all necessary measures, including legislative measures," to ensure for all women "the genuine possibility of exercising the rights" established in the Convention.[9] Other delegates opposed these changes on the grounds that ratification implied a country would take measures to comply and they were not approved.

The General Assembly adopted the Convention on December 20, 1952. It opened for signatures the following year, on December 22, 1953. The CPRW includes three substantive articles:

Article I. Women shall be entitled to vote in all elections on equal terms with men, without any discrimination.

Article II. Women shall be eligible for election to all publicly elected bodies, established by national law, on equal terms with men, without any discrimination.

Article III: Women shall be entitled to hold public office and to exercise all public functions, established by national law, on equal terms with men, without any discrimination.

[9] The term "states parties" is a technical term that refers to countries that have ratified or agree to adhere to a particular treaty or international agreement.

In 1953, the Commission passed a resolution urging states to ratify the CPRW, hoping to persuade others to join the eighteen countries that had already ratified it. Eleanor Roosevelt indicated that she expected that the Truman administration "would sign [it], although with certain minor reservations" (*New York Times*, February 25, 1953). But the United States did not ratify, due to "the feeling … that Washington is holding off to clarify its attitude toward all conventions that involve international obligations," a reference to the Bricker Amendment then pending in Congress (*New York Times*, April 4, 1953). The *Times* commended adoption of the CPRW in an editorial that lauded it as "an historic event" and reported that "the struggle for women's rights has almost been won; the struggle for equal opportunity and responsibility is at hand" (*New York Times*, April 5, 1953). The editorial further noted:

The United States has not yet signed the Convention. Though we have nothing to gain by doing so, since American women have achieved equality with men, we have much to lose by not signing. The fact that we have not approved this document and that the Soviet Union and its satellites have (though with reservations) makes it more difficult for us to defend our claim to championship of democracy.

In other words, ratification of the CPRW was critical for the United States not because American women lacked rights, but in order to maintain global leadership in the context of competition with the USSR. This rhetoric would become a mainstay of debates about ratification of CEDAW in the 2000s.

DEDAW, PRECURSOR TO CEDAW

The new countries that joined the UN in the 1960s proved to be a powerful constituency in support of ending racial discrimination. Participants at the Non-Aligned Movement's first conference in Belgrade in 1961 viewed racial discrimination as their highest human rights priority. The UN Sub-Commission on Prevention of Discrimination and Protection of Minorities drafted the CERD in 1963. Universal condemnation of racial discrimination in the developing world helped CERD move quickly through the UN system: the General Assembly approved it unanimously two years later, in 1965.

Progress on women's issues lagged behind progress on racial issues. In 1962, the General Assembly passed a resolution inviting a range of UN agencies "to strengthen and expand their programmes designed to meet the needs of women in developing countries and seek new methods to achieve this purpose" and to "study ... the possibility of providing and developing new resources aimed especially at the initiation and implementation of a unified long-term United Nations programme for the advancement of women" (UN General Assembly 1962). In July 1963, all but nine UN member countries had extended formal political rights to women – but the percentage of women who held political office remained close to zero nearly everywhere. In an effort to close the gap between de jure and de facto political equality, the CSW had repeatedly requested that the General Assembly and the Secretary General urge member-states to provide biannual reports on the numbers of women appointed to government positions and elected to parliament. Increasingly urgent entreaties by the CSW to the General Assembly over the years suggest that their requests for reporting went largely unheeded.

The speedy success of CERD created momentum and inspired delegates on the CSW to follow suit. Delegates from the USSR, Hungary and Poland proposed that the CSW draft a declaration on the status of women that would be modeled on CERD. In November 1963, the General Assembly responded to this pressure by formally charging the CSW with drafting a Declaration on the Elimination of Discrimination against Women (DEDAW).

The Commission devoted two sessions over two years to drafting the Declaration. The main point of contention during these two sessions concerned its scope. CSW delegates divided into two camps: those who wanted the Declaration to obligate states to take action to address discrimination against women, and those who envisioned the Declaration as a general statement of support. Delegates from the socialist countries sought to have the Declaration, like CERD, require governments to take action to advance women's rights. The Polish delegate, Mrs. Dembinska, submitted a draft of the Declaration that reflected this goal. She remarked that existing conventions on various aspects of women's rights "had been signed and ratified by relatively few countries," a "situation [that] showed that women needed a new instrument to help them to encourage signatures and ratifications of existing instruments" (UN Commission on the Status of Women 1965, 12). Delegates from Soviet Bloc countries also used the deliberation process to highlight the advanced status of women in socialist countries and envisioned DEDAW as providing a model for other countries to follow. Mrs. Mironova, the delegate from the USSR, energetically broadcast the high level of equality that women had achieved in the Soviet Union, affirming that "her own country had ratified the Convention [on the Political Rights of Women] immediately it has been adopted [sic] in 1952, and was consistently applying all the principles set forth in it" (UN Commission on the Status of Women 1965, 12).[10]

Mrs. McKay, the delegate from the United Kingdom, proposed a second draft that sought to articulate general principles of women's rights and prioritized women's political and legal rights. As McKay asserted, the Declaration "was not a convention, recommendation or resolution. The purpose of a Declaration was to establish principles, not to impose legal obligations, but the Polish draft seemed to follow the latter course" (UN Commission on the Status of Women 1965, 13). Mrs. McKay modeled her draft of DEDAW on the Universal Declaration of Human Rights rather than on the Declaration on the Elimination of Racial Discrimination (UN Commission on the Status of Women 1965, 13). The first article of the UK draft emphasized political rights and affirmed that "all women have the right to vote in elections, to be eligible for election in publicly elected bodies, to hold public office and to exercise all public functions on equal terms with men" (UN Commission on the Status of Women 1965, 8–9). Gladys Tillett, the U.S. representative, supported this version on the grounds that "political rights ensured the preservation of all other rights" (UN Commission on the Status of Women 1965, 11). Tillett had served as assistant chair of the Democratic National Committee from 1940 to

---

[10] Mironova inundated the committee with figures documenting the vast magnitude of women's participation in political life in the USSR: 390 delegates to the Supreme Soviet, 27 percent of the total representing 49 different nationalities of the Soviet Union, 23 percent of all magistrates and officials in the office of the Public Prosecutor, and a thirty-four-fold increase in the number of women employed as "experts and specialists in various branches of the national economy." She finished with the mention of Soviet astronaut Valentina Tereshkova, "who circled the world 48 times in the spaceship Vostock" (UN Commission on the Status of Women 1965, 8–9).

1950, a position that was at the time the highest rank any woman had achieved in the party (*New York Times*, October 3, 1984).

Once the two versions were resolved, the General Assembly distributed a draft version of the declaration to UN member countries for comment, and made it clear it would not consider a resolution until the CSW reviewed all the suggestions made by states' parties. Thirty countries responded, most with brief statements that suggest a shallow level of engagement with the topic. Many of the statements took up less than a page; China and Cambodia offered a single paragraph. Hungary and Romania provided the most extensive comments, with five pages of specific alternative provisions and suggestions for amendments. Nearly all of the statements affirm their commitment to the draft declaration on the basis of their participation in existing treaties or the degree to which their domestic laws already adhered to basic principles of equality. Argentina's remarks, for example, stressed that its existing legal protections for women in the areas of health, maternity, dismissal because of marriage, economic exploitation, and equality in private and family law made an international declaration unnecessary. The statement from the USSR highlighted the importance of the declaration for other countries. None of the governments that responded expressed any opposition to the declaration (United Nations October 30, 1964).

Support for affirmative action measures came from a surprising constituency: secular leaders of Muslim countries. The Royal Government of Afghanistan offered five comments. One item reads: "It should be specifically stated that it is not enough to establish equality between men and women and to grant them equal opportunities. Amends must be made to women by granting them certain privileges. (A higher wage rate. A higher and compulsory percentage in regard to their appointment or election to various posts.)" (United Nations October 30, 1964, 4). Arvonne Fraser, who would become a leading CEDAW advocate, later interpreted this statement as "anticipating the idea of affirmative action" that appeared in CEDAW (Fraser 1995, 80). A statement from Iraq also stressed the need for de facto equality: "Although often discrimination does not exist by law, it is in fact applied and practised. Such de facto discrimination against women is often accepted and believed in by both men and women. Tradition and ignorance are at the roots of such beliefs" (United

Nations, October 30, 1964, x). The comment by the Afghan government resonated with growing support for the idea that legal equality had to be accompanied by real, substantive equality. Mrs. Hussein, a CSW member from United Arab Republic, recalled the remark by Afghan government that "amends had to be made to women by granting them certain privileges" and further noted that the Government of Iraq "laid stress on the need for education in the matter so that de facto discrimination, as opposed to legal discrimination, might be eliminated" (UN Commission on the Status of Women 1965, 12). The CSW forwarded a revised draft to the General Assembly in 1967, where UN delegates introduced sixty-six additional amendments to the text, eleven of which were adopted. The Assembly finally voted to adopt the Declaration on November 7, 1967.

The preamble to DEDAW affirms the UN's limitations to date in addressing women's rights:

Despite the Charter of the United Nations, the Universal Declaration of Human Rights, the International Covenants on Human Rights and other instruments of the United Nations and the specialized agencies, and despite the progress made in the matter of equality of rights, there continues to exist considerable discrimination against women. (UN General Assembly 1967)

Following CERD, DEDAW frames gender equality in terms of discrimination, rather than rights. Article 4 incorporates the three main provisions of the CPRW: the right to vote and be eligible for elections, the right to vote in all public referenda, and the right "to hold public office and to exercise all public functions." Article 5 reprises women's equal rights to "acquire, change or retain their nationality," as stipulated by the Nationality Convention. The Declaration incorporates measures already guaranteed in other documents ("political and nationality rights, freedom of choice in marriage, equal rights in education and employment, traffic in women") and includes some new rights as well, such as "the abolition of discriminatory customs and practices as well as laws and regulations, equal rights in marriage and discrimination in penal law" (Reanda 1992, 285). It guarantees equal rights "in the field of economic and social life," including "equal remuneration with men and to equality of treatment in respect of work of equal value." DEDAW stopped short of calling for positive action measures, despite expressions of support from developing countries that sought redress for "inherited laws, traditions and customs that stood against women's advancement" (UN General Assembly 1967). The committee that drafted it considered including affirmative action measures, but ultimately decided to make the Declaration a general statement of principles, rather than a treaty that required governments to take action. DEDAW articulated a legal framework for women's rights, and did not require signatories to take action. As a result, "the level of response from Governments was low" (United Nations 2007, 7). Among the countries that signed DEDAW, few adhered to the reporting requirements. The CSW never adopted a coherent system of review of the reports it did receive (Reanda 1992).

CONCLUSION

American delegates who helped draft the Charter at the San Francisco Conference in 1945 opposed the inclusion of women's rights in the UN Charter and argued strenuously against the creation of a separate CSW within the UN. These measures passed nonetheless because the U.S. delegation could not sway delegates from other countries and did not have the votes to impose its agenda. American efforts to prevent the UN from devoting resources to women's rights did not end at the San Francisco conference, however. Unable to thwart the creation of a stand-alone CSW, the U.S. government sought to ensure that the new organization would be ineffectual in promoting substantive change in the status of women in UN member countries, particularly not within the United States. For the next several decades, U.S. delegates to the Commission did what they could to make sure that the organization would have only nominal power. The reasons behind such a stance can be traced to divisions within women's movements in the United States, as well as U.S. concerns about rising Soviet influence and UN interference in domestic matters.

The limited success of the CSW can be explained in part as a consequence of U.S. obstructionism, which was motivated by a desire to limit the power of the UN overall in the context of the Cold War. The U.S. government consistently sought to prevent the Commission from exercising real power to improve the status of women, or to demand that states take action to achieve it. Faced with ideological competition from the Soviet Union, the United States wanted the CSW to limit itself to studying the status of women and drafting non-binding declarations of commitment to women's rights that required no action on behalf of UN member nations. Despite these constraints, the CSW erected a series of international agreements that would form the institutional scaffolding for future advances in women's rights.

3

Geopolitics and Drafting the UN Treaty on Women's Rights

Despite interference due to Cold War struggles between the superpowers, the CSW quietly passed a series of limited measures that laid the groundwork for future progress on women's rights. Conflicts between the United States and the USSR limited the CSW's ability to require UN members to take decisive action on women's rights. As Chapter 2 illustrates, U.S. and Soviet delegates used the CSW to broadcast the superiority of their progress on women's issues as well as their opposition to each other. Communist bloc countries wanted the CSW to adopt policies that required UN member states to take concrete action, whereas the United States and its allies envisioned the CSW as a source of general affirmations of support for women's civil and political rights.

In the early 1970s, however, the UN abandoned its obstructionist stance. It suddenly changed course and took the lead on two major UN initiatives for women – the IWY conference and the drafting of CEDAW. Changes in the balance of power within the UN made this change possible. The emergence of the developing world as a majority-voting bloc within the UN led to the increasing marginalization of the United States and the USSR within the UN. The U.S. government under the Nixon, Ford, and Carter administrations looked to human rights, and women's rights in particular, as a way to reassert declining U.S. power within the UN. These efforts did not immediately succeed in restoring American status within the UN; the United States would face humiliating diplomatic defeats at the World Conferences on Women in Mexico City in 1975 and Copenhagen in 1980. Nonetheless,

U.S. support for these conferences proved crucial for getting CEDAW off the ground.

As the power of third world countries within the UN grew, so did UN attention to the issues that most concerned the developing world. Social issues came to overtake security concerns as the power of third world countries within the UN increased, as Daniel Patrick Moynihan describes in *A Dangerous Place*, a memoir of his time in the UN:

> The huge irony, of course, is that just as the United Nations was being thus written off [by U.S. presidents], its "social, humanitarian, and cultural" committee came to be of enormous moment to its new members, now categorized as the Third World. At issue was nothing less than the legitimacy of Western political systems and democratic beliefs that the U.N. Charter embodied. This is to say, the low politics of the U.N. became the highest, most consequential politics of all. (Moynihan and Weaver 1978, 11)

In the 1970s, the UN began to hold global conferences on development-related themes, starting with the Environment Conference in Stockholm in 1972. These conferences were massive, chaotic affairs. They typically included two components: an official meeting attended by representatives from UN-member governments, UN agencies, and accredited international NGOs, and a parallel "forum" open to nonaccredited NGOs and anyone else who wanted to attend. The UN conferences embodied the "low politics" that Moynihan is talking about. The attendance of thousands of people at these conferences helped shift the UN agenda away from security concerns and toward issues such as poverty, food security, and population growth. Connections between these social issues and the status of women were not immediately obvious to many UN delegations, in no small part because so few women sat on the official delegations of their countries or participated in making high-level policy decisions. Activists in feminist movements in the United States and around the world began to challenge the exclusion of women, link those concerns to women's everyday experiences, and demand that women's issues be placed on government agendas. In this chapter we see how geopolitical context and relations among women's groups shaped the global women's rights agenda. Prior to the 1970s, the United States sought to limit the scope of UN agencies. The U.S. perspective changed as it embraced support for women's rights as a way to reassert its dealing power with the UN. Within the United States, the feminist movement enjoyed support from the Democratic and Republican parties alike until the end of the 1970s.

The account of U.S. interests in this chapter relies on primary accounts of these events drawn from diplomatic cables between the Secretary of State, U.S. ambassadors, and U.S. representatives to the UN. Records from the annual sessions of the CSW and the General Assembly, as well as in-person interviews, provide evidence of the drafting process for CEDAW.

THE DECLINE OF U.S. AUTHORITY WITHIN THE UN

In the 1970s, major shifts occurred in the global balance of power. The United States and the Soviet Union entered a period of détente and engaged in negotiations to limit the production of nuclear weapons, known as the Strategic Arms Limitation Talks. President Nixon opened relations with China with his historic visit in 1972. At the same time, the United States suffered from declining prestige in the world community as a result of international condemnation of the Vietnam War, the role of the Central Intelligence Agency (CIA) in the military coup in Chile in 1973, and the Watergate scandal. Détente produced a shift in the international balance of power, which in turn created an opportunity to break the Cold War stalemate on women's rights.

The thaw in relations between the two superpowers provided developing nations with a chance to assert their power in the international arena. First world countries had always been in the minority within the UN, but their voting power diminished year by year as new countries joined. In 1960 alone, seventeen new countries, formed as the result of wars of national liberation and independence, became members of the UN (Jackson 1983). Cold War struggles between the United States and Soviet Union prompted poorer, third world countries to organize on the basis of their shared identity as developing nations. In 1955, leaders of former colonies in Africa and Asia formed the Non-Aligned Movement. Led by Jawaharlal Nehru in India, Sukarno in Indonesia, and Gamal Abdel Nasser in Egypt, the Non-Aligned Movement sought to prevent developing countries from "becoming pawns in the struggles between the major powers" (Non-Aligned Movement 2001).

Within the UN, developing countries formed the Group of 77 in the hope of creating a wedge between the two superpowers.

The UN became a venue in which the third world countries could express opposition – and, often, hostility – toward the United States and (to a lesser extent) USSR. The China question graphically illustrated the decline of U.S. influence in the UN. At the end of World War II, the Kuomintang (KMT) or Nationalist Party controlled the government of mainland China and the island of Taiwan. When the Communist Party defeated the KMT in 1949, it declared the mainland as the People's Republic of China, but the KMT persisted in considering itself the legitimate government of China. During the Cold War, the world divided between those who recognized communist China and those who recognized Taiwan. Communist critics and the third world bloc had sought for decades to install communist China as the legitimate holder of China's seat at the UN (in the General Assembly and the Security Council), a move the United States opposed. On October 25, 1971, after years of failing to reach the two-thirds majority required to admit a new member, the General Assembly garnered enough support to eject the Taiwanese delegate and replace him with a representative of communist China.[1] When the Chinese delegation took the seat vacated by Taiwan, UN delegates erupted in celebration on the floor of the General Assembly. George H. W. Bush, then permanent representative of the United States to the UN, physically embodied U.S. dismay. Bush "sullenly watched assembly delegates literally dancing in the aisles in a circuslike anti-American demonstration" (Ostrower 1998, 131). The *New York Times* reported that "the United States had suffered a crushing defeat" and Bush himself "suffered a humiliating rebuff" (October 31, 1971). As historian Jocelyn Olcott describes this phenomenon, "Waves of decolonization had transformed the UN – and particularly the Economic and Social Council (ECOSOC) ... into a supranational advocate for postcolonial nations" (Olcott 2010, 282). The decline of U.S. power within the UN led to "a waning interest in the UN among the American public and Congress" (*New York Times*, January 27, 1972, p. 16).

The NAM's ability to control a majority of votes within the UN reached its height from 1973 to 1976, when the NAM countries voted

---

[1] Votes on matters that the General Assembly deems "important" require a two-thirds majority, whereas only a simple majority is required for other issues.

as a bloc. American delegates to the UN faced uniform resistance to their proposals: "U.S. diplomats, lobbying among delegates for support on key votes during the 1973 General Assembly session, were for the first time rebuffed with the explanation that states could not vote against consensus positions" that the NAM countries had reached at their 1973 conference in Algiers (Jackson 1983, 28). The Algerian delegation adopted the role of "whip," and the influence of Algerian Foreign Minister Adelaziz Bouteflika during his tenure as president of the General Assembly in 1974 helped keep the NAM countries in line (Jackson 1983). As a result, the non-aligned countries could basically impose their agenda on the General Assembly.

U.S. diplomats expressed a growing sense of concern about the increasing isolation of the United States within the UN. Although the UN wielded little power in terms of resources or influence, it had become the one international forum in which third world countries could unleash their enmity against the United States. In a diplomatic cable dated January 17, 1973, UN Representative Bush provided his annual assessment of U.S. performance in the UN. As Bush put it, the other delegations "recognized that we [were] seriously disappointed by lack of progress in difficult areas such as Middle East and African questions, [and] on terrorism but do not see US as having been humiliated" (United States 1973a). Bush attempted to put a positive spin on the situation – but his words unwittingly underscore the very limited nature of those successes.

U.S. officials continued to express concern about the power that developing countries exerted within the UN. In a cable dated December 26, 1973, the U.S. mission to the UN alerted the Department of State about a "marked intensification of [a] long-term trend towards greater coordination of non-aligned blocs' efforts within UN" (United States 1973a). The memo highlighted a disturbing movement toward greater unity among the developing countries, directed against the United States: "What is new and potentially alarming is the degree of mutual, unqualified, and generally effective support each group is giving the other" across a range of policy issues; non-aligned countries have a majority of votes and can "dominate" or "paralyze" the UN if they wish (United States 1973a). The same memo noted that coalescence among the non-aligned countries tended to benefit the Soviet bloc, with some notable exceptions. The language of the memo conveys a tone of contempt toward the USSR characteristic of the era: even though Soviets "often go at it with stomach-turning obsequiousness it is by no means inevitable that Soviets will always benefit" from the actions of the non-aligned nations (United States 1973a).

U.S. concerns grew over the coming year. A U.S. intelligence report from January 1974 provides an overview of the situation within the UN. The report notes that:

Deeply ingrained feelings about having been wronged, combined with a sharply honed sense of practical politics, thus have contributed to the emergence at the UN of a group of non-aligned states which embraces most of the existing African, Arab, and Asian members and about half of the Latin American nations ... The cumulative effect of such confrontations raises the specter of growing US isolation in the UN unless enough progress is made on these issues to satisfy the needs of an increasing number among the non-aligned. (United States 1974a)

A memo from the CIA considered the 1974 UN General Assembly to be a foreign policy disaster for the United States: "By the close of the ten-week session, Yasser Arafat had addressed the Assembly, Israel had been muzzled in open debate, South Africa had been suspended, and expropriation of foreign investments had been sanctified. LDCs [less-developed countries] achieved each of these victories by applying their two-thirds majority with considerable efficiency and little restraint" (United States 1975b).

These memos convey a growing sense of urgency about the status of the United States within the UN. The Nixon administration responded to the situation by initiating a proposal to limit U.S. financial contributions to the UN. Diplomatic cables to the U.S. Mission to the UN suggest that Secretary of State Henry Kissinger intended to address the problem of declining U.S. prestige by providing more foreign aid to individual countries in the hopes of pacifying the G-77. Kissinger initially recommended a "soft" course of action in response to this situation in the UN, expanding U.S. foreign aid "on peacekeeping, food security, development and science and technology" (United States 1973b). In addition, Kissinger suggested "we should seek to develop additional initiatives in such fields as human rights and disarmament, where there are prospects for moves which would be both substantively and cosmetically useful" (United States 1973b).

The State Department viewed the restiveness of the G-77 as a problem, and suggested increasingly pressing measures to address the issue. On May 17, 1974, the Department of State sent an urgent cable to all embassies requesting them to take immediate actions to revamp U.S. relations with G-77 countries. The State Department requested that embassy staff meet with host governments to emphasize "what we see as a serious risk to future effective work of UN organization" posed by the "steamroller" tactics of the majority (United States 1974d).

These efforts continued when President Ford took office in 1974. Ford adopted a "multilateral" approach that linked the provision of foreign aid to an aggressive campaign to monitor the voting behavior of LDCs at the UN. In June 1975, President Ford appointed Daniel Patrick Moynihan as permanent representative to the UN to spearhead this effort. Moynihan held the position for only nine months (he went on to become president of the UN Security Council in February 1976), but he spoke out forcefully against the erosion of U.S. status in the UN. Moynihan had publicly urged the United States to "go into the United Nations and every other international forum and start raising hell" in response to widespread anti-American sentiment expressed by third world countries (*New York Times*, February 26, 1972, p. 3). He condemned what he characterized as U.S. withdrawal from world leadership in the wake of international condemnation of Vietnam: "Like Lyndon Johnson's 'jackrabbit in the hailstorm' ... we were 'hunkered down and taking it'" (Moynihan and Weaver 1978, 12). Moynihan challenged what he saw as the hypocrisy of third world leaders spouting anti-U.S. rhetoric: "Throughout 1974, U.N. assemblies were almost wholly given over to assaults on Western positions by combined Communist and Third World blocs ... The Maharajah of Jammu and Kashmir found himself denouncing 'colonial denudation' of the East and (curious from a man with a swimming pool in his living room) the 'vulgar affluence' of the West" (Moynihan and Weaver 1978, 31). Moynihan also decried a bureaucratic mindset among U.S. officials working within the UN, whom he implied were in denial that the country faced any problems at the UN. Moynihan proposed to track UN votes on issues relevant to the United States. In a meeting with Ford and Kissinger in September 1975, Moynihan affirmed that he perceived the situation in the UN as "a dangerous erosion of our diplomatic position in the world" (United States 1975a). Collecting information about how other countries voted in the UN would allow U.S. officials to hold them accountable and increase the political costs of voting against the United States. As President Ford put it, "We have to keep a record so we can go to them and say we won't take this abuse and have you [UN member states] come back bilaterally for help" (United States 1975d). On December 29, 1975, Kissinger sent a memo to all regional assistant secretaries of state regarding the position of the United States in international organizations. He characterized the UN as unfriendly to the United States:

An increasing share of American foreign policy is being conducted in international organizations and conferences, and a substantially larger proportion of my own time is being devoted to the preparation and presentation of our position in these forums. Yet the mood and conduct of many in the United Nations and other international gatherings have become increasingly hostile to us. (United States 1975e)

Kissinger intended to "give greater attention to multilateral relations and do more to gain support for [US] positions" and direct ambassadors "to take greater personal interest in multilateral diplomacy" (United States 1975f).

KISSINGER'S RHETORICAL EMBRACE OF HUMAN RIGHTS

In this context of irritation about the UN criticism of the United States, Secretary of State Kissinger began to express support for human rights. On August 22, 1974, just a few weeks after Gerald Ford assumed the presidency in the wake of Nixon's resignation, Kissinger (still secretary of state) sent a cable to all diplomatic posts in which he stated, "It is our desire at 29th GA [General Assembly] to demonstrate our concern about human rights in all areas of world in ways which can lead to effective measures, but avoid putting undue strains on bilateral relations" (United States 1974e). The measures Kissinger had in mind included passage of the Declaration of Elimination of All Forms of Religious Intolerance, "which we strongly support but which has been delayed by Communist States" (United States 1974e).

Kissinger's statements served American interests in several respects. He capitalized on changes in domestic public opinion about human rights. Democrats in the U.S. Congress, under the leadership of Congressman Donald Fraser from Minnesota, held a series of hearings on human rights violations in 1973 that prompted Republicans in the White House to take the issue more seriously (Vogelsgang 1978). Fraser's hearings drew attention to systematic violations of human rights then being committed by military regimes that the U.S. government supported, particularly in Latin America. By framing U.S. interests in terms of human rights, one of the defining issues within the UN since its founding, Kissinger hoped to regain moral leadership within that institution. Kissinger also sought to gain leverage in negotiating with the Soviets at the Conference on Security and Cooperation in Europe, a series of talks that would produce the Helsinki Accords, a set of principles aimed at reducing conflict between Western countries and the Eastern bloc. Finally, by embracing human rights, even only at a rhetorical level, the United States could appear to accede to the demands of developing nations for greater equality without supporting their calls for the radical redistribution of economic resources from wealthy to poor countries.

Thus, by 1975, the United States had endured several years of growing humiliation and frustration with the UN and endeavored with increasing urgency to reverse the situation. The Nixon and Ford administrations sought to reassert U.S. power over the G-77 countries. Although it must be stressed that Kissinger's affirmations of support for human rights existed purely at the level of rhetoric, this call for U.S. ambassadors to support human rights initiatives in the UN did have concrete consequences and would prove critical to getting CEDAW off the ground.

INTERNATIONAL WOMEN'S YEAR AND INITIAL PLANS FOR CEDAW

All UN member-states had global and domestic interests in advancing the status of women in the early 1970s, although women's issues remained a relatively low priority until mid-decade. The United States sought to preserve its claim as the undisputed world leader in protecting women's rights and establishing equality for women, a goal it exploited to improve its standing within the UN. Domestically, women's rights legislation enjoyed strong bipartisan support in the early

1970s. Congress responded to the feminist movement by passing a wave of women's rights legislation during this period: the ERA, which then went to the states for ratification; Title IX of the Educational Amendments Act (1972), which prohibits sex discrimination in education; the Revenue Act of 1971, which allowed parents to deduct child care costs from their taxes; and the Comprehensive Health Manpower Training Act of 1971 and the Nurses Training Act of 1971 prohibited sex discrimination in the training of health care professionals (Costain 1992; J. Freeman 2000). Congress passed a Child Development Act that would have provided publicly funded day care (President Nixon vetoed it). Both the Democrats and the Republicans adopted affirmative action measures for party leadership positions. Women were engaged in battles to expand women's rights in both parties and many of them would later be appointed to the committee that drafted CEDAW.

Among the countries in the Non-Aligned Movement, secular leaders had long seen the liberation of women as key to modernization. Some leaders in the developing world saw the expansion of women's rights as a way to achieve modernization. For others, focusing attention on women was a way to address population growth, then perceived as a hindrance to economic underdevelopment. The 1967 Charter of Algiers, one of the founding documents of the Non-Aligned Movement, affirms that "the virtual stagnation in the production of food-stuffs in developing countries, in contrast with the rapid increase in population, has aggravated the chronic conditions of under-nourishment and mal-nutrition and, combined with the distortion of production and trading patterns by artificial means, threatens to give rise to a grave crisis" (Group of 77 1967). Women fought in movements for national independence from colonial powers, demanded greater inclusion in the governments of their new nations, and insisted that they participate in the process of development. International development efforts had begun to focus on areas that women inhabited: agriculture, the informal sector, and population growth. "For women of newly independent countries, however, male-female issues could not be rightly resolved while oppression of whole societies – men and women – prevailed" (Schneider 2008, 623). Female leaders in developing nations had played important (although largely ignored) roles in movements of national liberation, and many of them would also serve as delegates to the UN CSW and help draft CEDAW.

Population control was a major global issue in the 1970s and a "top priority national policy" for Nixon, as demonstrated by his efforts to link foreign aid to population policy (Connelly 2008, 254). Population growth in the developing countries stoked fears that Americans were outnumbered and could be overrun (Connelly 2008, 255). Paul Ehrlich articulated these sentiments in *The Population Bomb*, a popular and influential book that "by 1974 had gone through twenty-two printings and sold two million copies" (Connelly 2008, 255). It seems hard to believe today, but at the time few people viewed population control as an issue that was relevant to women. Former CSW Chair Helva Sipila acknowledged that the UN's effort to develop a coordinated approach to development and the growing awareness of population growth made the moment ripe to mobilize for the drafting of a convention on women's rights. She wryly remarked that women had not previously been seen as relevant to population policy "perhaps due to the lack of knowledge of the interrelationship between the status of women and the size of the family" (UN Commission on the Status of Women 1974, 9).

Latent connections between feminism and the population control movement became manifest at the World Population Conference, held in Bucharest, Romania, in August 1974. The exclusion of women from the official delegations and the absence of women's concerns from the draft plan galvanized the few women in attendance. A handful of well-known feminist leaders, including Germaine Greer, Betty Friedan, and Margaret Mead, initiated conversations that resulted in the incorporation of women's perspectives and participation into the Plan of Action. They even got population-control advocate Nelson Rockefeller to concede that women must play a role in making decisions about family planning (Connelly 2008).

Despite détente, the spirit of cooperation and reduced conflict over nuclear weapons between the two superpowers did not extend to women's issues. The U.S. and the USSR continued to battle for dominance of the global women's rights agenda within the UN throughout the 1970s. Women's issues remained a low priority within the UN in the 1970s. Leticia Ramos-Shahani, one of the drafters of CEDAW, recalled:

At that time, the dominant thinking was that women's issues was a marginalized topic that was just one of the concerns of the social welfare sector. It was not worth placing the women's issue in the international agenda alongside "more serious" subjects like disarmament, the nonproliferation treaty, the new international economic order, and gross violations of human rights. (Quoted in Tripon 2007, 22)

As Chapter 2 describes, UN commitment to women's rights had increased over the decade of the 1960s but remained weak. The delegates to the CSW became keenly aware of DEDAW's ineffectiveness as they reviewed its implementation. Most countries ignored the Declaration and few women were even aware of the rights that they did or did not have. Several CSW members expressed dismay that the Declaration to Eliminate Racial Discrimination had been codified as a convention within two years, but seven years had passed since converting the women's declaration into a convention even made it onto the UN agenda.

In 1972, some CSW delegates proposed to hold an international conference to commemorate a global year for women and begin drafting an international convention on women's rights – but the Commission voted down both measures. The idea for a conference came, ironically, from the WIDF, the organization that had been at the center of a dispute during the CSW's very first meeting in 1946 as I discussed in Chapter 2. WIDF leaders persuaded the Romanian delegate to the CSW to propose holding an international conference, but the proposal did not pass; instead, "the Warsaw Pact countries began to plan [their own] conference in East Berlin in October 1975" (Schwelb 1966, 283). At the 1972 session, the USSR also tabled a motion that would have had the CSW draft a convention on women's rights. The Commission decided instead to write to member governments asking for their input on such a convention (Reanda 1992).[2]

In 1974, the CSW took two giant steps forward by voting to hold a global conference to celebrate IWY and beginning to draft a binding convention on women's rights. The CSW revisited the idea of holding a UN-sponsored conference when the U.S. delegate, Pat Hutar, "pointed out that the only major IWY event would take place in East Berlin" (Schwelb 1966, 283). Hutar reintroduced a proposal to hold a UN conference for IWY. The Soviet delegate, Tatiana Nikolaeva, strenuously objected and offered a series of arguments against the U.S. proposal. Nikolaeva insisted there was not enough time to organize a conference, that the conference would represent an additional cost "at

[2] See E/CN.6/Min.573, 579, 588 (1972).

a time when the Secretary-General was appealing for economies to be made," that women's issues were not as important as other issues such as nuclear disarmament, and finally, that women's issues should be considered not on their own merits, but instead in the context of "the struggle against racism and racial discrimination" (UN Commission on the Status of Women 1974, 160). Her Byelorussian colleague, Mrs. Marinkevich, concurred, on the grounds that "measures that directly or indirectly related to the question of the status of women would be adopted" at other conferences, obviating the need for a women's conference per se (UN Commission on the Status of Women 1974, 160). It is ironic that the communist countries opposed holding a separate conference for women given that they had insisted on a separatist approach to women's rights for decades in the CSW. They remained resolute; CSW member Leticia Shahani recalls that "The Soviet Union ... filibustered until nine o'clock at night to prevent passage of the resolution" (quoted in Fraser and Tinker 2004, 30). U.S. government documents suggest that the USSR opposed the women's conference because it had already scheduled an international women's conference that would take place in Moscow in October 1975, and it did not want to compete for the spotlight with a UN conference (United States 1974b). Others have suggested that the Soviets feared holding an international conference on the status of women would cause "the Soviet Union to weaken its grip on the women's issue among its allies and thus lose a powerful tool of control and propaganda" (quoted in Fraser and Tinker 2004, 30; see also Ghodsee 2010). Repetition of these arguments failed to dampen the enthusiasm for a conference among the CSW delegates, and the measure to hold a conference passed by a wide margin (UN Commission on the Status of Women 1974, 173).

The United States seized Soviet opposition to the IWY conference as a grand opportunity. UN Ambassador John Scali framed the meeting in dramatic terms, heralding it as a major foreign policy victory for the United States. In a cable summarizing the meeting for the State Department, Scali wrote:

Session characterized by emergence of the US in new human rights leadership role on issue of equal rights for women. Soviet opposition to US-LDC sponsored resolution asking UN to call women's conference during IWY revealed clear Soviet bias against equality for women. Timely release of presidential IWY proclamation during session further underlined US dedication to equal rights principles. Created added support for US IWY res[olution] and effectively stalled Soviet drive designed to focus world wide attention on single communist women's year conference scheduled for Moscow in 1975. US initiatives in integration of women in UN programs for development, family planning, observance of IWY widely supported.(United States 1974c)

Ambassador Scali's words read like a direct response to Kissinger, who had instructed ambassadors to "demonstrate our concern about human rights in all areas of the world." Scali characterized the CSW meeting as marking the "emergence of the US in a new human rights leadership role." Scali further remarked that the IWY conference proposal precipitated "a realignment of old commission voting patterns with support from LDCs and PRC [People's Republic of China] for the US against socialists" (United States 1974c). Scali argued that the Soviets lost support not only because they opposed holding a conference on women, but because their negotiating style alienated the other members of the Commission. When the substance of their arguments proved ineffective in persuading the other delegates, the Soviets brought in a *man* to do the negotiating:

Substitution of male member of soviet [sic] delegation in chair during a futile filibuster effort created widespread antagonism among delegates. Generous and warm-hearted position subsequently adopted by USSR delegate [Nikolaeva] who had been temporarily replaced by male colleague reversed trend somewhat before session ended but did not materially affect wide propaganda advantage gained by the US move and the soviet [sic] blunder. (United States 1974c)

Scali's account suggests that the Soviet delegation was aware of the high stakes of the decision and sought aggressively to oppose conference proposal. On January 30, 1974, in the middle of the CSW session, President Nixon called for IWY to be commemorated at all levels of government. The announcement scored additional points for the United States during the CSW meeting.

The reading of president Nixon's IWY proclamation, the first by any chief of state, in concluding days of session and prior to vote, added momentum to favorable vote and US leadership and served as put-down for Soviet position against equality. Requests poured in from all delegations for copies of proclamation for use by governments in preparation of similar instruments further strengthening propaganda impact of US initiative. (United States 1974c)

The USSR also opposed a CSW resolution on family planning calling for the right of individuals "to decide freely and responsibly on the number and spacing of their children, establishment of national population commissions, introduction of population education, and equal representation of men and women on delegations to the 1974 World Population Conference" (United States 1974c).

CSW delegates also took the initiative to begin drafting a women's rights convention. During the CSW's 1974 session, several of the delegates of the CSW formed an informal working group to draft a convention. They did so without official permission to act on behalf of their official delegations. The working group that composed the initial draft included Mrs. Hussein from Egypt, Mrs. Kolstad from Norway, Mrs. Cockcroft representing the United Kingdom, and Mrs. Bruce, an American. Mrs. Marte de Barrios, the delegate from the Dominican Republic, chaired the Working Group.[3] They met for five days from January 7 to 11, and again on January 18, 1974. They did not vote on the draft as a group, leaving many unresolved issues in the text. The group considered a document that consolidated the replies of UN members regarding the prospects for drafting a convention on women.

No one delegation wanted to step forward to take charge of compiling a formal draft that would be attributed to their country. The developed Western countries were "lukewarm" about an international treaty they saw as duplicating or perhaps overriding existing domestic laws, the Soviet Union was hesitant to give up its monopoly claims to represent women's issues in the global arena, and representatives from other countries lacked the expertise to write a draft (Fraser and Tinker 2004). With time running short, Shahani, then chair of the CSW, took the initiative to develop a draft herself. As Shahani remembers it, she persuaded the Soviet delegate, Tatiana Nikolaeva, to help her get Committee approval:

At the time our two countries had no diplomatic relations, but women could be ahead of their time. Since she did not always ask for instructions and was ready to take initiative, Nikolaeva readily said, "Yes." For my part, I knew I was taking a risk, for I had not cleared the draft with my government … The next day I received a telegram from my foreign secretary reprimanding me

[3] UN documents refer to the women as "Mrs" and do not provide their first names.

for not having sought the permission of the government ... I knew, however, that if I had gone through the intricate process of clearing the draft ... I would never have finished it on time for the session of the commission. (Quoted in Fraser and Tinker 2004, 32)

Shahani's willingness to circumvent formal channels in order to "get things done" proved critical to drafting CEDAW. Shahani's family connections may have prevented her from getting fired for breaking with diplomatic protocol.[4]

In another break with customary UN practice, the Working Group adopted Shahani's draft "without attributing it to any individual delegation" (Shahani 2004, 30). Arvonne Fraser portrays the initial draft as an exemplar of feminist practice: "The draft would not bind governments represented on the working group ... the speed and efficiency of this process was extraordinary, suggesting that a well-connected, politically effective group of women were again collaborating in their own free space" (Fraser 1995, 84). The summary records of the CSW provide a slightly different account of the origins of the draft document. Mrs. Cockcroft, the UK delegate, maintained that Mrs. Shahani and Mrs. Nikolaeva both submitted drafts. They tried to combine the two into a single document, but were unable to resolve all their differences, so they bracketed articles on which they disagreed (UN Commission on the Status of Women 1974, 9). After completing a first draft, the CSW took a one-year hiatus to focus its energies on the Mexico City Conference in 1975. It would return to consideration of the draft convention at its 1976 meeting in Geneva.

---

[4] Shahani's family was very well connected within the Marcos regime. Her father, Narciso Ramos, served under Marcos as a member of congress, as the secretary of the Ministry of Foreign Affairs, and as an ambassador. Shahani's brother, Fidel Ramos, served as chief of the Philippine constabulary under Ferdinand Marcos for sixteen years (1970–1986); in 1992, Ramos would succeed Corazon Aquino as president. Although Shahani credits the partnership to women's sisterly ability to transcend political conflict, it is plausible that Shahani acted under instructions from the State Department. As Beth A. Simmons (2010) notes, Shahani represented the Philippines, one of the United States' strongest allies at the time. But given the power of the G-77 within the UN, a delegate from the Philippines would have been well positioned to negotiate between the two superpowers. Although the Philippines was a reliable U.S. ally, Shahani did not always support the U.S. position. U.S. representative to the UN, John Scali, noted that "LDC reps, such as Amb Shahani of Philippines, who had supported US position in last year's Commission on Status of Women, were not sympathetic to US on issue of CERDS," referring to the Charter of Economic Rights and Duties of States adopted by the 29th UN General Assembly (United States 1975e).

1975: THE MEXICO CITY CONFERENCE

The UN gave the CSW "six months and less than $350,000" to plan IWY and the Mexico City conference, compared to "over two years and a budget of $3 million" for the Population Conference held the previous year (Zinsser 2002, 146). The funding for the Mexico City conference was low because the decision to hold the Conference was not finalized until October 1974. By that time, "the UN budget for the 1974–75 fiscal year had already been approved and it did not include provisions for the IWY conference" (Garner 2010, 218).

U.S. officials viewed the proposal to hold the IWY Conference as a victory, but it soon became clear that the Conference itself would present the United States with difficult political challenges. Conflict among nations threatened to derail the feminist agenda at every juncture at Mexico City. First world feminists wanted to prioritize a women's rights agenda. Second world nations (the Socialist countries) insisted they had already achieved equal rights and whatever problems existed in other countries were due to capitalism. Third world nations believed that enhancing economic development would resolve women's problems (Stephenson 1982). The theme of the Mexico City conference – Peace, Development, and Equality – conveyed a rhetorical commitment to all three perspectives, but in reality third world interests dominated the agenda. Women in the developing world resisted Western feminists efforts to prioritize any issues that did not pertain directly to economic development and basic human needs, on the grounds that people who were hungry could not afford to focus on "luxury" issues such as affirmative action, equal pay, abortion, or rape. Unable to agree, "the delegates enshrined rather than reconciled their ideological differences" (Zinsser 2002, 147).

In addition to the main work of approving the Conference document, the World Plan of Action, delegates brought a bewilderment of issues to Mexico City; they introduced "800 amendments to the Plan of Action and 168 additional resolutions" (Zinsser 2002, 147). The National Security Council feared that the Mexico City conference would be a venue for communists to spout anti-American sentiment and consequently directed Secretary of State Henry Kissinger to prevent First Lady Betty Ford from attending (Ghodsee 2010).

Western conceptions of feminism did not prevail in Mexico City. Ideological differences between the two superpowers continued to divide them on women's issues. Soviet and Eastern-bloc women portrayed women in essentialist terms as uniquely able to promote peace amidst global conflicts. Western women criticized the degree to which "political" issues predominated over feminist concerns with equality and rights:

> While the feminists from the advanced capitalist countries wanted the conference to focus exclusively on women's equality with men, women from the Eastern Bloc countries and the developing world pushed the idea that women were inherently different from men, and that they had a biological predisposition to be less violent.... As a result, they considered things like neo-colonialism, apartheid, racism and Zionism to be uniquely male forces in the world that could, through women's increased participation in international affairs, be challenged and defeated. (Ghodsee 2010, 6)

The Mexico City conference produced two documents: the Plan for Action and the Declaration of Mexico. The Declaration of Mexico reflects the view that "a reordering of the economic order to correct the imbalances between rich and poor countries must be undertaken before equality can be considered. Otherwise, full partnership will mean only shared poverty" (U.S. Department of State 1980, 3). The Declaration also condemned Zionism, which the United States opposed as a challenge to the legitimacy of Israel.[5] When considered in the context of the Vietnam War, parts of the Declaration of Mexico read as a direct attack on U.S. foreign policy. Paragraph 29, for example, states, "Peace requires that women as well as men should reject any type of intervention in the domestic affairs of States, whether it be openly or covertly carried on by other States or by transnational corporations" (quoted in Ghodsee 2010, 6). The U.S. delegation voted against the Declaration, but a huge majority of the delegates supported it: eighty-nine countries voted in favor, three against, and eighteen abstained (Ghodsee 2010, 6).[6]

---

[5] Conflicts over Zionism raged at each of the first three conferences, with the United States strenuously opposing any mention of the term in the final document. The United States did not get its wish until the third World Conference on Women in Nairobi in 1985, when at the eleventh hour Kenyan conference officials brokered a compromise, replacing "Zionism" with the phrase "all forms of racial discrimination" (Ghodsee 2010, 9).

[6] Ghodsee (2010) and perhaps U.S. officials as well overstate the degree to which the Declaration fails to reflect U.S. feminist concerns. Nine of the thirty articles of the Declaration call for equality in various arenas. Paragraph 28 affirms that "women

Attending the Mexico City conference, U.S. political scientist Jane Jaquette "found North American feminists surprised to discover that not everyone shared their view that patriarchy was the major cause of women's oppression, and that Third World women held views closer to Marx than Friedan" (quoted in Fraser and Tinker 2004, 197). In Mexico City, "The U.S. delegation was successful in strengthening the World Plan [of Action] by adding the concept of equal pay for work of equal value. However, its effort to add 'sexism' to the official list of forms of oppression failed. Several delegations argued that the word did not translate into their language" (U.S. Department of State 1980, 3).

At the end of the Mexico City conference, tensions remained high, but the United States remained committed to the process. One issue that generated widespread support at the Mexico City conference was drafting a convention on women's rights. As article 197 of the Plan for Action stated: "High priority should be given to the preparation and adoption of the Convention on the Elimination of Discrimination Against Women, with effective procedures for its implementation." This expression of support broke the stalemate in the CSW and allowed plans for CEDAW to move forward.

AMERICAN INPUT INTO THE OFFICIAL FIRST DRAFT OF CEDAW, 1976

Members of the Commission supported the idea of converting the Declaration into a binding convention on women's rights, but none could get permission from their official country delegations to let them take the lead in drafting such a document. The Working Group revised the draft on the basis of comments from forty UN member countries, ten NGOs, the International Labor Organization, the Educational, Scientific and Cultural Organization, and the Food and Agriculture Organization.[7] In the process of consulting UN countries about the

---

all over the world should unite to eliminate violations of human rights committed against women and girls such as: rape, prostitution, physical assault, mental cruelty, child marriage, forced marriage and marriage as a commercial transaction." Inclusion of these issues does not conform to the view that socialists viewed such problems as stemming only from capitalism.

[7] A summary of these comments is available in UN Commission on the Status of Women 1976.

draft, only one – Norway – expressed the view that "a convention on women's rights is unnecessary" because other treaties already expressed the most important rights. Norway and Sweden suggested that the convention should address discrimination on the basis of sex, which would include men as well as women (UN Commission on the Status of Women 1976, 7). The comments raised the most questions about the creation of a committee to oversee implementation of the convention. Most felt that the CSW should oversee the convention and that adding a new committee was unnecessary and too expensive. Others wanted to see a committee comprised of independent experts on women's issues.

The U.S. delegation to the Working Group that drafted the Convention in 1976 included six women: Patricia Hutar; Elizabeth (Betty) Athanasakos, a municipal judge from Florida; Shirley B. Hendsch, director of International Women's Programs at the Department of State; Nan Frederick, coordinator of the Women In Development Office at the Agency for International Development; Marguerite Rawalt, a former president of the National Association of Women Lawyers; and Florence Perman, an administrator at the Department of Health. The American delegation represented both parties and brought considerable expertise on women's issues to Geneva. Hutar had demonstrated her negotiating skills at the Mexico City conference.[8] Betty Athanasakos had been a Nixon appointee to various commissions on women. Marguerite Rawalt was one of the founding members of the National Organization for Women. The diverse members of this group reflected the bipartisan nature of feminist politics that predominated in the United States at the time.

The State Department urged the U.S. delegation to collaborate with other delegations in introducing proposals. As one cable advised: "Make every effort to work with and through other appropriate delegations in seeking proposal of amendments cited below, with U.S. as a co-sponsor.

---

[8] U.S. Ambassador to Mexico John Jova reported in a cable that "Ms. Hutar handled stream of most diverse and sometimes difficult speakers at microphone with poise and confidence" (United States 1975c). Hutar's diplomatic skills won her accolades in the Nixon administration. In a letter to the White House, State Department Executive Secretary George S. Springsteen wrote, "We believe [Hutar] will be as successful in winning approval for [global observance of IWY] as she was at the recent meeting of the Commission." Hutar's role in the CSW proved critical given Soviet opposition to the proposed Convention (United States 1974b).

(likely prospects would be: Egypt, Dominican Republic, Costa Rica, the Philippines, India, Indonesia, Thailand, Finland, and United Kingdom)" (United States 1976c). In a telephone interview, Athanasakos confirmed that the Americans persuaded representatives from other countries to introduce U.S. proposals. Her recollections suggest that the U.S. delegates faithfully complied with their instructions and always tried to work behind the scenes in order to avoid Soviet opposition:

> If the US was seen to be behind it, the Soviets were against it. We didn't want to cross them in any way ... we were so afraid of the Russians. If the US delegate said it, right away it would send up a signal that [the Soviets are] against it. We did not initiate anything. We worked through other countries to solve the problem. (Athanasakos 2011)

Several State Department cables advised the delegates to pay particular attention to U.S. policy on issues relating to population control. A background paper on "population matters" directed the U.S. delegates to "be au courant with U.S. international population policy as it relates to the status of women and the involvement of women in socio-economic development" (United States 1976). Cables sent to the delegates emphasized the centrality of population issues to U.S. foreign policy:

> The United States government has been concerned at the highest level with international population policy ... and the United States recognizes that population growth is inextricably linked to all phases of socio-economic development, including unemployment/underemployment, environmental degradation, food production, problems of rapid urbanization, and improvement in the status of women and their active participation as beneficiaries and as agents of change in community and national life. (United States 1976, 1)

State Department officials instructed the U.S. delegates to stress the global consensus reached at the previous UN conferences in Bucharest and Mexico City, and not back down from the accords reached at those meetings:

> The main thrust of U.S. Delegation argumentation should be that over 135 nations agreed to the principle of family planning at the World Population Conference and the World Conference on International Women's Year as related to socioeconomic development and elevation of the status of women. In no way should this language be weaker than at these two Conferences. The World Plans of Action of both Conferences set forth the correlation of

population factors with socioeconomic development and improvement in the status of women; both Plans are mutually reinforcing. (United States 1976, 2)

The State Department provided clear and adamant instructions to the delegates regarding women's rights to family planning. The United States wanted CEDAW's preamble to include specific language on family planning that would "reflect rights and responsibilities as contained in the World Population Plan of Action and in the World Plan of Action of International Women's Year" (United States 1976, 5). The language that the State Department wanted the delegates to incorporate into the preamble, from Paragraph 19 of the Plan of Action, reads as follows: "Individuals and couples have the right freely and responsibly to determine the number and spacing of their children and to have the information" and the means to do so (United States 1976, 5). State Department instructions frame this right in explicitly feminist terms that link family planning to women's equality: "The exercise of this right is basic to the attainment of any real equality between the sexes and without its achievement women are disadvantaged in their attempt to benefit from other reforms" (United States 1976, 5). The delegates did not succeed in getting this language into the preamble, but it does appear in various places in the text of CEDAW itself. Article 10(h) obligates states to provide "access to specific educational information to help to ensure the health and wellbeing of families, including information and advice on family planning." It also guarantees women "the same rights to decide freely and responsibly on the number and spacing of their children and to have access to the information, education and means to enable them to exercise these rights." Article 14(b) reinforces these rights for women in rural areas.

The State Department instructed the delegates to frame potentially controversial provisions for family planning in terms of precedent set by the CSW in the 1960s. They reminded the delegates that the 1967 DEDAW indirectly referred to family planning, well before the issue became a global priority: "Such reluctance in language used [in DEDAW] is understandable in the time frame of 1967 but not in 1976 following the progress made over the past decade. It would be appropriate for the U.S. Delegation to mention this fact in discussion of the agenda item" (United States 1976, 2).

Since 1980, the Republican Party has opposed the expansion of women's reproductive rights and supported limits on abortion and contraception. Thus, it is striking that a Republican administration is largely responsible for including family planning as a woman's right in CEDAW. The CEDAW Committee would later interpret these clauses of CEDAW as ensuring that abortion cannot be criminalized or so difficult to obtain as to threaten a woman's life. Ironically, these very passages would become the focus of opposition from social conservatives within the Republican Party, and would become a roadblock for U.S. ratification of CEDAW.

In a 2011 interview, Betty Athanasakos expressed surprise, as well as disappointment, that the United States has not yet ratified CEDAW. The fact that even she, one of the women who traveled to Geneva to draft the Convention, was not aware that the United States had not ratified CEDAW attests to the Convention's very low profile in the United States. Athanasakos affirmed that State Department officials approved every decision that she and the other delegates made on the drafting committee: "I would call the person in DC, to ask them what's the [US] position. Everything we did was approved." That is to say, the U.S. government authorized all the measures that the U.S. delegates negotiated on CEDAW. Athanasakos recalled that President Ford and his wife were very particularly supportive: "They would have supported [CEDAW] but they got voted out and the government got more conservative" (Athanasakos 2011). Here, Athanasakos is referring not to President Carter, who succeeded President Ford, but to social conservatives who won control of the Republican Party. State Department officials had U.S. ratification in mind in the instructions they provided to the CSW delegation.

The U.S. government wanted to build as much support as possible for the Convention:

The Draft Convention on the Elimination of Discrimination Against Women was concluded with a minimum of politicization in an attempt to make possible widest number of ratifications ... If small number of modifications can be made in the substantive articles when text is present to the ECOSOC and the GA, US ratification may well be possible. (United States 1976b)

Conflict over the structure of the committee that would oversee implementation of the Convention proved one of the most contentious issues. The American and Western European delegations preferred to appoint the treaty committee from representatives of states parties to the Convention, rather than a subset of members of the CSW, but the latter proposal won out (United States 1976a). It does not appear that any of the delegates supported a committee made up of independent experts rather than officials appointed by governments; this provision was added during the later revisions.

CEDAW'S LONG ROAD TO THE GENERAL ASSEMBLY

The General Assembly voted, in Resolution 3521, that the CSW would complete a draft Convention in 1976.[9] The CSW met this goal: on December 17, 1976, the CSW approved the draft and forwarded it to the Economic and Social Committee. The ECOSOC then presented the draft Convention to UN member countries on May 12, 1977, urging them to "present their comments on the draft Convention as soon as possible before 15 July 1977, so that they may be transmitted by the Secretary-General to the General Assembly well in advance of its thirty-second session" in December 1977. This statement suggests that the members of the committee believed the General Assembly would approve the draft Convention quickly and easily. However, the process was still far from over. The General Assembly delegated consideration of the draft Convention to the Third Committee, one of six standing committees within the General Assembly. A working group of the Third Committee then sent it to member states, and received comments from forty governments and ten NGOs. This would be the third working group that worked on CEDAW, so a clarification of the sequence is in order here. In 1974, several delegates of the CSW formed an informal working group to write a preliminary draft. In 1976, the CSW created a formal working group to write a formal draft, which they presented to the General Assembly. The General Assembly delegated the work of revising the draft convention a third time to the Third Committee. For the sake of clarity, I will refer to this last group as WG3 in the sections that follow.

WG3 deliberated on the draft Convention for the next two years, meeting twelve times in 1977 and twenty-one times in 1978 before they

---

[9]   Retrieved from http://www.un.org/documents/ga/res/30/ares30.htm.

returned the draft to the Third Committee as a whole for a vote (Galey 1979; Reanda 1992). In 1977, they managed to cover only the preamble and the first ten articles, thus requiring a second year of meetings.[10] WG3 amended the draft by adding Article 8 on women's participation in international organizations, but rejected proposals for creating an optional protocol that would give individuals and organizations the right to petition in cases of discrimination.[11] The preamble gave WG3 particular trouble, primarily because it encompassed so many issues that are not germane to the Convention itself. The language of the preamble reflected the highly political views of the NAM and proved particularly difficult for WG3 to reconcile. Delegates from developing nations wanted to preserve the relevance of geopolitical context to women's rights, whereas delegates from the developed countries wanted to emphasize the issues that all women faced regardless of context (Jacobson 1992).

Most of the revisions that the WG3 made to the draft Convention during this period are relatively minor changes in wording to make the document more consistent with other UN treaties and clarify the language. It revised the nationality article to conform different notions of citizenship, and changed "the sexes" to "men and women," for example. Requirements for membership of the CEDAW Committee, known at the time as "the body which considers progress in implementing the convention," raised the greatest concern and required the most time to discuss. WG3 failed to resolve this issue before handing the draft Convention back to the Third Committee, and so presented three competing proposals. The first proposed an ad hoc committee made up of "10–15 members of the CSW." A second proposal populated the CEDAW committee with twenty-three members of the Economic and Social Council. The rationale behind these two proposals was that the Committee would draw from government representatives already

---

[10] The Working Group included representatives from Argentina, Austria, Belgium, Byelorussian Soviet Socialist Republic, Canada, Cuba, France, India, Iran, Ireland, Japan, Jordan, Kenya, Morocco, Netherlands, New Zealand, Nigeria, Oman, Pakistan, Philippines, Romania, Sweden, Syrian Arab Republic, Union of Soviet Socialist Republics, United Kingdom, United States, and Yugoslavia (UN General Assembly November 30, 1979).

[11] The UN General Assembly adopted an optional protocol to CEDAW in 1999 (see http://www.ohchr.org/EN/ProfessionalInterest/Pages/OPCEDAW.aspx). I discuss the optional protocol in Chapter 4.

associated with the UN and would cost less to implement. The third proposal most closely resembles what the General Assembly would ultimately approve; it called for eighteen and later twenty-three "experts of high moral standing" elected by CEDAW ratifying countries (UN General Assembly 1979). As I will argue in Chapters 4 and 5, the independent nature of the CEDAW experts is one of the main reasons that CEDAW has evolve into a powerful international institution.

Another issue that provoked a lot of discussion was Article 23, which allowed for the International Court of Justice, the judicial branch of the UN, to resolve international disputes over interpretation of the Convention. The United States proposed this article on the grounds that CERD had included a similar clause. Many countries opposed this measure because they did not feel an international court would ever be necessary to resolve issues that were primarily domestic in nature, but the United States won out. Ironically, the Clinton administration proposed a reservation on this clause when it tried to get the Senate to ratify the treaty in 1994.

Why did it take the WG3 so long to review the draft Convention? Their reports do not indicate much in the way of political controversy. Rather, the work at hand involved painstaking efforts to phrase each paragraph of the Convention in ways that acknowledged the differences in the status of women across many different countries but still articulated shared aspirational goals. The General Assembly voted to extend the work of the Working Group twice because it had not been able to get through all of the articles. These measures suggest that the work was arduous.

Finally, in December 1979, after two years of work, WG3 brought the revised draft to the Third Committee, which devoted two days of discussion to it before voting to approve the draft (December 6–7, 1979) and sending it along to the General Assembly. Once again, the preamble prompted a lot of debate. The delegates from the UK and France proposed striking the preamble altogether and replacing it with a shorter version. Mr. Whomersley, the delegate from the UK, argued that "the existing wording was inappropriate and unprecedented for a legal instrument," was too long, and contained material that was "unquestionably politically controversial" as well as irrelevant to the Convention itself (UN Third Committee of the General Assembly 1979, 4–5). At the same time, other delegations proposed adding *more* paragraphs to the existing proposal to strengthen its opposition to imperialism. The Algerian representative proposed that "the right of self-determination" should be replaced with "the right to self-determination and the realization of the right of peoples to self-determination and independence." The Indian delegate proposed an amendment that would add the text "peoples under alien and colonial domination" (UN Third Committee of the General Assembly 1979, 7). The delegate from Syria chided his British colleague, saying, "It was hardly appropriate to propose an entirely new wording" of the preamble, but then went on to propose that the words "aggression" and "interference" be added to the preamble before the words "in the internal affairs of States." The heated tenor of the discussion prompted the Mexican delegation to propose postponing the vote, which not surprisingly prompted more conflict. On December 7, 1979, the Third Committee nonetheless approved the draft Convention and sent it to the floor of the General Assembly.

The General Assembly desperately wanted to vote on the Convention by the end of the 1979 session so that it could be opened for signature at the second World Conference on Women scheduled to take place in Copenhagen in June 1980. After six years in the drafting process, CEDAW moved very quickly through the General Assembly. The delegates agreed that they could vote on most of the document without discussion, given that the Working Group had already devoted so much time to it (Galey 1984, 481). Nonetheless, debate on the draft in the General Assembly was heated, with some countries still insisting they needed more time.

The General Assembly vote ultimately hinged on a single issue: the structure of the committee that would oversee implementation of the treaty. The question was whether the committee would be made up of CSW delegates or an entirely separate committee. In the end, the General Assembly approved CEDAW with 130 in favor, none against, and 11 abstentions. The eleven delegations that abstained from voting did so on the grounds that the draft Convention had been prepared too hastily. After the vote was taken, those delegations took the floor to explain that they had abstained because they did not have enough time to consider how the Convention would be implemented back home. Many expressed concern that the lack of consensus would translate into a high number of reservations that would ultimately impede implementation of CEDAW (United Nations 1984, 40).

INTERNATIONAL WOMEN'S YEAR IN THE UNITED STATES:
THE END OF BIPARTISANSHIP

From 1974 to 1979, the draft Convention quietly made its way through the UN, out of the public eye. Meanwhile, IWY had dramatic and very visible effects within the United States. American feminists, Congress, and the federal government embraced IWY and the ensuing Decade for Women as a way to expand U.S. commitments to the rights of women at home and abroad. The United States undertook major initiatives to celebrate the UN Decade for Women. In 1973, the State Department held a workshop on IWY that generated interest among members of Congress and led to the drafting of the Percy Amendment of the Foreign Assistance Act of 1973, which created the Women in Development program. At the same time, Congress passed the Helms Amendment to the Foreign Assistance Act, which stipulated that "no foreign assistance funds may be used to pay for the performance of abortion as a method of family planning or to motivate or coerce any person to practice abortions" (Center for Health and Gender Equity 2014). On January 9, 1975, President Ford issued an executive order creating the National Commission on the Observance of IWY (NCOIWY). In December 1975, Congress passed legislation funding conferences for women in each of the fifty states as well as a national women's conference to be held in Houston in 1977. Congress allocated $5 million for the effort – a nickel for every woman in the United States. The IWY Commission used the funds to provide low-cost transportation, lodging, and child care to allow low-income women to attend the conferences. Federal funds thus supported the massive organization of feminists at the grassroots level across all fifty states. President Ford also sought to strengthen gender equality within the federal government itself: he "established an Interdepartmental Task Force that included a woman and a man from each federal department and agency to examine the treatment and status of women in the Federal sector" (U.S. Department of State 1980, 12).

The NCOIWY recommended U.S. ratification of the Convention on the Political Rights of Women, an international agreement affirming women's right to vote and run for public office that the UN General Assembly had approved in 1952. The Senate Committee on Foreign

Relations gave its advice and consent to the treaty and the Senate approved it in January 1976. IWY events also facilitated coalition building among women's organizations. In a review of IWY activities for the U.S. Mission to the UN, the State Department reported that "the National Commission on the Observance of IWY helped bring together the many organizations supporting ERA to support a single organization, called ERAmerica, to coordinate their efforts and to unify the many existing ERA educational and public information programs in the country" (U.S. Department of State 1976). IWY thus had a direct impact on domestic women's rights policy in the United States. The declaration of 1975 as IWY galvanized the U.S. women's movement and spurred the U.S. federal government to adopt feminist policies.

IWY programs also galvanized efforts to collect data about the status of women. The reports that the government prepared in order to attend the Mexico City conference "pointed up serious deficiencies in data collection and analysis in all government agencies. To correct this situation, the IWY Commission has recommended to the President that all Federal agencies be required to collect, tabulate, cross-tabulate and analyze data relating to persons by sex, ethnicity, race and where appropriate by age, income and other indicators of disadvantaged conditions" (U.S. Department of State 1976). In April 1976, the Census Bureau published a report on women, which the State Department heralded as "a landmark step in documenting the degree to which women are integrated in the social and economic life of the country" (U.S. Department of State 1976).

Moderates within the Republican Party embraced feminist issues in an effort to revive the party in the wake of the Watergate scandal. Social conservatives had gained influence within the party during the Nixon administration, but their power evaporated when Nixon resigned on August 9, 1974. The moderates who took control of the Republican Party at that point – including President Gerald Ford, Vice President Nelson Rockefeller, and Republican National Committee Chair Mary Louise Smith – sought to restore the party's legitimacy by moving it toward the center (Melich 1998). Support for feminist concerns and IWY constituted a key part of their strategy. Republican support for feminism also expanded feminism's popular appeal. As author

Tanya Melich writes, "With the Republicans in charge, the IWY had a less radical image than it would have had with the Democrats. They have given the women's movement a centrist cachet and a mainstream legitimacy that was needed, for most Americans knew little about the movement beyond the more radical headlines it had attracted in the early 1970s" (Melich 1998, 82).

When President Carter took office in 1977, he sustained the Ford administration's commitment to IWY. Carter continued Ford's precedent of appointing people from outside his party to the Commission. Carter's Republican appointees included Senator Charles Percy (R, IL), Congresswoman Margaret Heckler (R, MA), Elizabeth Athanasakos, and Gerridee Wheeler, a member of the Republican National Committee (National Commission on the Observance of IWY 1978a). Republicans remained actively engaged in the national conferences, even as the leadership of the IWY effort and substance of the issues debated at the conferences moved to the left. Carter appointed former Congresswoman and feminist leader Bella Abzug as presiding officer of the National Commission on the Observance of International Women's Year. Abzug's appointment struck some as an unfortunate decision, on the grounds that she would alienate moderates. IWY programs and agenda became more radical at the Houston Conference in 1977 as the attendees supported planks on abortion rights and the ERA. Feminist leader Betty Friedan herself moved to the left during the Houston Conference when she reversed her longtime anti-gay stance and espoused support for lesbianism.

The 1977 Houston Conference was the centerpiece of the U.S. celebration of IWY. More than 150,000 people attended the preliminary conferences held in each of the 50 states. One of the most dramatic and well-publicized events of the conference was the Torch Relay, in which more than 2,000 women carried a lighted torch from Seneca Falls, New York, to Houston, Texas (National Commission on the Observance of International Women's Year 1978b). Delegates at the National Conference debated twenty-six proposals, including support for the ERA. They approved all but one, a Cabinet-level position for women's affairs: "The almost unanimous and spontaneous feeling of the delegates was that such a position ran counter to the goal of equality because the Cabinet position would be special treatment under the law and not equal treatment" (U.S. Department of State 1980, 13).

The IWY conferences showed how strongly American women supported women's rights issues and demonstrated how easily women could be mobilized into action.

Not everyone supported these initiatives, however. Conservative women mobilized aggressively to oppose the National Women's Conference on many fronts. Fundamentalists found the government's explicit support for women's rights and creation of government programs to expand those rights threatening in the extreme. Phyllis Schlafly, prominent Republican and leader of an anti-feminist organization called StopERA, filed nine lawsuits accusing the NCOIWY of illegally using federal money for lobbying. Although all of the suits were ultimately thrown out, the need to mount a legal response diverted resources and time away from the planning process. Hundreds of conservative men and women registered for the state conferences on the day they took place with the sole aim of voting down all the proposals. Anti-feminists made up the majority of delegates in fourteen states. Conservative opponents created the IWY Citizens' Review Committee in response to what they perceived as predetermined agendas of the state conferences. Senator Jesse Helms, a conservative Republican from North Carolina who would later become one of the most outspoken opponents of U.S. ratification of CEDAW, worked with this committee to hold congressional hearings on September 14–15, 1977. Helms denounced the use of federal funds to hold the IWY conferences in a hearing held in the Old Senate Office Building, which is also federal property. He denounced the conferences as "rigged" – although he allowed only anti-ERA partisans to speak. At Helms's hearings, "conservative women from across the nation testified that they had been victims of discrimination at the state conferences" (Spruill 2008, 84). Helms's efforts did not persuade Congress to launch an investigation into IWY or prevent the Houston Conference from taking place, but did "achieve his main objective: reminding his constituency of anti-feminists that he would steadfastly support them and pursue their cause" (Spruill 2008, 85). On the basis of Helms's hearing, conservative political leaders authored a "minority report" in which they claimed to "speak for the majority of women, the homemakers and professional women of the United States who, by design of the IWY national and State committees, are represented in Houston at the National Women's Conference by a minority of the delegates"

(Joan Gubbins et al. 1978). The report opposed all efforts that required federal funding or involved the UN:

The World Plan of Action, adopted at Mexico City, June 1975, was not drafted by American women but rather by the United Nations Secretariat ... therefore it is in no way representative of the thinking or wishes of the majority of American women.... Further, we deplore the deliberate and invidious discrimination against women who hold views contrary to the stated World Plan of Action and the National Plan of Action by virtually eliminating representation of their views during the planning and execution stages of the IWY Women's conferences, both at the national and State levels. (Joan Gubbins et al. 1978)

In an effort to appease opponents, the IWY Commission appointed former Congresswoman Martha Griffiths (D-MI) as chair of the Homemaker Committee. Griffiths commissioned a series of studies that examined how laws affected homemakers in each of the fifty states, including "domicile, support, and alimony laws; employment laws; and court decisions" (Rawalt 1983, 70). Griffiths organized workshops and initiated proposals aimed at enhancing the status of homemakers, but women in the opposition showed little interest in dialogue. Opponents who attended the conferences "voted against every resolution considered, even those to enhance the legal status of homemakers" (East 1983, 43).

The conflicts that emerged over the course of the IWY conferences quickly found their way into partisan politics, and the brief era of bipartisan support for feminism came to an end. During the 1980 elections, Democratic candidates differed starkly from Republican ones on the ERA and abortion. Carter supported the ERA but Republican candidate Ronald Reagan did not, reversing his party's longstanding support (Wolbrecht 2000). This became patently clear at the 1980 Democratic National Convention, which took place in New York August 11–14. The *New York Times* reported that the "battle for women's rights ... moved where it belongs, to the center of American politics," but erroneously predicted that "the Republicans clearly seem to be on the losing side" (August 20, 1980, p. A18). The environment for women's rights changed once Ronald Reagan became president and Republicans gained control of the Senate. Carter had lost decisively, winning 41 percent of the popular vote to Reagan's 50.7 percent on November 4. The Democratic Party lost control of the Senate for the first time in twenty-eight years.

Government-sponsored IWY events helped set in motion the partisan realignment on women's issues that occurred in 1980. IWY activities, along with struggles over abortion and the ERA, simultaneously strengthened popular support for feminism in the United States and catalyzed the formation of a powerful antifeminist countermovement. The deep divisions that emerged on women's issues in the context of IWY conferences continue to spur conflict between the Democratic and Republican Parties today. These disputes are a core reason why the United States has not ratified CEDAW.

The events surrounding the commemoration of IWY in the United States helped seal CEDAW's fate even before the UN opened the Convention for signature. In 1977, CEDAW was still making its way though the revision process in various committees of the UN. Two years before the General Assembly approved CEDAW, bipartisan support for women's rights in the United States had begun to evaporate. The mobilization of conservatives against the Houston Conference would bring the era of Republican leadership on women's rights – leadership that made CEDAW possible – to a close.

CEDAW DEBUTS ON THE WORLD STAGE

In July 1980, the UN opened CEDAW for signature at the second World Conference on Women in Copenhagen. The UN convened the Copenhagen Conference to review the progress made in achieving the goals agreed upon at the Mexico City Conference and develop specific strategies for the second half of the UN Decade for Women. The United States was one of fifty-two countries that signed the treaty on July 17, bringing the total to sixty-five signatories.[12] Although signing a treaty is not the same as ratifying it, initial support for CEDAW looked promising. Maryland Senator Barbara Mikulski described the joy she felt while attending the Copenhagen Conference as member of Congress: "There was such buoyancy, such enthusiasm, such optimism, such hope that we were going to end discrimination around the world and we were going to do it through a legal document, through the United Nations" (U.S. Senate 1990, 32). President Carter delegated the honor of signing to Sarah Weddington, who worked for him as

---

[12] Thirteen countries had signed the Convention prior to July 17.

special assistant. Weddington had become famous as one of the lawyers who had argued on behalf of Jane Roe in the *Roe vs. Wade* abortion case before the Supreme Court in 1973. Neither Carter's signing the Convention nor the Conference itself got much media coverage in the United States. The U.S. government report on the Conference affirmed that "several newsworthy events" overshadowed the Conference, including "the return to the United States of the ailing U.S. hostage released by the Iranians, the Republican National Convention [at which Ronald Reagan won the presidential nomination], the Special Session of the UN General Assembly on Palestinian Rights, and the Bolivian coup" (U.S. Department of State 1980, 132). One-third of the 1,264 journalists attending the Copenhagen meeting were from the United States, yet press coverage in the U.S. media was minimal (U.S. Department of State 1980, 132).

The State Department had committed substantial time and resources to prepare for the Copenhagen Conference. It organized nine regional conferences and one national conference to raise awareness about the Copenhagen agenda (U.S. Department of State 1980). The official delegation held nine meetings with American attendees to the NGO Forum during the conference itself, which 400 women attended. The U.S. delegates had envisioned CEDAW as the centerpiece of the Copenhagen Conference, but once again, as they had in Mexico City, "political" issues dominated the agenda and pitted the United States against the rest of the world. The G-77 negotiated en banc during the conference, issuing proposals and recommendations as a group. This was how the G-77 typically operated during this era: they would pursue their specific interests across all of the UN agencies, regardless of how relevant the venue was (Gregg 1993). The non-aligned country delegations focused the Copenhagen agenda on the participation of women in liberation movements in Palestine and South Africa, ignoring the fact that "17 million Iranian women were being returned to medieval segregation and several hundred million women in other non-aligned countries remained circumscribed by tribal or religious customs" (Jackson 1983, 176). Representatives from the Palestine Liberation Organization (PLO) attended every meeting and PLO leader Leila Khalid gave a keynote address. Khalid had won global notoriety in 1969 when she and fellow PLO members hijacked a plane they believed the Israeli ambassador to the United

States would be aboard (Jackson 1983). Although Americans insisted that women's issues were distinct from "political issues," the presence of Leila Khalid "the Palestinian superactivist," blurred the distinction (Fraser and Tinker 2004, 32).

The World Conferences on Women were particularly vulnerable to being overtaken by the non-aligned countries because they did not command significant resources and women's issues were not yet a high priority on the agenda of most UN member countries. Moreover, "individual delegates were committed to women's rights, but tended to be from private life and unfamiliar with political trade-offs of the United Nations and NAM. They were thus vulnerable to an organized lobby of non-aligned activists that forced through its own political agenda, unrelated to women's issues" (Jackson 1983, 176). Additionally, as U.S. delegate to Copenhagen Vivian Lowery Derryck recalled, "Women delegates often didn't have the political savvy, knowledge of their own political systems, or the political will to fight the professional diplomats," referring to the male diplomats who took their seats when final negotiations took place (quoted in Fraser and Tinker 2004, 157). The conference ended without consensus about how to proceed in the second half of the UN Decade for Women.

The United States tried but failed to prevent the Copenhagen Plan for Action from including planks that opposed Zionism and apartheid in South Africa (U.S. Department of State 1980, 104). Members of the U.S. delegation to Copenhagen acknowledged the setbacks they faced. In an interview with the *New York Times*, Sarah Weddington stated, "We knew before we left for Copenhagen that it would be a difficult conference but we were still terribly disappointed that the collective will of women there did not operate to focus on women's issues from a woman's perspective" (August 9, 1980). In a follow-up report, the State Department harshly condemned the politicization of the Conference. The substance of the report reveals conflicting loyalties between foreign policy goals and feminism: "The U.S. delegation … understood that politicization is more than discussing political issues in a political context. It is invidious and unconscionable, particularly in the case of the feminist movement, when the structures of power that suppress women, use and exploit the women's cause to assure that these structures do not change" (U.S. Department of State 1980, 111). The State Department report attributed the dominance

of political issues over women's concerns not to the political maneu-
vers of the Non-Aligned Movement but to the absence of women in
positions of political power. The language is extraordinary for a State
Department document: "Feminism ... was a mere whisper in the din of
political concerns that dominated the conference ... [that was] looking
for opportunities to assert itself in a system and in a political situation
developed, orchestrated, and maintained almost entirely by men" (U.S.
Department of State 1980, 125).

Delegates who attended the convention drew this conclusion on the
basis of observing numerous occasions in which "men held their country's chair and openly scoffed at women's attempts to include feminist language or issues into the Program" (U.S. Department of State
1980, 138). The report acknowledged the frustrations of members of
the U.S. delegation who "sometimes felt they were being forced to
choose between upholding their official responsibilities, and pursuing
the goals of women all over the world" (U.S. Department of State
1980, 126).

CONCLUSION

A changed geopolitical context prompted the U.S. government to take
a leadership role in women's issues in the UN, reversing a decades-
long policy of obstructionism. U.S. initiatives to hold an international
conference to commemorate IWY and draft CEDAW would dramatically change the landscape for global women's rights. Advocates of
U.S. ratification of CEDAW often mention the leading role that the
United States played in drafting the treaty itself. Women active in
the Democratic and Republican parties during the second half of the
1970s, at the tail end of the Ford administration and throughout the
Carter administration, represented the United States on the UN CSW
and participated in the drafting of CEDAW. Female party leaders came
to the CEDAW drafting process fresh from struggles to empower
women nationally and within the parties themselves.

U.S. efforts did not succeed in reestablishing American leadership
in the UN, however. At both the Mexico City and Copenhagen conferences, Third World countries dominated the agenda and sidelined
U.S. concerns (Ghodsee 2010). The politicization of women's issues
forced the United States to vote against the Platform for Action that

came out of the conference. Congress responded to the Copenhagen Conference by cutting funding for two key UN programs for women: the International Research and Training Institute for the Advancement of Women (INSTRAW) and the Development Fund for Women (UNIFEM) (Fraser and Tinker 2004, 158). IWY had a huge impact in the United States at the domestic level, however. The federal government launched a series of initiatives to gather information on the status of women, strengthen gender equity in federal agencies, and dedicate more resources to improving the rights of women in the United States. The Houston Conference in 1977 and the state-level conferences that preceded it mobilized tens of thousands of women across the country, many of whom had not previously supported the feminist movement. These efforts legitimized feminism and broadened support for feminism – but at the same time triggered a backlash.

The UN had high hopes for CEDAW, but those hopes would not be realized yet. The countries of the Non-Aligned Movement, with their majority in the UN, kept the focus on other issues that initially overshadowed attention on CEDAW and the state-focused approach to rights that it represented. The people who attended the Mexico City and Copenhagen Conferences gained valuable experience about how to navigate in the UN world – how to lobby official delegations, how to maneuver politically, and how to keep the focus on issues they cared about. Beginning with the third World Conference on Women in Nairobi in 1985, global women's rights advocates began to see how CEDAW could help them pursue their goals and exert pressure on government officials.

4

An Evolving Global Norm of Women's Rights

Members of the UN have signed scores of statements, platforms, declarations, and resolutions that articulate a commitment to women's rights. Among them are the Beijing Platform for Action, which outlines "an agenda for women's empowerment" (UN Women 1995); UN Security Council Resolution 1325, which "urges" and "calls upon" countries to incorporate women and women's needs into conflict resolution (Office of the Special Adviser on Gender 2000); and the Declaration on the Elimination of Violence against Women, which "urges that every effort be made" to address domestic and sexual violence (United Nations 1993). What sets CEDAW apart from other international agreements on women's rights is that CEDAW has the force of international law. Ratification of CEDAW legally obligates countries to take "all appropriate measures" to eliminate discrimination against women.

Today CEDAW is one of the most important instruments for advancing women's rights in the international arena, but it did not start out that way. Although the formal text of CEDAW has not changed since the General Assembly adopted it in 1979, its meaning has evolved over time in terms of how it is interpreted, implemented, and supported. In the thirty years since it came into force, CEDAW has grown in global visibility, relevance, and influence. It has gained prominence within the UN system, within the countries that have ratified it, and among activists in the transnational women's movement. Several factors have strengthened CEDAW. Over time, the Committee that oversees the Convention has developed an increasingly clear interpretation of what constitutes discrimination against women, has become more effective in administering the treaty, and has greater legitimacy, as demonstrated by a growing number of domestic laws and judicial decisions that refer to CEDAW directly. Second, political considerations no longer trump women's rights in the way that governments and Committee experts interpret the treaty. Changes in the global balance of power, particularly the end of the Cold War, have reduced the degree to which ideological conflicts between the U.S. and the Soviet Union eclipse a focus on women's issues per se within the CEDAW Committee and in government reports. Politics continue to permeate the CEDAW process, but the nature of the political conflicts has changed. Third, greater NGO involvement has provided the Committee experts with access to better information about the status of women in individual countries and has expanded the audience for the Convention itself. Finally, a series of institutional reforms has allowed the Committee to operate more efficiently and effectively. As the result of these changes, the CEDAW of today is very different than the CEDAW of 1979.

I begin this chapter with a basic overview of the content of CEDAW, which contains a preamble and thirty articles divided into six parts.[1] I highlight some of the issues that have proven controversial in debates about U.S. ratification. My intention in this section is only to signal areas that could potentially arouse concerns in the United States, rather than provide a definitive assessment of their legal standing. Moreover, human rights treaties are currently understood to be non–self-executing in the United States, which means that Congress would need to adopt implementing legislation for specific articles of CEDAW in order for them to have effect in domestic law. In the brief treatment I provide here, I emphasize that CEDAW does not require governments to adopt particular policies and cannot impose policies upon countries that ratify, an argument I develop at length in Chapter 5.

CEDAW: THE BASIC TEXT

CEDAW begins with a preamble that makes the case for why CEDAW is necessary. It lists existing UN mechanisms that aim to achieve gender equality – the UN Charter, the Universal Declaration of Human Rights,

---

[1] Retrieved from http://www.ohchr.org/EN/ProfessionalInterest/Pages/CEDAW.aspx.

and the international human rights covenants. It also acknowledges their limitations: "Despite these various instruments extensive discrimination against women continues to exist." The preamble contains several paragraphs that defend the view that women's equality will come about as the result of economic development and end of colonialism. These paragraphs evince what might be called a developmentalist view and reflect the participation of countries in the nonaligned movement. As I discussed in Chapter 3, the text of the preamble proved very contentious. The result is an awkward compromise between general affirmations of support for women's rights and Marxist language that reflects the political climate that dominated the UN at the time CEDAW was drafted. Particularly arresting is the statement that "the eradication of apartheid, all forms of racism, racial discrimination, colonialism, neo-colonialism, aggression, foreign occupation and domination and interference in the internal affairs of States is essential to the full enjoyment of the rights of men and women." The tone and approach of the preamble differ dramatically from the main text. The preamble has had little impact on how countries comply with CEDAW or how it has been interpreted. In a comprehensive legal analysis of CEDAW, legal scholars Christine Chinkin and Beate Rudolf assure us that "the preamble is not an operative part of the treaty and thus does not directly create binding legal obligations" (Rudolf, Freeman, and Chinkin 2012, 37).

Part I comprises six general "covering" articles intended to guide interpretation and application of the specific substantive articles on political, social, and legal rights in parts II, III, and IV, respectively. Article 1 provides a definition of discrimination. The Convention defines discrimination as

Any distinction, exclusion or restriction made on the basis of sex which has the effect or purpose of impairing or nullifying the recognition, enjoyment or exercise by women, irrespective of their marital status, on a basis of equality of men and women, of human rights and fundamental freedoms in the political, economic, social, cultural, civil or any other field.

The phrase "effect or purpose" is perhaps the most significant phrase in this definition, as it conveys the treaty's exceptionally broad purview. The scope of state obligation is what makes CEDAW distinctive in relation to other human rights treaties and other declarations of support for women's rights: CEDAW obligates states to take positive action to eliminate de facto as well as de jure discrimination against women, intended and unintended, in every arena of society.

Article 2 commits signatories to adopt "all appropriate measures" to enact the treaty and eliminate laws that discriminate against women. It is one of the most important articles because it articulates the parameters of the proactive role the state plays in establishing equality. CEDAW places the responsibility for bringing about gender equality in the hands of the state; notwithstanding the Marxist language from the preamble, the substantive articles of the Convention do not regard the securing of women's rights to be epiphenomenal to economic growth or development. Article 2 contains seven provisions. Article 2 (a) enjoins states parties "to embody the principle of the equality of men and women in their national constitutions or other appropriate legislation." There is some question about the extent to which the United States already complies with this article. The U.S. Constitution guarantees sex equality through the 14th Amendment, but the formal text of the Constitution does not explicitly state that men and women are equal under the law, as many constitutions around the world now do. In Chapter 7, I return to the question of how fully the U.S. Constitution protects women's rights and whether an ERA would be required for full compliance. Article 2 (b) requires states to adopt legislation prohibiting discrimination against women, and Article 2 (c) requires *effective* legal protection for women's equality, both of which the United States has already done. Article 2 (d) establishes that women in public office must be treated equally, which also presents no obvious problems in the United States, as the United States has ample laws guaranteeing gender equality and the U.S. judicial system effectively upholds them. Article 2 (e) stipulates that governments will "take all appropriate measures to eliminate discrimination against women by any person, organization or enterprise." This is problematic in the U.S. context because it defines the state's jurisdiction more broadly than does the U.S. Constitution. This clause holds governments responsible for protecting women from discrimination committed by public actors as well as private individuals and organizations. The Supreme Court has interpreted the U.S. Constitution in terms of the "state action" doctrine, according to which the government is responsible for protecting individuals from harm done to them by state actors, but not from harm committed against them by private individuals. Article 2 (f) requires states to eliminate "regulations, customs and practices" that discriminate against women, and 2(g) requires the repeal of unequal penal codes. Article 2 emphasizes that states should take "all appropriate measures" to comply with these various provisions, language that gives ratifying countries substantial discretion in determining a course of action. Article 3 obligates states to promote the "full development and advancement of women." Chinkin maintains that the general nature of this statement is intended to address "matters that fall outside the express terms of other articles," but can also be read as "a notable statement of the importance of equality of women and men as a freestanding legal objective" (Rudolf, Freeman, and Chinkin 2012, 102, 121).

Article 4 has two parts. Article 4.1 calls for the adoption of "temporary special measures aimed at accelerating de facto equality between men and women." The intention is to require states to adopt affirmative action measures to correct past discrimination in various arenas and allow women to catch up with men, and then to eliminate those measures once equality is achieved. Although it could easily apply to education or employment, this article has been interpreted primarily to apply to political representation, in the form of gender quotas. Whereas gender quotas would likely arouse concern in the United States, more than 100 countries have adopted measures to require that women constitute a certain percentage of candidates for political office. Article 4.2 provides for protective maternity legislation.

Article 5 addresses the transformation of gender stereotypes. Issues of interpretation are perhaps most relevant to Article 5(a), which enjoins states parties to "take all appropriate measures ... to modify the social and cultural patterns of conduct of men and women, with a view to achieving the elimination of prejudices and customary and all other practices which are based on the idea of the inferiority or the superiority of either of the sexes or on stereotyped roles for men and women." Initially, the CEDAW Committee interpreted Article 5 narrowly as a provision that "would obligate states only to launch information and education campaigns" (Rudolf, Freeman, and Chinkin 2012, 143). Although critics of CEDAW view Article 5 as condemning women's roles as mothers, "the drafters of the Convention stressed the need to see maternity as a positive value instead of a ground to discriminate against women, and they were fully aware that a change in the traditional role of men and women in society is a prerequisite for achieving full equality between men and women" (Rudolf, Freeman, and Chinkin 2012, 142). Article 6 calls for the "suppression" of trafficking and prostitution. CEDAW is one of many international treaties that seek to prevent and punish human trafficking. What makes CEDAW different is that it "offers unique potential to address the underlying root causes of women's and girls' particular vulnerabilities to trafficking" (Rudolf, Freeman, and Chinkin 2012, 172).

Part II of the Convention addresses three aspects of political rights. Article 7 requires governments to ensure that women and men have an equal right to vote, serve in public office, and participate in nongovernmental organizations. This is a slightly modified version of the CPRW from 1952. Article 8 requires governments to "take all appropriate action" to provide equal opportunities for women to represent their countries in the diplomatic corps and international organizations. Article 9 incorporates the provisions of the 1957 Convention on the Nationality of Married Women, which guarantees that women's citizenship status is independent of her husband's and men and women have equal rights in determining their children's nationality.

Part III focuses on social and economic rights and includes five articles. Article 10 addresses equality in various aspects of education, including educational attainment at all levels of schooling, quality of schooling, access to scholarships, and participation in sports and physical education programs. Article 11 focuses on employment. Two of the clauses in Article 11 would raise some concerns in the American context. Article 11(1)(d) establishes women's "right to equal remuneration, including benefits, and to equal treatment in respect of work of equal value, as well as equality of treatment in the evaluation of the quality of work." Legislation to establish equal pay or comparable worth policies in the United States has been controversial. Some have argued that the United States would require a reservation to exempt the United States from adhering to this article, whereas others, including the American Bar Association, maintain that existing U.S. law is already in accord with this article. Article 11(2)(b) calls for paid maternity leave, which the United States does not provide as a matter of public policy. Private employers may provide paid maternity leave at their own discretion, and the Family and Medical Leave Act allows all workers to take unpaid leave for a range of reasons that goes beyond maternity leave. Article 12 enjoins states to provide equal "access to health care services, including those related to family planning." This provision could prove controversial in the United States given that abortion could be construed as an aspect of family planning. Article 13 guarantees (a) the right to family benefits; (b) the right to bank loans, mortgages, and other forms of financial credit; and (c) the right to participate in recreational activities, sports, and all aspects of cultural life. Article 14 represents an effort to address the specific needs of women in rural areas. Part IV covers the rights of women in the legal arena (Article 15) and in marriage and the family (Article 16). Many countries have reserved parts of both of these articles on the grounds that they conflict with religious law.

The articles in Part V commit countries that sign the Convention to a system of regular reporting on their compliance with the Convention and describe the operation of the CEDAW Committee, which oversees implementation. Article 17 defines the membership of the CEDAW Committee and stipulates that the twenty-three Committee members "serve in their personal capacity." They must be citizens of the state party that nominates them, but, unlike many UN delegates, they do not represent their governments in an official capacity. As I discuss in Chapter 5, this provision gives the Committee more autonomy than it would otherwise have. The institutional autonomy of the Committee has allowed it to develop an extremely progressive understanding of women's rights, one that outpaces the status of women or women's rights in any UN member country. The requirement that experts are of "high moral standing and competence in the field covered by the Convention" has meant that Committee members bring expertise in women's rights to their work with CEDAW. Article 18 requires states to submit periodic reports on their progress toward compliance. Signatories must provide an initial report within one year of ratifying the convention, periodic reports every four years after that, and additional reports "whenever the Committee so requests." Articles 19–22 define other guidelines for the operation of the Committee: "The Committee shall adopt its own rules of procedure," and experts serve a two-year term (19); the Committee meets for two weeks per year at UN headquarters, pending approval of an amendment to confirm the Committee's current practice of meeting three weeks twice a year

(20); the Committee reports annually to the ECOSOC and the General Assembly and it "may make suggestions and general recommendations based on the examination of reports and information received from States Parties" (21); and specialized agencies within the UN may attend CEDAW sessions (22). I shall examine Part V of the Convention in more depth in my discussion of the reporting process in Chapter 5.

The first article in Part VI, Article 23, defines the relationship between CEDAW and existing domestic law and addresses the possibility that countries have adopted policies that are more progressive than the Convention. It says, "Nothing in the present Convention shall affect any provisions that are more conducive to the achievement of equality between men and women" in existing legislation or the provisions of other international treaties or domestic agreements. According to Article 24, "States Parties undertake to adopt all necessary measures at the national level aimed at achieving the full realization of the rights recognized in the present Convention." Article 25 describes the process by which CEDAW enters into force, and Articles 26 and 27 lay out the provisions for amending, disputing, and distributing the Convention.

Article 28 allows signatories of CEDAW to exempt themselves from a particular part of the treaty by adopting reservations. A country may also ratify the treaty along with statements of "understandings" and "declarations" that clarify the terms on which a country is willing (or unwilling) to implement the treaty provisions. Together, reservations, understandings, and declarations are known as RUDs. CEDAW enjoys the dubious distinction of having the highest number of RUDs of any UN human rights treaty. Although CEDAW formally prohibits reservations that are "incompatible with the object and purpose" of the treaty, neither the Committee nor individual states parties have the power to decide whether a reservation is incompatible or punish states that make incompatible reservations. The liberal use of reservations by countries ratifying the treaty in the mid-1980s prompted some signatories to object strenuously, but nothing came of their protests (Clark 1991).

The relative flexibility of the CEDAW reservations regime has benefits and limitations. The weak reservations process has probably led more countries to ratify the treaty, making it more universal, but it also reduces the weight of ratification (Cartwright 1997). The majority of CEDAW reservations are to articles that the CEDAW

Committee considers to be core provisions: Articles 2, 5, 7, and 16.[2] As the CEDAW Web site maintains, "The Committee is particularly concerned at the number and extent of reservations entered to those articles" (UN Women 2000).

The CEDAW Committee has urged states parties to withdraw their reservations. As of 2010, of the fifty-two countries that had ratified CEDAW with reservations, thirteen have removed all of them and nineteen have removed some of them (Byrnes and Freeman 2012, 10). Four additional countries removed their reservations in 2011. Members of the Committee exert pressure on states parties to withdraw their reservations and thus do not necessarily treat reservations as though they were off the table for discussion. "The dialogue with States Parties on reservations, as well as an uncompromising insistence on the universal validity of CEDAW norms, has contributed to the review of reservations" and has prompted many countries to withdraw them (Goonesekere 2007, 54). The Committee's treatment of reservations is particularly relevant to the debate about CEDAW in the United States. Placing a reservation on a particular article, a strategy urged by many supporters of ratification, does not preclude the Committee from asking about it during the reporting sessions.

The last two articles of CEDAW are Article 29, which outlines the provisions by which the International Court of Justice can adjudicate disputes among states parties, and Article 30, which calls for CEDAW to be made available in Arabic, Chinese, English, French, Russian, and Spanish. Finally, in 1999, the UN General Assembly approved an Optional Protocol to CEDAW. The Optional Protocol (OP) is a separate treaty that 104 states have ratified to date.[3] Ratification of the OP, which is permitted only for countries that have ratified CEDAW, allows any individual or organization within that country to present a claim of rights violation before the CEDAW Committee.[4] CEDAW itself applies only to governments, not individuals or organizations. There has to date been very little public discussion about the prospect of the United States ratifying the OP.

[2] Retrieved from http://www.un.org/womenwatch/daw/cedaw/reservations.htm.
[3] Current ratification data for the Optional Protocol is available at United Nations 2013b.
[4] Five other human rights treaties have Optional Protocols: ICESCR, ICCPR, CRC, CAT and CRPD.

CEDAW'S EVOLVING JURISPRUDENCE

After the initial fanfare introducing CEDAW to the world at the Copenhagen Conference in 1980, the Convention remained largely irrelevant to the transnational women's rights movement. In its early days, CEDAW was weak and did not operate effectively. It had an anemic operating budget and was governed separately from the other human rights conventions. Initially, the Division for the Advancement of Women oversaw CEDAW and the Office of the High Commissioner for Human Rights in Geneva oversaw the other treaties. It was a low priority for those states that had ratified it and countries submitted their initial reports slowly. By 1984, less than half of the ratifying countries had submitted initial reports (twenty-one of fifty) and only thirteen of those had presented their reports in a session with the CEDAW Committee (Galey 1984). People continued to view women's inequality as the result of "general backwardness" rather than the effect of weak, ineffective, or nonexistent government policy (Corti 2007, 38). These were inauspicious origins for the Convention that would eventually become the world's foremost guarantor of women's human rights.

It took a while for the treaty body to get off the ground. The CEDAW Committee held its first session from October 18 to 22, 1982; it devoted the entire session to adoption of rules of procedure, which it presented to the General Assembly in 1983. At its fifth session, held in 1986, the Committee heard reports from five countries: Mongolia, Vietnam, Ecuador, the Czech Republic, and El Salvador. The delegation from each country included only one or two government officials. A lack of statistical information prevented the experts from ascertaining the de facto status of women; as a result, the constructive dialogue between government officials and CEDAW experts focused on information that had *not* been provided, rather than on the quality of existing legal guarantees and programs. Statements from government officials reflected exaggerated claims about the degree to which they complied with the treaty. The representative from Mongolia, for example, began his presentation by asserting that "full equality between men and women in all aspects of life" had been realized in Mongolia and that "any attempt to deny women's rights was punishable by law" (United Nations 1986, 10). Some of the questions from some members of the Committee reflected a low level of sophistication about gender inequality. One expert, in a question to the delegate from Mongolia regarding Article 5, "asked specifically if the superiority of the male sex still prevailed" (United Nations 1986, 12). The Mongolian official responded to all the questions by affirming "that equal rights were guaranteed in his country and that the solution of women's problems was inseparable from the general advancement of his Government" (United Nations 1986, 13). These exchanges typify CEDAW's early sessions: government officials provided a low level of information, Committee experts exhibited an insufficient knowledge about women's rights, and the government delegations included only a few officials.

In the early years of CEDAW, experts from the Soviet Union and Eastern European countries used the Committee as a vehicle to praise the progress of communist countries with regard to women's rights, mute criticisms, and excoriate capitalist countries for their lack of progress. Eastern bloc countries ratified early and had strong representation on the Committee in the early 1980s. Elizabeth Evatt, a former CEDAW expert from Australia, recalls that in the 1980s,

My colleagues and I spent much energy on the struggle between competing ideologies. Members from the Soviet Union and the Eastern bloc countries, which dominated the Committee, insisted that women could achieve equality only under their centrally controlled socialist economies. Members from Western countries did not agree. This led to many hotly contested debates. Now, however, that struggle between competing ideologies is over. (Evatt 2007, 106)

Former CEDAW Committee expert Hanna Beate Schöpp-Schilling echoes Evatt:

Not only did those [socialist] countries believe that they fully complied with the Convention – which they undoubtedly did in almost all aspects of women's *formal* equality with men; they were also convinced, as were the Committee's experts coming from these countries, that their laws and equality policies as well as the nature of their reports under Article 18 of the Convention could serve as "models" for other countries. (Schöpp-Schilling and Flinterman 2007, 163)

Désirée Patricia Bernard, an expert from Guyana, served on the Committee starting in 1982 and chaired it from 1985 to 1988. She recalled that

[w]hen the Committee was inaugurated, many of the experts were from socialist countries – Cuba, Bulgaria, China, German Democratic Republic, Hungary,
Mongolia, Poland, USSR, Vietnam, and Yugoslavia – with many belonging to
the Soviet bloc. Most of these experts invariably presented a united position
on important aspects of the Committee's work, and experts from the Soviet
bloc looked to the USSR expert for guidance in deciding how they should
approach any issues that came up for discussion. (Bernard 2007, 267)

Since the collapse of the Soviet Union in 1991, the CEDAW experts
have demonstrated a more uniform willingness to put women's rights
over ideological considerations, and acknowledged the actual situation of women in their countries more openly. Again, Bernard:

After 1989 the composition of the Committee changed ... [which] resulted in
a shift in the types of questions that experts posed to representatives of States
Parties in dialogue with them. Hitherto, the criteria used by the Soviet bloc
experts tended to reflect women's responsibilities as wife and mother, and the
protection and glorification afforded them by the state. The reports of these
States also reflected only positive aspects of women's lives and denied the existence of any negative situations found in Western countries such as prostitution. In later years, the reports received from the majority of the former Soviet
bloc States Parties were more open and frank, with admissions of negative
situations as well as discussions of positive progress made in implementing the
Convention. (Bernard 2007, 267)

These statements reveal that the CEDAW Committee initially faced
the same kinds of ideological conflicts that the CSW had confronted in
its first few decades, as I discussed in Chapter 2. When the Cold War
came to an end in 1991, the need for communist countries to tout the
party line on the status of women diminished and country representatives spoke more freely about the problems women in those countries
faced.

THE GENERAL RECOMMENDATIONS

Although the formal text of CEDAW has not changed since the
General Assembly approved it in 1979, the way the Committee interprets it has evolved continuously. General recommendations (GRs)
are the formal mechanism that have facilitated a progressive interpretation of the Convention over time, as stipulated by Article 21.
Since 1986, the CEDAW Committee has issued twenty-nine general

recommendations that explain how states parties should interpret various articles.[5] Taken together, the GRs constitute the evolving jurisprudence of the Convention. The GRs seek to resolve areas of ambiguity and correct areas that have presented multiple countries with implementation difficulties. They are general in that they provide guidance to *all* states about how to report on issues not fully specified within the Convention and instruct governments on general issues of compliance and interpretation. Although the text of CEDAW is legally binding, the GRs themselves are not. As the CEDAW Web site makes clear, the "general recommendations are addressed to States parties and usually elaborate the Committee's view of the obligations assumed under the Convention." The operative word here is "view"; the GRs do not reflect the Committee's ruling or judgment (UN Women 2013b).[6]

The Committee has used its ability to write general recommendations to define a progressive jurisprudence of the Convention. Changes in global understandings of women's rights inform the GRs. According to former CEDAW Committee member Dorcas Coker-Appiah, "the CEDAW Committee is consistently interpreting the Convention to take into account new forms of discrimination as they are emerging" (quoted in Hayes 2011). Teng Beng Hui, a women's rights advocate in Malaysia, observes, "This allows the Convention to remain relevant to changing circumstances and histories and to be utilized in response to emerging issues" (Tan Beng Hui 2007, 7).

The first thirteen GRs stand out for their brevity and vagueness. Each is one to two paragraphs long and covers less than a page of text. As former Committee expert Silvia Rose Cartwright notes, these early GRs, all written in the late 1980s, provide little guidance about actions that a state might take to respond to a specific issue (Cartwright 2007). One example is GR No. 3, which addresses Article 5 on stereotypes. Article 5 is perhaps the most vague and confusing part of the treaty, but the general recommendation offers little help in elucidating its meaning. The recommendation merely "urges all States parties effectively to adopt education and public information programmes, which will help eliminate prejudices and current

---

[5] Retrieved from http://www.un.org/womenwatch/daw/cedaw/recommendations/index. html.

[6] I thank Stephanie Farrior for this insight.

practices that hinder the full operation of the principle of the social equality of women." In other words, GR No. 3 instructs countries to adopt public awareness campaigns in order to change gender stereotypes but does not clarify what constitutes violations of Article 5. Many of these early recommendations merely urge governments to heed existing guidelines. GR No. 5, for example, "recommends that States Parties make more use of temporary special measures such as positive action, preferential treatment or quota systems to advance women's integration into education, the economy, politics and employment." In other words, GR No. 5 simply instructs governments to implement Article 4.1.

Beginning with GR No. 14 on female circumcision, the GRs offer more specific direction and aim to incorporate the "Committee's accumulated knowledge" about the type of information government officials should provide in a particular area (Cartwright 2007).[7] Drafted in 1990 and 1991, GR Nos. 14–18 go well beyond the text of the Convention to define a series of specific issues as forms of discrimination against women: female circumcision (14), AIDS (15), employment in the informal sector (16), unpaid household labor (17), and disability (18). Each explains how the issue in question is relevant to a particular article of the Convention, recommends that governments collect data on the problem, urges governments to include that data in their periodic reports, and identifies other UN entities that have addressed the issue. Each of these five recommendations is approximately one page in length.

Beginning with GR No. 19, written in 1992, the recommendations become much longer and more detailed. GR No. 19 addresses violence against women and is thus one of the most important recommendations. The text of CEDAW does not address violence against women explicitly, reflecting the era in which the Convention was drafted. Sexuality and violence against women did not appear on the

---

[7] As the CEDAW Web site indicates, "At its tenth session in 1991, the Committee decided to adopt the practice of issuing general recommendations on specific provisions of the Convention and on the relationship between the Convention Articles and what the Committee described as 'cross-cutting' themes. Following this decision, CEDAW issued more detailed and comprehensive general recommendations which offer States parties clear guidance on the application of the Convention in particular situations." Retrieved from http://www.un.org/womenwatch/daw/cedaw/recommendations/index.html.

international agenda until the 1980s (Keck and Sikkink 1998). The prominence of this issue in contemporary transnational feminism makes this omission stand out. Over time, the CEDAW experts came to see prevention of violence as central to eliminating discrimination against women. GR No. 19 articulates the ways in which violence against women is relevant to each of the specific articles of CEDAW, identifies specific measures that states might take to eliminate it, and affirms that "the full implementation of the Convention requires States to take positive measures to eliminate all forms of violence against women." GR No. 19 evolved out of a CEDAW session held prior to the 1993 World Conference on Human Rights in Vienna. After the Vienna Conference, which I discuss later in this chapter, the CEDAW Committee conducted a systematic review of the parts of the Convention that related to violence against women. GR No. 19 defines violence against women as a form of discrimination, "placing it squarely within the rubric of human rights and fundamental freedoms, and making clear that states are obliged to eliminate violence perpetrated by public authorities and private persons" (Ramaseshan 2007, 11). GR No. 19 reaffirms that CEDAW's definition of discrimination applies to both public and private action:

Discrimination under the Convention is not restricted to action by or on behalf of Governments (see articles 2 (e), 2 (f) and 5). For example, under article 2 (e) the Convention calls on States parties to take all appropriate measures to eliminate discrimination against women by any person, organization or enterprise. Under general international law and specific human rights covenants, States may also be responsible for private acts if they fail to act with due diligence to prevent violations of rights or to investigate and punish acts of violence, and for providing compensation. (Office of the United Nations High Commissioner for Human Rights 2013a)

Accordingly, "States parties should take appropriate and effective measures to overcome all forms of gender-based violence, whether by public or private act." This is highly relevant to the question of private jurisdiction, an issue I return to in Chapter 7. During the CEDAW sessions, the experts now routinely ask specific questions about the measures that states have adopted to combat violence against women. In this area, CEDAW has had a significant impact on the General Assembly, which formalized its commitment to the issue when it adopted the Declaration on the Elimination of Violence Against Women in 1993.

GR No. 21 on equality in marriage and family relations was developed at a conference convened by Committee expert Hanna Beate Schöpp-Schilling. It addresses discrimination as it relates to three articles: Article 9 concerning nationality rights; Article 15 on equality before the law; and Article 16, which seeks to ensure equality "in all matters relating to marriage and family relations." Its purpose is to update the convention to address the need for equality among "various forms of family," "whatever form it takes, and whatever the legal system, religion, custom or tradition within a country." The GR singles out polygamous marriages as a family form that "contravene[s] a woman's right to equality with men." GR No. 22 recommends that governments approve the proposed amendment to CEDAW that will allow the CEDAW Committee to meet for three weeks twice a year. The CEDAW Committee has already adopted this change to its working procedure, despite the fact that the amendment has not yet been approved. GR No. 23 provides a sophisticated analysis of the obstacles that women face in participating in public life and have contributed to "the gap between the de jure and de facto" status of women that is the "critical issue" surrounding a range of factors affecting women, including stereotypes, the double burden of paid and unpaid labor, less access to political information, and the design of electoral systems.

GR No. 24 addresses Article 12 on women's health. It identifies a list of specific women's health statistics that states should provide in their report. It goes well beyond the substance of Article 12 to stipulate that full compliance with the treaty requires an adequate institutional framework in the government overall, one that "ensures effective judicial action. Failure to do so will constitute a violation of article 12." The GR makes explicit links between Article 12 and GR No. 19 on violence against women, for example, in its call for "fair and protective procedures for hearing complaints and imposing appropriate sanctions on health-care professionals guilty of sexual abuse of women patients." The language of the recommendation reflects feminist theoretical claims about gender power imbalances. In a description of the way in which sexual mores can compromise women's health, it states: "As a consequence of unequal power relations based on gender, women and adolescent girls are often unable to refuse sex or insist on safe and responsible sex practices. Harmful traditional practices, such as female genital mutilation, polygamy, as well as marital rape, may also expose girls and women to the risk of contracting HIV/AIDS and other sexually transmitted diseases." GR No. 24 embraces an intersectional approach to women's health, calling for "special attention to be given to the health needs and rights of women belonging to vulnerable and disadvantaged groups, such as migrant women, refugee and internally displaced women, the girl child and older women, women in prostitution, indigenous women and women with physical or mental disabilities."

GR No. 24 specifically mentions abortion. It calls upon states to "prioritize the prevention of unwanted pregnancy through family planning and sex education and reduce maternal mortality rates through safe motherhood services and prenatal assistance. When possible, legislation criminalizing abortion could be amended to remove punitive provisions imposed on women who undergo abortion." This statement articulates the position that the Committee has sought to maintain across all states parties, which aims to reduce the degree to which legal limits on abortion threaten women's health. It asserts that severe restrictions on abortion constitute a violation of women's right to health. CEDAW Committee expert Carmel Shalev, who took the lead in formulating this GR, affirms that abortion remains contentious:

Despite the fact that many [members of the Committee] consider freedom of choice in abortion to be key to women's autonomy over their lives and their social status, there has never been a consensus among the members of the Committee on this issue, except for the understanding that – if performed at all – abortion should take place under safe conditions. (Shalev 2007, 202)

The word "abortion" does not appear in the formal text of the Convention – but this general recommendation makes it clear that the Convention is not "abortion neutral," as some advocates of CEDAW in the United States have claimed. At the same time, the CEDAW Committee does not advocate abortion on demand or define abortion as a basic human right, as conservative opponents of CEDAW in the United States have attested.

The more recent GRs have provided extensive meta-level guidelines on how governments should interpret the Convention overall. GR No. 25, for example, affirms that

The Convention is a dynamic instrument. Since the adoption of the Convention in 1979, the Committee, as well as other actors at the national and international levels, has contributed through progressive thinking to the clarification and understanding of the substantive content of the Convention's articles and the specific nature of discrimination against women and the instruments for combating such discrimination.

The Committee experts who drafted GR No. 25 used it as an opportunity to articulate the Committee's vision of the main purposes of the treaty, and the text is thus worth quoting at length:

A joint reading of articles 1 to 5 and 24, which form the general interpretative framework for all of the Convention's substantive articles, indicates that three obligations are central to States parties' efforts to eliminate discrimination against women. These obligations should be implemented in an integrated fashion and extend beyond a purely formal legal obligation of equal treatment of women with men. Firstly, States parties' obligation is to ensure that there is no direct or indirect discrimination against women in their laws and that women are protected against discrimination – committed by public authorities, the judiciary, organizations, enterprises or private individuals – in the public as well as the private spheres by competent tribunals as well as sanctions and other remedies. Secondly, States parties' obligation is to improve the de facto position of women through concrete and effective policies and programmes. Thirdly, States parties' obligation is to address prevailing gender relations and the persistence of gender-based stereotypes that affect women not only through individual acts by individuals but also in law, and legal and societal structures and institutions. (Office of the United Nations High Commissioner for Human Rights 2013a)

The Committee thus identifies three points that are central to compliance with CEDAW. First, the state is obligated to eliminate public and private discrimination. Second, de jure equality is insufficient. CEDAW requires countries to go beyond legal guarantees of women's equality to ensure that women enjoy de facto equality with men. Let me emphasize that no country in the world has achieved this. Thus, while countries can provide evidence that they are moving toward this goal, no country will get a glowing report card from the CEDAW Committee when it comes to its evaluation of the actual status of women. Substantive equality, or equality of results, matters as much as formal legal equality. Finally, changing – eliminating – gender stereotypes is not (simply) a matter of changing the way in which individual people think about women, but transforming the norms imbedded in institutions. In this recommendation, the Committee experts address erroneous claims that people have made about the notion of equality espoused by the

Convention. They take particular care to emphasize that CEDAW does not aim to treat men and women exactly the same:

Rather, biological as well as socially and culturally constructed differences between women and men must be taken into account. Under certain circumstances, non-identical treatment of women and men will be required in order to address such differences. Pursuit of the goal of substantive equality also calls for an effective strategy aimed at overcoming underrepresentation of women and a redistribution of resources and power between men and women.

GR No. 25 also provides an exegesis of Article 4.1, which calls for states to adopt "temporary special measures" to bring about de facto equality, generally called affirmative action in the U.S. context. GR No. 25 provides an extensive analysis that draws upon the founding documents of the Convention (the *travaux préparatoires*) as well as previous general recommendations. The GR explains the philosophical principles that undergird the call for affirmative action measures, provides a glossary of the terms used in the article, and outlines precise recommendations to states parties about how to implement the article.

Through the GRs, the guidelines for interpretation of CEDAW have become both more precise and more expansive over time. The GRs have allowed CEDAW to remain dynamic and address new ways of understanding gender discrimination and new challenges that did not exist or were thought about differently at the time that CEDAW was drafted. This information should reassure critics who worry that CEDAW's vision of equality reflects a 1970s-style feminism, no longer relevant to the problems that women face today. Through the GRs, CEDAW's vision is continuously informed by contemporary discussions about discrimination against women. At the time same, the evolving jurisprudence of CEDAW is likely to raise serious concerns among critics who do not agree with the basic principles of the Convention in the first place.

INSTITUTIONALIZATION OF NGO INVOLVEMENT

In the 1980s, the number of transnational women's rights NGOs exploded, and the UN became a focal point for women's engagement (Keck and Sikkink 1998). Activists' attention focused on the World

Conferences on Women in Mexico City, Copenhagen, Vienna, and Nairobi. However, women's rights activists in the transnational arena paid little attention to CEDAW until the late 1980s. Not until the creation of the International Women's Rights Action Watch (IWRAW) did NGOs begin to understand how CEDAW could benefit them.

Plans for IWRAW began to take shape at the NGO Forum for the Third World Conference on Women in Nairobi, Kenya, held the summer of 1985. As in Mexico City and Copenhagen, the World Conferences on Women consisted of two parts: an official conference for government delegations and a parallel conference of nongovernmental organizations, known at Nairobi as the NGO Forum. Arvonne Fraser was one of the thousands of participants at the NGO Forum. Fraser had been active in the Democratic-Farmer-Labor Party in Minnesota (essentially the Democratic Party), for many decades. She moved to Washington, DC, in 1963 when her husband, Donald Fraser, was elected to Congress from Minnesota's Fifth District (he served from 1963 to 1979). In 1972, Arvonne founded the Women's Equity Action League. She directed the Women in Development Office at the U.S. Agency for International Development from 1977 to 1981. She became a senior fellow at the Humphrey Institute of Public Affairs at the University of Minnesota when she returned home in 1982. At the NGO Forum, Fraser and Rebecca Cook, a Canadian lawyer for the International Planned Parenthood Federation, held a series of workshops to teach NGOs how to use CEDAW to achieve their goals. Several hundred women from as many as fifty countries, including several CEDAW Committee members and people who would later be elected to the Committee, attended the daily sessions that Fraser and Cook organized (Connors 2007, 283). At the official conference, "almost all representatives agreed that a major achievement of the U.N. decade was the adoption of CEDAW" (U.S. House of Representatives 1986). Nonetheless, CEDAW appears just six times in the 38,000-word Conference document, the Forward Looking Strategies, the plan for action agreed upon by the governments that attended.

After the Nairobi Conference, Arvonne Fraser created IWRAW to provide the CEDAW Committee with higher-quality information about the status of women worldwide. As Fraser recalls in her memoir, *She's No Lady*, "Too few people knew about [CEDAW]. I was appalled that, now an international treaty, its significance and potential drew little interest and even less attention" (Fraser 2007, 227). IWRAW pioneered the development of "shadow reports" that provide an alternative view of the information in the official government reports submitted to the CEDAW Committee. As Fraser put it, "Governments tend to paint rosy pictures of themselves. CEDAW Committee members couldn't know what was going on in every country. They needed alternative or 'shadow reports' from non-governmental groups" (Fraser 2007, 248). IWRAW staff conducted the research for the shadow reports using publicly available sources (such as Lexis/Nexis searches), interviews with experts, and information from NGOs in particular countries. IWRAW Executive Director Marsha Freeman affirmed that "proper citation was key so that activists could back up the info" and identify its source; the quality and verifiability of the research enhanced the legitimacy of the reports in the eyes of skeptical and often defensive government officials (M. Freeman 2008).

IWRAW sought to increase the visibility of the Convention by publishing it in English, French, and Spanish and distributing it worldwide. It edited *Women's Watch*, a quarterly newsletter that reported on violations of women's human rights, and cited examples of how organizations had used the treaty to change government policy (Fraser and Tinker 2004, 174). *Women's Watch* told the stories of individual activists and women personally affected by discrimination, a tactic long used by human rights activists to raise awareness. Fraser put her political instincts and organizing skills together on behalf of IWRAW; she maintained her contacts by sending them information and materials on a regular basis. She hired Freeman, "a lawyer with a Ph.D. in English," as executive director. IWRAW also sought to disseminate information about CEDAW by publicizing what the CEDAW Committee actually said and did. As Fraser wrote: "The UN doesn't like to alienate its member governments. IWRAW had less compunction. We were bent on telling the world in simple language that said 'there's a new treaty on women's rights. A CEDAW Committee monitors its implementation. Here is information about that Committee, who is on it, what it does and did this session' (Fraser 2007, 248).

IWRAW is headquartered at the Human Rights Center of the University of Minnesota Law School in Minneapolis. It continues to operate today, participating in the CEDAW process and coordinating research and publication of material related to the Convention. It no longer produces shadow reports; that work has passed to country-level NGOs.

In 1993, IWRAW gave rise to an offshoot organization called IWRAW Asia Pacific. Malaysian women's rights activist Shanthi Dairam came up with the idea after she attended an IWRAW seminar that trained advocates how to use CEDAW to address reproductive rights policy. Dairam's experience at that meeting inspired her to found her own organization and deepen the involvement of NGOs at the domestic level. As she stated in an interview, "No one knew about CEDAW. No one was bringing women into the review [process] at the national level when they didn't even know what all that was about. I wanted constituencies of women who would work on the ground, so that was how the whole program started" (Dairam 2011). Dairam wanted to forge stronger links between CEDAW and grassroots advocacy at the domestic level.[8]

IWRAW Asia Pacific initially focused on linking domestic activism with CEDAW in twelve countries in South and Southeast Asia. It now trains national organizations how to write shadow reports, use CEDAW to address their specific concerns, and monitor their country's compliance with CEDAW. The organization works with 15 countries in Southeast Asia and has provided training for women's groups in more than 117 countries worldwide (IWRAW Asia Pacific 2013). IWRAW Asia Pacific publishes materials that support advocacy and capacity building among NGOs. A series of very user-friendly manuals are available on its Web site. Each of these reports begins with a clear explanation of a particular policy issue, defines international legal terms in straightforward language, describes key debates, and lays out the contours of international law that are relevant to particular issues. IWRAW Asia Pacific also provides informal oversight of the CEDAW process, sometimes reporting on

---

[8] Dairam named her group IWRAW Asia Pacific to capitalize on the reputation of the existing organization. The two organizations share the same name but are autonomous from one another. Dairam tipped her hat to Fraser during her remarks on the 30th anniversary of CEDAW at the UN headquarters in New York in 2012: "It was [Arvonne's] pioneering work that first created the realization of the significance of the relationship between the work of the Committee and women's groups as early as 1985. She initiated the creation of an international network of women activists, motivating them to take an interest in the Convention and in the reporting process at the United Nations" (Dairam 2012).

misinterpretations or misuses of the Convention (see Facio and Morgan 2009).

The relationship between IWRAW Asia Pacific and the CEDAW Committee has become formalized, such that any NGO wanting to participate in a reporting session must submit a request through IWRAW Asia Pacific. On the Web site for each of the sessions of the CEDAW Committee, the following text appears:

Representatives of non-governmental organizations and national human rights institutions may also provide information orally on the States parties under consideration directly to the Committee at informal meetings scheduled for this purpose. Organizations wishing to make oral interventions at these meetings should contact IWRAW-AP at iwraw-ap@iwraw-ap.org or iwraw_ap@ yahoo.com, or the Secretary of CEDAW (Office of the United Nations High Commissioner for Human Rights 2013b).

Thanks to IWRAW Asia Pacific, NGOs now have formal opportunities to participate in the meetings at which government officials present their reports to the CEDAW Committee, which I discuss at length in Chapter 5.

GEOPOLITICS AND THE UN WORLD CONFERENCES

With the collapse of the socialist world in the 1990s, a rights-based agenda came to dominate the global women's movement. Socialists could no longer credibly trumpet their superiority when it came to the status of women. Arguments linking women's oppression with economic inequality lost power as market economics swept across the globe. In this context, the UN hosted the World Conference on Human Rights in Vienna from June 14 to 25, 1993. The Vienna Conference changed the way that people thought about women's issues in the UN community. Former CEDAW expert Jane Connors recalls that until Vienna "the emphasis of the international women's movement was on issues relating to women and development, with little attention being paid to human rights" (Connors 2007, 283). What emerged in Vienna was a "consensus of UN member States" on the idea that women's rights were properly understood as human rights. This change "gave [CEDAW] a new global relevance," observed Savitri Goonesekere, a CEDAW expert from Sri Lanka (Goonesekere 2007, 52).

Women's rights advocates came to the Vienna Conference having done the kind of preparatory work that allowed them to seize the post–Cold War moment effectively. Prior to Vienna, American activist Charlotte Bunch held a series of small conferences at the Center for Women's Global Leadership at Rutgers University (Joachim 2003). The groups that attended these preparatory meetings, such as the Women's Rights Project of the Human Rights Watch, the women's project of the International League for Human Rights, and the women's program of the International Human Rights Law Group, "played key roles in the organizing and lobbying that resulted in the inclusion of a section on women's human rights in the Vienna Declaration and Programme of Action" (M. A. Freeman 2008, 71). The actions by women's groups were part of the "thousands of preparatory documents and position papers, contributions by 95 international organizations, expert bodies, national human rights institutions and approximately 900 non-governmental organizations" that participated in the process (UN General Assembly 1998). CEDAW's significance changed with the formal affirmation that "the human rights of women and of the girl-child are an inalienable, integral and indivisible part of universal human rights" (United Nations 1993 para. 18, cited in Corti 2007, 39).

The parallels between the Vienna Declaration and Programme of Action and the language of CEDAW "put CEDAW on the world's human rights agenda and further strengthened it. The [CEDAW] Committee was given universal recognition as a human rights treaty body, and the doors of the manifold UN entities … were finally thrown open to begin a new and productive period of cooperation" (Corti 2007, 39). Former CEDAW expert Cees Flinterman recalls, "With hindsight the year 1993 can be regarded as a catalyst in the development of human rights of women" (Flinterman 2007, 286).

The momentum generated at the Vienna Conference carried over to the Fourth World Conference on Women, held in Beijing in 1995. It was the largest conference yet, with more than 6,000 government delegates and more than 4,000 accredited NGO representatives. The parallel NGO Forum held in Huairou near Beijing drew some 30,000 participants (UN Women 2011). The Beijing Conference sparked a new wave of interest in CEDAW and prompted the UN General Assembly to initiate efforts to strengthen the Convention. Aurora Javate de Dios, a CEDAW expert from the Philippines, recalled, "Interest in the Beijing

Conference and the discussions on the draft Beijing Platform for Action brought renewed attention and interest in the Convention, as evidenced by most intense discussions and new documents produced by international organizations, governments, and NGOs focusing on the work of the CEDAW Committee" (Javate de Dios 2007, 310).

In one of many memorable moments of the conference, Hillary Clinton, then First Lady, gave a speech in which she declared, "Women's rights are human rights, and human rights are women's rights" (YouTube 1995). Beijing was the largest UN women's conference yet, but it was not only memorable for its size. Intense conflicts emerged between feminists and religious conservatives over a range of issues, including reproductive rights, gay rights, and use of the term "gender" (Baldez 2002). The threats that fundamentalists posed to women's rights prompted people to see CEDAW from a new perspective; they began to value its importance as a legally binding document that guaranteed certain rights. As Javate de Dios recalled, "The challenges and difficulties posed by conservative countries and groups during the negotiations in Beijing crystallized the strategic importance of the CEDAW Convention as the only legally binding human rights instrument for women that a majority of UN member States have committed to implementing" (Javate de Dios 2007, 310). Advocates saw CEDAW as a way to prevent existing rights from erosion.

The UN made a big push to get more countries to ratify CEDAW prior to the Beijing Conference. Malaysia was one of twelve countries that ratified in 1995, the year that the conference took place. Malaysian women's rights advocate Ivy Josiah explains that Malaysia reserved Article 16 because taking a controversial issue (family rights) off the table allowed the government to act quickly and ratify the treaty in time for the conference: "We didn't have time to argue about these things. Just reserve the whole thing and we'll lobby to remove the reservations after." Countries that attended the Beijing Conference without having ratified the Convention risked losing face in the international arena. As Josiah recalled, "What was really good about that UN conference was that they already said they would have a chart or a board of the countries that have signed on, or the countries that have not signed on. The conference itself was the trigger factor" that prompted many countries to ratify (Josiah 2011).

The Beijing Platform for Action added to the responsibilities of the CEDAW Committee by calling on the CEDAW experts to monitor implementation of the Platform's goals. Former expert Schöpp-Schilling notes that "the Platform for Action is not a legally binding document"; it merely "invites" states parties to report on "measures taken to implement the Platform for Action," but does not require them to do so (Schöpp-Schilling 2007, 251). The CEDAW Committee has facilitated this process by "linking the Platform for Action's twelve areas of concern to the articles of the CEDAW Convention. Thus, in the view of the Committee, the contents of the Platform recommend *programmatic* details to States Parties for implementing *rights* articulated in the Convention" (Schöpp-Schilling 2007, 261). The CEDAW Committee later did the same thing with regard to the Millennium Development Goals (MDGs), a campaign initiated by the UN in 2002 to achieve concrete progress in reducing poverty: "In 2005 [the CEDAW Committee] added a paragraph to its concluding comments pointing out that the achievement of the MDGs depends above all on the complete and effective implementation of the Convention" (Ibid.).

INSTITUTIONAL REFORMS

In the years since 1979, CEDAW has been strengthened by a series of reforms to the operation of the CEDAW Committee. CEDAW is weaker than other human rights conventions in terms of enforcement mechanisms. Weak capacity and inadequate resources initially prevented the CEDAW Committee from working effectively. Members of the CEDAW Committee experienced profound marginalization within the UN itself. Former Committee chair Ivanka Corti describes her frustration at having to attend the Vienna Conference at her own expense, for example (Corti 2007, 39).

In 1995, in response to demands to strengthen CEDAW generated at the Beijing Conference, the UN General Assembly passed a resolution (51/68) allowing the Committee to meet twice a year for three weeks each (UN General Assembly 1997).[9] Lengthening the time of the sessions and increasing their frequency has allowed the Committee

---

[9] As I mentioned in the discussion of GRs, this change requires a formal amendment to the text of CEDAW, the status of which is currently pending. Sixty-four countries have approved the amendment, of the 125 countries required (Office of the United Nations High Commissioner for Human Rights 2012).

to dispense with a backlog of reports. The UN provided additional resources to the Division for the Advancement of Women, which created a Women's Rights Unit to oversee CEDAW. Under the leadership of Australian lawyer Jane Connors, CEDAW brought its practices into line with the other human rights treaties.

In 2008, the UN made a number of institutional changes to the CEDAW process. After twenty-five years under the Division for the Advancement of Women, operation of CEDAW moved to the Office of the High Commissioner for Human Rights (OHCHR) in Geneva, Switzerland. The move has integrated the Committee more fully into the UN human rights community and has "facilitated the process of harmonization and cross-fertilisation" among the treaty bodies (Byrnes 2010, 2). Before this reform, the treaty bodies of the other human rights treaties tended to eschew women's rights on the grounds that "it was the CEDAW's job to deal with women"; now they work together to address women's issues from a range of perspectives (Otto 2002, 24). Working more closely with other treaty bodies has proven particularly important in adjudicating cases that involve competing human rights. In some cases of domestic violence, for example, protecting the victim's right to "life and physical and mental integrity" potentially conflicts with the need to protect the perpetrator's right to freedom from arbitrary detention (Byrnes 2010, 2).

The OHCHR adopted a new set of reporting guidelines for all the human rights treaty bodies in 2008. Countries are now required to submit a "common core document" that provides general background information on human rights within the country, as well as a treaty-specific report that addresses each of the specific treaties that the country has ratified. The new guidelines provide extremely specific instructions for the structure of the reports, including lists of statistical indicators, page length (common-core document no more than sixty pages and treaty-specific report maximum of forty pages), and even the font size that should be used (12-point Times New Roman).[10]

The treaty-specific guidelines for CEDAW ask that countries discuss any measures adopted in response to the Committee's previous

---

[10] The guidelines and the common core documents for all countries are available at http://www2.ohchr.org/english/bodies/coredocs.htm.

concluding comments and provide information on "remaining or emerging obstacles" to achieving full equality. The guidelines request that reports should indicate how a country plans to implement the convention "with respect to different groups of women, in particular those subject to multiple forms of discrimination." In this group, the guidelines include lesbian, bisexual, and transgendered women; migrant women; refugees; and asylum seekers. The guidelines request that periodic reports explicitly discuss how countries have implemented the Beijing Platform for Action and the Millennium Development Goals.

Finally, in 2008 the CEDAW experts implemented a third reform that aims to strengthen oversight over states parties during the period between sessions. The Committee now identifies three country-specific priority issues in each set of concluding observations it provides to state parties and requests that governments provide a "follow-up report" on those issues within two years. The follow-up reports are posted on the CEDAW Committee Web site. As of 2013, the Committee has requested follow-up reports from forty-three countries; all but four (Egypt, Haiti, Panama, and the United Arab Emirates) have submitted them (Committee on the Elimination of Discrimination against Women 2013).

In 2010, four of the UN organizations that deal with women's issues were consolidated under a single institutional umbrella, called UN Women: the Division for the Advancement of Women; the International Research and Training Institute for the Advancement of Women; the Office of the Special Adviser on Gender Issues and Advancement of Women; and the United Nations Development Fund for Women (UNIFEM). This initiative occurred as an effort to strengthen UN programs for women and as part of a more general set of reforms intended to make the UN operate more effectively and efficiently.[11]

CEDAW DEFINES AN INTERNATIONAL NORM

A large number of laws and court cases that cite CEDAW suggest that CEDAW has become a global norm. Let me cite a few examples. China incorporated the exact wording of Article 1 of CEDAW into

---

[11] The way in which the creation of UN women has affected the CEDAW process is an important issue that warrants further research.

the Law of the People's Republic of China on the Protection of Rights
and Interests of Women, which was revised in 2005 (Dairam 2007,
326). The Australian Law Reform Commission recommended that
CEDAW's definition of equality be incorporated into domestic law:
"Equality in law, as required by CEDAW, needs to be understood in a
different and more substantial sense than merely equality before the
law. Any understanding of equality must take account of the social
and historical disadvantages of women and how that has affected the
law" (Byrnes 2010, 12). The Hong Kong Law Reform Commission
and the Philippines Magna Carta for Women also cited CEDAW. In a
sexual harassment case that came before the Supreme Court of India in
1997 "the petitioners made repeated reference to the CEDAW, which
has been ratified by India, arguing that the definitions of gender equality in this document" addressed the parts of the Indian Constitution
that spoke to violations of women's rights (Nussbaum 2001, 56).
The Court not only decided in favor of the claimants, but also used
CEDAW to develop a series of measures that employers should undertake to prevent sexual harassment in the workplace. In their legal
analysis of CEDAW, Rudolf et al. (2012) identify scores of cases that
cite CEDAW specifically, but acknowledge that their count is not comprehensive. The Global Justice Center maintains a CEDAW case bank
that provides information on legal cases relevant to CEDAW brought
in individual countries and international courts (Global Justice Center
2011). The large number of cases that cite CEDAW constitute evidence
for the central claims made in this chapter – that the Convention has
grown in international significance over the years.

Many studies on the impact of CEDAW cite domestic policies, laws,
constitutions, and judicial decisions as evidence that the Convention
has influenced domestic policy, but the impact of CEDAW on specific
legal reforms cannot be isolated by other factors that shape domestic
policy, such as lobbying or preferences of politicians, a point I made
in Chapter 1. What we can say, however, is that CEDAW has gained
significance as a central point of reference for women's rights policy
worldwide. Countries around the world have made explicit reference
to CEDAW in public policy, judicial cases, and legislation. These cases
provide evidence that CEDAW has become more legitimate as a tool
of international law. The more frequently CEDAW is mentioned in
domestic policy, the stronger the Convention becomes.

CONCLUSION

Over its thirty-year history, CEDAW has become increasingly effective as a result of efforts by the Committee experts to develop an expansive and coherent jurisprudence, NGO participation, and institutional reforms undertaken by the UN. The global women's rights community paid little attention to CEDAW until the late 1980s when women's rights advocates began to participate directly in the CEDAW process. This work began in earnest as a result of the efforts of Arvonne Fraser and the IWRAW in 1985 and expanded thanks to the work of IWRAW Asia Pacific. NGO participation has made governments pay more attention to the process, knowing they would be accountable to their CEDAW promises at home as well as in the international arena. As a result, CEDAW enjoys global visibility, high salience within the transnational women's movement, and relevance as a reference point for women's rights policy around the world. The CEDAW Committee has sought to make the process more efficient and effective over time, but it remains imperfect. The three-week sessions provide insufficient time to delve into complex issues. Often, neither the CEDAW experts nor the government officials have enough expertise to discuss particular problems in depth. CEDAW has nonetheless become an increasingly powerful instrument for advocating for and advancing women's rights.

U.S. debates about ratification of CEDAW must take the dynamism of the Convention into consideration. It is easy to imagine how the ever-changing interpretations of the articles of the Convention would unnerve conservatives who are more prone to "originalist" interpretations of judicial documents. At the same time, the evolutionary nature of interpretations in CEDAW jurisprudence should prove very attractive to women's rights advocates concerned that the text of the Convention itself is inadequate to address contemporary concerns about the status of women.

5

CEDAW Impact: Process, Not Policy

In 2009, a Malaysian NGO posted a short video about CEDAW on YouTube. The video begins with black and white footage of three teenagers, two boys and a girl, jumping rope. A second girl stands hesitantly to the side. She tries to jump in but falls, then refuses help from the others. As this footage unfolds, these words flash across the screen:

BEFORE CEDAW
Violence in the home was not a crime
Married mothers were not the guardians of their children
Federal constitution did not prohibit gender discrimination
50% of the population are women but less than 5% of politicians were women

Then the screen goes black and we read:

Malaysia ratified CEDAW in 1995.

The screen cuts back to the kids jumping rope, this time in color. The second girl, now happy and confident, jumps in with one of the boys. We read:

Domestic violence is now a crime.
Non-Muslim married men and women are equal guardians of their children.
Gender discrimination is forbidden under the Federal Constitution.
Government plans for 30% women to be decision makers (Women's Candidacy Initiative 2009).

The video depicts CEDAW as the key variable that made the difference between weak and strong rights for women. Before Malaysia ratified CEDAW, the government did not protect women from discrimination; after Malaysia ratified CEDAW, the government moved quickly to adopt laws guaranteeing women's rights. Before CEDAW, women were weak and vulnerable; after CEDAW, women participate fully in civic life and everyone is happy. In the video, CEDAW is like a light switch: ratifying it has an immediate and powerful effect on state policy.

In suggesting that the presence or absence of CEDAW has a direct impact on the status of women's lives, the Malaysian video portrays an idealized vision of the treaty. This is the view that CEDAW advocates promise and CEDAW opponents warn against. It is a compelling view, but a misleading one. Ratification of CEDAW does not lead automatically or instantaneously to changes in the status of women or the adoption of laws protecting women's rights. Instead, ratification of CEDAW precipitates a dynamic process by which domestic political actors can work to bring about change. By ratifying CEDAW, countries take on a legal obligation to comply and make a public commitment to the standards articulated in the Convention. This commitment empowers citizens and NGOs to demand that their government make good on its promises. In and of itself, the Convention lacks the power to transform women's lives. In the context of the domestic political process, however, the Convention can strengthen efforts to eliminate discrimination against women.

In the 187 countries that have ratified CEDAW, women's rights advocates have a clear interest in portraying the Convention as exerting direct impact on government policy. Amplifying the power of CEDAW legitimizes claims for change and intensifies the stakes of inaction. Within the United States, however, these claims have had an altogether different effect. The vision of CEDAW as exerting a direct impact on policy outcomes has impeded the prospects for ratification in the United States. Opponents of CEDAW in the United States have misconstrued the effect of the Convention by exaggerating its potential impact. Recall from Chapter 1 that Concerned Women for America presents CEDAW as requiring the United States to adopt policies that will have a dramatic and detrimental effect on American women. These arguments have contributed to a twenty-five-year deadlock over ratification. Furthermore, claims that CEDAW necessitates

the adoption of a particular set of policies fly in the face of a growing consensus within the literature on international organizations that
human rights treaties work primarily by empowering domestic political actors to demand change at home.

Chapter 1 reviews existing research on socialization to show that
it has overlooked the main mechanism by which CEDAW affects
policy outcomes in signatory countries: the reporting process. From
a socialization perspective, the reporting process is perhaps more
important than the substance of the text of CEDAW because it is
during the reporting sessions that government officials, NGO leaders, and CEDAW experts engage in face-to-face discussion about the
Convention and deliberate about how it applies to particular countries. Engagement with the reporting process teaches government officials and citizens about women's rights. It also teaches the Committee
experts about the particular conditions and policy innovations in various countries and provides them with the opportunity to share their
expertise with other countries. Participation in the CEDAW sessions is
essential to the dissemination of the norms that CEDAW represents.
The process of gathering information on the status of women and
demonstrating compliance with the committee engages states parties
in a process by which they come to value "doing a good job" when
it comes to women's rights. Even if government officials are painting
an unrealistically rosy picture by giving the CEDAW committee what
it asks for, they come to understand what the norms governing the
status of women are. The participation of NGOs in the reporting process by writing shadow reports and meeting with CEDAW committee
members ensures that government officials will take the process as
seriously as they can in order to avoid the risk of negative publicity or
unfavorable press coverage back home. Jo Goodhew, New Zealand's
Minister of Women's Affairs, describes the periodic report as a "report
card" (Scoop News July 13, 2012). Countries want to avoid getting a
bad report card from the CEDAW Committee in the form of concluding comments that highlight the persistence of discrimination against
women at the domestic level.

My aim in this chapter is to correct misconceptions and clarify how
the treaty works. I show that participation in the reporting process is
where much of the action of CEDAW takes place. I describe the various components of the reporting process in the order in which they

occur. First, a country writes its periodic report and submits it to the CEDAW Committee. The CEDAW Committee reviews the report and generates a list of questions that the country delegation must answer in writing. Second, a CEDAW session takes place during which government officials and CEDAW experts engage in a critical dialogue about the country's compliance with the Treaty. The Committee experts meet separately with representatives from NGOs from the country in question. In the final stage of the process, the CEDAW Committee issues its concluding observations, which assess the strengths and limitations of a country's efforts to address its CEDAW obligations. I provide an ethnographic analysis of a CEDAW session in action by describing the session at which the Russian Federation presented its periodic report on July 15, 2010. I conclude by discussing what the reporting process might mean for the United States.

THE CEDAW COMMITTEE

Article 17 of CEDAW stipulates that compliance with the Convention is overseen by a committee comprised of twenty-three experts on women's rights elected by the states parties to the Convention. The experts serve four-year terms, with nine members rotating off every two years. Each state party can nominate one person. Elections are held by secret ballot and the nominees with the highest number of votes and an absolute majority of votes win. Most, but not all, of the experts have been women. Article 17 requires that election of the Committee experts must strive to achieve "equitable geographical distribution and ... the representation of the different forms of civilization as well as the principal legal systems." Compensation for experts on the Committee is low:

According to Article 17(8) of the Convention the members of the Committee shall receive emoluments from UN resources on such terms and conditions as the General Assembly may decide having regard to the importance of the Committee's responsibilities. Initially CEDAW experts received $3,000 US per year. But from 2003 the emoluments were limited to $1 (one) US per year. The same was done for other treaty bodies. (Melander 2007, 346)

Committee experts customarily take the lead in discussions based on their individual areas of expertise (Byrnes 2010). They occasionally initiate efforts to educate their colleagues on particular topics outside the formal work of the committee. Hungarian expert Krisztina Morvai brought in outside experts to raise her colleagues' understanding of the reasons why women work in prostitution, for example (Morvai 2007). Filipina expert Rosario Manalo convened a workshop on migrant women during a CEDAW session in August 2004 that led to the formation of a CEDAW Working Group of Experts on Migrant Women, in the hopes that the working group would propose a GR on migrant women (Manalo 2007, 186). The Committee continues to learn about how discrimination against women works, thanks to the expertise that members bring to the table.

The experts do not represent their countries in an official capacity, a factor that has provided the Committee with considerable autonomy within the UN system. Because they are independent, the CEDAW experts are more willing to challenge claims made by government officials about national policy than they would be if they represented the states parties themselves. As longtime CEDAW expert Hanna Beate Schöpp-Schilling affirms, "The Committee is, after all, an organ of the States Parties, not of the United Nations" (Schöpp-Schilling 2007, 262).

A couple of measures provide the expert Committee with some leverage over states parties. One is the iterated nature of the reporting process: "The obligation to appear again and again before the Committee has the potential for motivating a State Party to show progress" (Dairam 2007, 319). In addition, Article 18 (1)(b) gives the Committee the power to request reports beyond the initial and periodic reports "whenever the Committee so requests." Countries that fail to file periodic reports may trigger the committee to take the initiative and commission its own report (Farrior 1997). The Committee has used this power to demand reports on gender-based violence in the former Yugoslavia in 1993, impact of the genocide on women in Rwanda in 1995, and impact of the Argentine crisis on women in 2002 (Schöpp-Schilling 2007, 260, fn. 5).

PERIODIC REPORTS

Article 18 of CEDAW requires states parties to submit periodic reports on the progress they have made toward "giving effect" to the

Convention. Ratification requires governments to gather data, compile reports on compliance with the treaty, and present those reports to the CEDAW Committee. Countries must file an initial report within a year of ratification and a subsequent report every four years after that. According to Article 18, the periodic reports should address "the legislative, judicial, administrative or other measures which they have adopted ... and on the progress made in this respect." The report "may indicate factors and difficulties affecting the degree of fulfillment of obligations." Periodic reports generally have two sections. The first provides an overview of the status of women in specific detail, as specific as the country can muster. The idea behind this section is to allow the committee to assess the de facto status of women: to what extent do women enjoy equality and freedom from discrimination in their everyday lives? The committee requests precise, statistical detail to provide as comprehensive a picture as possible. In the second section, the country reports on the de jure status of women with regard to each of the substantive articles of the Convention (1–16), describing legislation, public policy, and court action taken to bring about the expansion of women's rights in the way envisioned by the Convention.[1]

Compiling the periodic reports constitutes an important part of the treaty process. The reports in and of themselves, although not a replacement for stronger enforcement mechanisms, require governments to take a diagnostic look at the status of women and identify the strengths and weaknesses of their existing policy. The Committee sets high standards for states parties. The experts are not reluctant to challenge government officials about the quality of the data included in the reports. The reporting requirements alone have generated voluminous amounts of data about the status of women, increasing awareness about discrimination against women, and weakening claims that equality had already been achieved. The reporting process by itself may be sufficient to prompt states to take action by changing laws or "implementing enforcement mechanisms" to existing laws (Farrior 1997, 237).

---

[1] As I discussed in Chapter 4, the current practice is for states parties to submit a Common Core Document to each of the treaty bodies, and then a treaty-specific document addressing the issues specific to each individual treaty.

To a large extent, the effectiveness of the CEDAW process rests on the willingness of state parties to submit reports on time and the quality of the information they provide. Preparing reports imposes a significant burden on ratifying governments:

A State which has ratified all the core human rights treaties is expected to produce more than 20 human rights reports over a ten-year period: that is one every six months. States must also produce responses to lists of issues and prepare to attend treaty body sessions, and then perhaps will need to submit further reports on follow-up to concluding observations.(Office of the United Nations High Commissioner for Human Rights n.d.a, 33)

As more governments ratify more human rights treaties, the treaty bodies or committees that oversee the process face the problem of dealing with a backlog of reports. At the end of a session, the Committee meets for a week to discuss the reports that will be presented at the next session. They prepare lists of questions for the states parties that will appear at the next session. The states parties then have several months to prepare written responses before they appear before the Committee. Government officials have only a limited amount of time to respond.[2] The Committee now allows governments to submit two or more reports in a single session so that the country can catch up on delayed reporting. This informal practice, although expedient, has raised concerns that "some States Parties utilize this informal rule to 'normalize' their reporting schedule into an eight-year reporting cycle" (Schöpp-Schilling 2007, 254).

THE CEDAW SESSIONS

CEDAW tethers the process of socialization to a regularized pattern of interaction between states, the CEDAW Committee, other international

---

[2] Egyptian Mervat Tallaway saw the process from both sides: she served on the committee and later, as minister of insurance and social affairs, presented Egypt's report to the committee. She acknowledged the voluminous work required of states parties: "When I was responsible for presenting my country's report, the Ministry received over sixty written questions on the report submitted from the Committee's pre-session group before we actually appeared in front of the Committee. Approximately forty additional questions were asked in the oral constructive dialogue with the Committee. Over twenty Committee members inquired about all aspects of a woman's life in Egypt." (Tallaway 2007, 272)

organizations, and domestic NGOs. The reporting sessions constitute the central axis of this system of engagement. They provide a formal venue in which governments exhibit and enact their commitment to the norms articulated by the Convention. The sessions can be thought of as a stage on which norms are performed and embodied. The Committee experts invariably subject this performance to a stringent critique.

Each session last three weeks. Between seven and twelve countries present their reports at each session. The Committee devotes one day of its three-week session to each country; that session opens with a thirty-minute statement by the head of delegation, followed by a "constructive dialogue" in which the Committee experts ask questions and the delegation responds. The constructive dialogue between government officials and experts on the CEDAW Committee is limited to five hours, from 10 AM to 1 PM and from 3 PM to 5 PM. The introductory statement by the head of a delegation can last no more than thirty minutes. This was not always the case as Swedish expert Göran Melander recalls, "During my first year in the committee this could go on for hours" (Melander 2007, 346). Experts have three minutes to ask a question, which the Committee chair strictly enforces. Setting time limits for various parts of the reporting – and hewing to them – has streamlined the process. The CEDAW experts meet with NGOs on the first day of the first and second week of each session and allocate five to seven minutes for NGOs to make oral presentations to the Committee, followed by a short dialogue between the NGOs and the members of the Committee. NGOs may attend the entire session, and have several opportunities to meet informally with members of the Committee, for example, during lunch or in between sessions. At the end of a session, the rapporteur assigned to that country drafts "concluding observations" on the basis of the constructive dialogue and governments' responses to questions. These comments acknowledge the country's progress in implementing the treaty, express concerns about areas of limited improvement, and recommend actions to take in the future. The CEDAW Committee sessions are open to the public. All written materials, including summary records of the discussions that take place during the open sessions, are publicly available on the Web site of the Office of the United Nations High Commissioner for Human Rights.[3]

---

[3] Retrieved from http://www2.ohchr.org/english/bodies/cedaw/sessions.htm.

During the constructive dialogue, members of the committee aim to strike a balance between critical review and diplomatic respect for the government delegation: "While experts point to what they consider a lack of implementation, they do not act as a court and do not pass 'verdicts' on a State Party. Rather, the Committee develops specific guidance for each State Party, suggesting the adoption of a variety of measures, legal and otherwise" (Schöpp-Schilling 2007, 254). The experts strive to be as diplomatic as possible in their deliberations with government officials. As former CEDAW expert Emna Aouij from Tunisia recollected: "We needed to establish trust and a constructive dialogue with [the States Parties], not to judge them but to inspire them to negotiate and thus to improve the status of women in the country concerned, to us the measurement of success" (Aouij 2007, 86).

At the same time, the experts sometimes find themselves unable to contain their astonishment at the statements that government officials make. Again, from Aouij:

A discussion comes to mind that occurred during the presentation of one report of a State Party concerning the personal status of a married woman who could be divorced by her husband ... by his simply giving her a "present." I reacted immediately by saying: "Mr. Representative, women need justice and dignity, not a sweetener or a gift!" (Aouij 2007, 87)

Hungarian expert Krisztina Morvai, recalled:

In my very first question ever as a CEDAW member, I tried to address the members of the reporting government in a very diplomatic way. It went something like this: "May I ask the distinguished delegation why, of all professions, did you identify and choose 'cabaret dancing' as a basis for a special visa status for women? Why not brain surgery, civil engineering, or opera singing, for example?" The delegation members looked embarrassed, and the representatives of nongovernmental organizations (NGOs) in the room were laughing. It was obvious that the government spokespersons had never before considered this issue as problematic from a sex-equality point of view (Morvai 2007, 141).

Questioning between the members of the CEDAW Committee and representatives of governments during the constructive dialogue can assume a pointed tenor. Committee members have on occasion directly challenged government representatives on their interpretation of Islamic law. "To the Government of Pakistan, for example, a Committee member pointed out that 'Islamic law did not prohibit joint custody agreements'" (Musawah 2011, 10). Former expert Sjamsiah Achmad, from Indonesia, noted that "some [Committee] members seemed to forget, at times, that the Committee is not a court but rather serves to educate governments about women's rights and encourage them to pursue its adoption" (Achmad 2007, 335).

CONCLUDING OBSERVATIONS

At the end of the reporting session, the CEDAW Committee makes a series of recommendations to states parties called concluding observations. Under no circumstances could the concluding observations themselves be construed as requiring a country to take action. Rather, they provide a focus for NGO work and supply information that legislators can use in formulating legislation or asking pointed questions of government officials in oversight hearings. As IWRAW Asia Pacific founder Shanthi Dairam suggests, "Concluding comments provide the basis for a national collaborative process to be set up between governments and NGOs for the implementation of the Convention, thus indicating conscious efforts by government to pursue the Committee's recommendations as well as to build collaborative relationships with NGOs" (Dairam 2007, 315). Women's rights advocates can use the concluding comments in their advocacy work. "Concluding comments by the Committee or any other treaty body are not legally binding, but if women can persuade courts to take note of the comments, the positive ruling of the court can help create new standards or interpret existing standards" (Dairam 2007, 324). Writing in 2007, Schöpp-Schilling observed that "the Committee's biggest – and so far unresolved – challenge has been to achieve a balance between acknowledging a specific country's situation on the one hand and the consistency of its formulations in all concluding comments on the other" (Schöpp-Schilling 2007, 254).

Regardless of how diplomatic the CEDAW experts are, conservative opponents of CEDAW in the United States monitor the words of the Committee carefully. In Chapter 1, I mentioned that Concerned Women for America capitalized on a statement that the CEDAW Committee made to Belarus about Mother's Day in its concluding observations in 2000. That statement became the centerpiece of U.S. opposition to CEDAW and would frame opposition activity for the next ten years. Concerned Women for America is paying extremely close attention to the activities of the CEDAW Committee.

NGO PARTICIPATION IN THE REPORTING SESSIONS

The text of the Convention provides no formal guidance about the role of NGOs in the reporting process, but over time, the CEDAW Committee has formalized and expanded the opportunities for NGO participation. NGOs submit shadow reports, make oral statements during the committee sessions, offer comments on official reports, and propose questions that committee members might ask of official representatives (Farrior 1997). NGOs are encouraged to participate as consultants in writing the periodic reports, either in collaboration with government officials or as contractors. The CEDAW Committee relies heavily on shadow reports prepared by NGOs in its evaluation of government reports. UNIFEM provides funding to NGOs to travel to CEDAW sessions to interact with the Committee.

NGO involvement provides valuable information to the expert Committee, but also strengthens the capacity of activists to use CEDAW in their work at home (Goonesekere 2007). Participation in the reporting sessions can enhance the legitimacy and authority of NGOs in the eyes of government officials. CEDAW strengthens NGOs by providing them with a high-profile arena in which to promote change, one with the imprimatur of the UN. Shanthi Dairam cites a specific example in which NGO participation in the CEDAW process made a concrete impact on the domestic policy process. During its eighteenth session in 1998, the Committee praised Zimbabwe for passing a law that granted legal status to women over the age of eighteen: "On the Government's return home, however, it announced that it was going to repeal the Act. Drawing on their experiences from the review process in New York, four women from Zimbabwe ... were able to publicize the contradictory action effectively. The Government subsequently withdrew its intention to repeal the Act" (Dairam 2007, 318).

NGO participation in the CEDAW reporting process has increased NGO clout, prompting governments to acknowledge their existence, invite them to participate in future meetings, and consult them in formulating policy. Participation in the CEDAW process provides a focal point for domestic NGOs and facilitates coalition building. The involvement of NGOs in Bangladesh dramatically increased the quality of the state's report to the CEDAW Committee. In 1995, women's groups in Bangladesh mobilized to educate the community about CEDAW in the lead up to the Beijing Conference. They held a preparatory NGO forum, organized a series of workshops to discuss CEDAW, distributed newsletters about women's issues, and organized a media campaign to make people aware of the upcoming conference. UNIFEM funded Bangladeshi NGOs and IWRAW Asia Pacific trained them how to lobby the Committee experts. At least initially, NGOs were better funded than the government agency charged with writing the periodic reports. The government agency for women and children, for example, "had no computers or fax machines," whereas NGOs did (Afsharipour 1999, fn. 151, 156). As a result of these efforts, the quality of Bangladesh's third report to the CEDAW Committee improved dramatically: "Rather than making blanket statements regarding the degree to which Bangladesh has complied with the Convention, the New Report acknowledges the country's weaknesses and lays out a plan of action for its future" (Afsharipour 1999, 160).

Many domestic organizations initially approach the prospect of working on CEDAW with skepticism. As Malaysian NGO leader Ivy Josiah commented in an interview, Malaysian women's groups initially saw the Convention as irrelevant to their work at the domestic level, but they eventually came around: "They started understanding that if we want to have government accountability, and most governments want to look good in the international arena, this is the way to do it" (Josiah 2011).

Organizations active in the transnational arena can also exert pressure for compliance in other international organizations because the reporting session has standing in the international community. As Josiah reported, "The Malaysian delegate to the Human Rights Council was embarrassed by no reports on CEDAW. He was asking NGOs to get the government to do its reports" (Josiah 2011). In Malaysia, the shadow reporting process brought groups in civil society together. The CEDAW process provides a focal point for NGOs to collaborate with one another and CEDAW provided a blueprint for their efforts:

We are all coming together to produce a report, to produce a baseline report, and in so doing, we are really surfacing where are the areas for reform. So we may never go to NY or Geneva. It doesn't matter. The point is, we have in our hands a comprehensive document that we can use to see and to keep coming back to CEDAW to see where we're at. I've always been convinced that the process itself, the interaction with the committee itself, is not the end. It's one of the ends, but one of the objectives is how to build civil society within Malaysia and to really use what we're finding. (Josiah 2011)

In some cases, NGOs devote so much time and energy to the CEDAW sessions that some worry the sessions have become an end in themselves. Getting caught up in the CEDAW process in New York or Geneva can be a problem for NGOs, as well. Dairam worries that NGOs lose sight of the importance of the less glamorous work of applying CEDAW back home:

Even we [IWRAW Asia Pacific] don't push the NGOs hard enough once we have finished the review. The review itself is so glamorous. To be there is so exciting. It's a once in a lifetime opportunity to go in and watch all of this. But you get so caught up in that moment, and it's like you've achieved everything once you come back. (Dairam 2011)

Dairam emphasizes the need to conceive of CEDAW as a tool rather than an end in itself. People tend to see IWRAW's main goal as "increase[ing] the capacity for the implementation of CEDAW," but Dairam thinks the mission would be better understood as "the application of international standards for the realization of rights" (Dairam 2011).

NGO participation in the CEDAW process is no guarantee of progress. Bangladesh, for example, has been a model participant. It has submitted reports on a regular basis and appeared at CEDAW sessions five times in twenty years. Civil society groups have been engaged in the process and "indeed the Committee generally relies heavily on NGOs to provide additional detailed information about shortfalls in treaty implementation." Nonetheless, progress in Bangladesh has been slow to non-existent (Byrnes and Freeman 2012, 39).

THE CEDAW SESSION IN ACTION

When I first learned about CEDAW, I was skeptical that it was an issue worth paying attention to, from an academic perspective as well as a policy perspective. Given the pressing needs of American women at home, I questioned whether expending energy to ratify CEDAW, or to prevent its ratification, was time well spent. My views changed dramatically once I attended a CEDAW session in person. I made my first visit to a CEDAW session at UN headquarters in New York in June 2010. What I saw astonished me.

CEDAW has an impressive virtual presence. All the documents that are produced in the context of the reporting process are available online on the Web site of the OHCHR. With one click I can read the government's assessment of its own policy, evaluate that report in light of shadow reports provided by NGOs, and compare my own assessments to those that the CEDAW experts offer in their Concluding Observations. I can read summaries of the exchanges that take place between an official delegation and the CEDAW Committee experts. I can readily see which countries have presented their reports at CEDAW sessions and which are scheduled to appear over the next couple of years.

Yet the value of being able to access this information pales in comparison to the experience of seeing it put to use in real time during the CEDAW sessions themselves. In these sessions, countries are represented by human beings who express their views with diplomatic dignity, but also, in some instances, emotion. The stakes involved are revealed by the silence and then quick scurrying of papers and delegates back and forth to generate a response to a question for which a delegation is insufficiently prepared. The presence of NGO activists in the same room as government officials sometimes poses a security risk that creates a palpable tension. In short, the reporting process reveals many unscripted moments that reveal so much about a country's dedication to the goal of eliminating discrimination against women. Participation in the process has value in and of itself, in addition to the reams of paper and bytes of information provided by the various players. It is in the process of engaging in a dialogue, in person, where socialization to the norms defined by CEDAW occurs.

I chose to focus this section on the Russian Federation to highlight how changes in the geopolitical context, specifically the end of the Cold War, have affected women's rights generally and Russia in particular. This allows me to draw comparisons between the role that the Soviet Union played in the early days of the CSW, which I discussed in Chapter 2, with the current gender politics of the CEDAW Committee and the Russian Federation.

The Russian Federation had initiated the reporting process by submitting its periodic report the previous year, on March 9, 2009. The sixty-four-page document combined the sixth and seventh periodic reports and included activities between 1999 and 2007. Russia, and before that the Soviet Union, had previously presented its reports on time and at regular intervals. The CEDAW Committee reviewed the periodic report and delivered a list of thirty-one questions back to the government on September 9, 2009. The questions requested additional information on a broad range of topics, including plans to adopt equal opportunities legislation, cultural practices that "hamper women's advancement," data on domestic violence, measures to address domestic violence, and government resources to implement programs to prevent domestic violence (Committee on the Elimination of Discrimination against Women 2009). The questions asked about violence in Chechnya; measures to combat trafficking of women and girls; low numbers of women in office; and murders of female journalists, as well as education, employment, contraceptive use, and sex education; rural women's awareness of their rights; and the status of women who faced intersecting forms of discrimination such as ethnic minorities, disabilities, or asylum seekers.

The government responded to the list of questions on March 22, 2010, with 129 pages of answers (Committee on the Elimination of Discrimination against Women 2010c). The responses reveal, among other things, that the Russian Federation does not systematically collect data on violence against women, but instead derives domestic violence data from crime statistics. Moreover, the data appear to undercount the number of cases: "In the first half of 2009, 16,101 women became victims of a crime committed by a family member, in 8,217 of these cases the perpetrator being the husband of the victim. The corresponding figures for 2008 were: 26,531 and 13,942" (Committee on the Elimination of Discrimination against Women 2010c, 14).

Seven NGOs submitted shadow reports. A group called ANNA National Center for the Prevention of Violence maintained that, with regard to combatting domestic violence, "a systemic approach at government level does not exist" (ANNA National Centre for the Prevention of Violence 2010, 4). There is no separate law on domestic violence, and the Russian Criminal Code does not criminalize violence against women committed by family members. Another shadow report from a coalition called the Consortium of Women's Non-Governmental Associations challenged many of the claims made in the government report. It claimed that the official report "contains downright distortions" (Consortium of Women's Non-Governmental Associations 2010). Although the official report maintains that government machinery for promoting gender equality "went through radical changes," the shadow report stated that "in reality, the changes resulted in the liquidation of the machinery" (Consortium of Women's Non-Governmental Associations 2010). Two other groups, Front Line and the International Commission of Jurists, submitted a shadow report documenting the murders of women human rights defenders, blaming the "state party's failure to prevent, investigate and punish these attacks" (Front Line & International Commission of Jurists 2010). A shadow report by the Russian Lesbian, Gay, Bisexual, and Transgender (LGBT) Network, a self-described "Inter-Regional Social movement," condemned discrimination and violence against homosexual and bisexual women (Russian LGBT Network 2010).

The three-week session began on July 12, 2010. On the first day, the Committee spent its first hour reviewing reports. It met with representatives from UN agencies and then broke for lunch. In the afternoon, it spent two and a half hours in informal meetings with NGOs, an hour meeting national human rights institutions, and a half-hour in closed session. The Committee met with the delegation from Argentina on the second day, Fiji on the third day, and the Russian Federation on day four. Each of those days ended with an hour in closed session. The fifth day was devoted to hearing petitions related to the Optional Protocol. On day one of week two, the Committee continued its work on the OP, and then met with NGOs and national human rights institutions. The subsequent days were devoted to Australia, Turkey, Papua New Guinea, and India, respectively. On the first day of the third week, the committee met with the Albanian delegation. The remaining four days of that week were devoted to closed meetings (Committee on the Elimination of Discrimination against Women 2010b).

By 10 AM of the fourth day of the first week, July 15, 2010, the three columns of seats in Conference Room 4 of the temporary headquarters of the UN in New York were just about full. Members of the delegation of the Russian Federation – all twenty-five of them – sat at the desks on the left side of the room.[4] The CEDAW experts filled in the middle section of seats. Members of NGOs from Russia and the other countries presenting at this session took up most of the seats on the right side of the room. Naela Gabr, chair of the CEDAW Committee, sat on the dais at the front with the vice chairs and expert who had been selected as rapporteur for the Russian Federation. A group of students filled in the back rows, and I joined them. At 10:05 AM, Maxim Topilin, deputy minister of Health and Social Development from the Russian Federation, began to deliver his statement about Russian compliance with CEDAW. Here I quote from the summary records of the session, which are written in the third person. Topilin "said that his country took the implementation of the Convention very seriously," that "gender equality remained at the centre of his Government's attention," and that "Russian legislation was now inline with the provisions of the Convention" (Committee on the Elimination of Discrimination against Women 2010d, 2–4). He went on to describe the specific measures that Russia had adopted in order to comply with CEDAW, a list that included reforms to the Labour Code and Criminal Code, subsidies for women's health legal services, subsidies for unemployment, programs to combat domestic violence, and improved efforts to collect statistical data (Committee on the Elimination of Discrimination against Women 2010d). By the time Topilin finished speaking, an outside observer might have the impression that the Russian Federation was in full compliance with CEDAW.

Promptly at 10:30 AM, the CEDAW experts began to pose questions to Mr. Topilin. Thus began the constructive dialogue. The experts delivered their questions with diplomatic decorum, but their questions penetrated to the heart of limitations in the Russian Federation's presentation. Vinitha Jayasinghe, an expert from Sri Lanka, asked the first question: "Recalling that an earlier attempt to adopt equality

---

[4] The Russian delegation included representatives from the UN delegation, president's office, office of the prosecutor general, Ministry of Culture, Ministry of Education and Science, Ministry of the Interior, Federal Service of State Statistics, Department for Social Development, Ministry of Justice, and Ministry of Foreign Affairs.

legislation had been unsuccessful, [she] asked for information on the current status of that legislation, and whether the definition of discrimination it contained included both direct and indirect discrimination" (Committee on the Elimination of Discrimination against Women 2010d, 4). Jayasinghe asked this question fully aware (from the information provided in the periodic report, the response to the list of questions, and the shadow reports) that Russia had done little to create equal employment legislation despite being urged to do so by the CEDAW Committee in 2002. Nicole Ameline, an expert from France, "said that the increase in violence and impunity in some of the Republics in situations of internal conflict was a major concern, and she wondered what legal means were available to provide for the rights of the victims of such violence" (Committee on the Elimination of Discrimination against Women 2010d, 4). She asked her question knowing that Russia does not have any legislation criminalizing domestic violence, information she had learned from reading shadow reports submitted by Russian NGOs and meeting with members of those NGOs earlier in the week.

For the next two and a half hours, and then for two additional hours after a break for lunch, the CEDAW experts asked questions at a steady clip. Why were there not more women teaching in higher education? Why wasn't education data disaggregated by gender? Why didn't the Labour Code address sexual harassment? Why were there so few women in government? What had the government done to promote contraceptive use, given that only 27 percent of Russian women of childbearing age used modern contraceptives? Why did Russia "occupy 108th place in the Global Gender Gap Report of 2006," and what did the government plan to do in order to increase the number of women in political office? Topilin continued to answer questions from the CEDAW experts, but his growing agitation was evident by watching him and listening to his words as they were simultaneously translated from Russian to English. A moment came when Topilin appeared to drop the façade of diplomacy to articulate his thoughts on the issues being discussed. Here is what he said:

In all parts of Russia and among all ethnic groups, women and mothers were held sacred above all else. The attitude that women were of lower status simply did not exist in the Russian Federation, nor could it, as it was incompatible with national tradition. It was true that crimes were committed against women, and efforts were being made to combat that. In the Russian Federation, there were no traditions leading naturally to the violation of women's rights. That had never been the case, it was not currently the case and it could not be the case. (Committee on the Elimination of Discrimination against Women 2010d, 8)

Topilin's colleagues recognized that his statement violated CEDAW norms and they jumped into the breach, taking the microphone to reassure the Committee of Russia's commitment to gender equality. Here we see the head of the delegation articulating a set of beliefs about women that he believes reflect his nation as a whole. It appears he did not see these views as problematic, but rather was frustrated by the fact that the Committee members did not share his views and did not seem to value them.

The Committee published its concluding observations a month later, on August 16, 2010. The fifteen-page report praised the Russian Federation for its efforts, but also offered unstinting criticisms. In a comment about the delegation itself, for example, the Committee commended the state party for its high-level, large and multisectoral delegation, which was headed by the deputy minister of Health and Social Development and included a large number of women and men representing ministries and other governmental bodies with responsibilities for the implementation of measures in the areas covered by the Convention. The Committee appreciated the constructive dialogue that took place between the delegation and the members of the Committee, but it regretted that not all of its oral questions were answered (Committee on the Elimination of Discrimination against Women 2010a, 1).

The Concluding Observations requested that the government "submit the present concluding observations to all relevant ministries, to the Parliament (State Duma and Fed Council) and to the judiciary" and "to take the next steps with regard to the implementation of the present concluding observations." It raised "serious concerns" about increases in the rate of domestic violence and lack of effective mechanisms to address the issue. The Committee requested that Russia provide a follow-up report on the adoption of temporary special measures to increase women's participation in political life within one year and report on the situation of women and girls in the northern Caucasus region within two years. "The State party should take all necessary measures to end the impunity for violence against and killings of women and girls in the northern Caucasus, by ensuring that such cases are fully and promptly investigated and that perpetrators are brought to justice, regardless of whether they are State or non-State actors" (Committee on the Elimination of Discrimination against Women 2010a, 14).

Compare the 2010 dialogue between the Russian Federation and the CEDAW Committee to the interactions between Elzavieta Popova and Dorothy Kenyon at the CSW meetings in 1947, described in Chapter 2. Back then, little actual dialogue occurred during the CSW meetings. Discussion consisted of endless rounds of ideologically charged volleys among delegates who were competing to define international norms about the status of women. Delegates from other countries had little power to challenge the representatives of the two most powerful countries in the world for fear of international political repercussions. The power dynamics at the CEDAW sessions differ dramatically. At the 2010 CEDAW session I describe, no individual country determined the standards against which they or other countries would be judged. CEDAW, a document created by many countries and approved by the UN General Assembly, defines those standards. The CEDAW Committee, which does not represent any particular country and whose members do not even represent their own countries, interprets the standards that CEDAW sets out and applies them more or less evenly across all states parties.

What impact would this event likely have on the lives of Russian women back home? I would predict very little, given restrictions on press freedom and NGO activity in the Russian Federation. Although open to the public, what happens during the sessions tends to stay in the sessions. Awareness of what happens during them depends largely on the media. Press coverage of CEDAW sessions is unrestricted, but nonetheless limited by the fact that most of what goes on during them does not constitute "breaking news" and thus is not considered to be worthy of reporting.

CONCLUSION: IMPLICATIONS FOR U.S. RATIFICATION

By 2013, 187 countries had ratified CEDAW, which obligated them to take positive action to establish "the equal rights of men and women" in real terms in every arena of society. The vast majority of those countries have fulfilled the requirement of preparing an extensive report on the status of women's rights every four years and presenting it before an international panel of experts on gender equality. These countries have subjected themselves to strenuous questioning about the status of women and women's rights in their countries. Some countries send large teams of government officials to the sessions. Although none of the countries that have ratified CEDAW has reached the goal of completely eliminating discrimination against women, many have acknowledged their commitment to that goal publicly in the international arena and have taken concrete steps to achieve it. There is still a long way to go before women around the world enjoy all the rights that CEDAW establishes, but in the meantime, the process holds countries accountable to their promises to end discrimination against women.

What is perhaps most astonishing about the reporting process is to see experts on women's rights, representing an agreement that is more advanced in terms of women's rights than any nation in the world, asking pointed questions of government officials about their policies, and specifically about limitations to their existing policies. There is no country in the world, regardless of the laws it may have in place, in which women have achieved actual de facto equality with men. All the government officials that participate in the CEDAW process emerge at least somewhat bruised by the experience. The delegation from the Russian Federation was clearly in a defensive position. The presumption is that the government has resisted taking measures to comply with CEDAW or has declined to do so, and now needs to account for its shortcomings. It is uncomfortable to watch – and thrilling at the same time.

So what would participation in this process mean for the United States? The people with the most at stake are the NGOs that support and oppose ratification. If the United States ratifies CEDAW, the women's rights NGOs that have been supporting CEDAW for decades will write shadow reports assessing the government's official periodic reports about the status of women in the United States. The NGOs that oppose CEDAW will also write shadow reports assessing the status of women in the United States. When CEDAW opponents express concern about giving a panel of UN experts power over the United States, this is what worries them. Phyllis Schlafly has said, "It would be a circus, every four years" (Schlafly 2012). Indeed, U.S. participation in the CEDAW process would likely constitute another arena in which long-brewing conflicts about women's issues would be played out. At the same time, a quadrennial review of U.S. policy regarding the status of women could provide a welcome mechanism of accountability.

The research provided in this book cannot allow us to say whether participation in this process has led countries to adopt the policies that the CEDAW committee urges them to adopt. More research is needed to understand what happens once the CEDAW sessions end. What this analysis does suggest is that the CEDAW sessions provide an opportunity for countries to engage with the standards that CEDAW articulates. The CEDAW Committee experts assess the degree to which countries comply with those standards and make recommendations about future directions. The participation of NGOs in the process ensures that government officials will, at a minimum, be forced to consider the views of their own citizens on women's issues, as well as the judgment of international experts on the treaty.

Those who oppose CEDAW ratification in the United States insist that CEDAW would force the United States to adopt policies that a majority of Americans oppose. Even advocates of CEDAW reflect the view that CEDAW requires states to adopt certain policies when they assert that American women already enjoy all the rights that CEDAW guarantees. Many women's rights activists around the world espouse the same views, portraying CEDAW as obligating governments to adopt particular laws in order to comply with the Convention. These claims misapprehend how the Convention works. The CEDAW Committee does not have the power to force countries to take any particular measures. Ratification of CEDAW has not required any country to adopt a particular set of policies and it would not require the United States to do so. By ratifying CEDAW, countries agree to move toward a set of general standards of rights, collect information on the status of women and women's rights, make that information publicly available, and engage in a dialogue with global experts on women's rights about how best to bring about an end to discrimination against women. CEDAW, in other words, is more about process than policy.

6

Why the United States Has Not Ratified CEDAW

Few people in the United States have ever heard of CEDAW, yet ratification has been on the political agenda for nearly three decades. The key phenomenon this chapter seeks to explain is stasis – why the United States has not ratified CEDAW. During the period CEDAW has been pending, the geopolitical landscape has shifted in ways that might have been propitious for the Convention. The Soviet Union collapsed, Cold War ended, and United States emerged as a unilateral power in the global arena. Thousands of NGOs devoted to women's issues emerged around the world and the transnational women's movement became more visible and more powerful. A large coalition of NGOs supports U.S. ratification. CEDAW itself has grown more powerful. Yet none of those changes has provided sufficient impetus for ratification, primarily because these factors also heightened the motivations for anti-feminist and pro-life advocates within the United States to oppose CEDAW. As conservative organizations in the United States realized that CEDAW had become a powerful tool to effect change on the international and domestic levels, they sharpened their efforts to oppose it. Focused and wellorganized grassroots opposition has prevented legislation recommending ratification of CEDAW from making it to a vote on the Senate floor. Ultimately, the answer to the question of why the United States has not ratified CEDAW is that the stakes of doing so are high for both sides. CEDAW matters.

Not only is there significant opposition to CEDAW, but the institutional rules governing treaty ratification in the United States magnify

opposition where it exists. As I discussed in Chapter 1, it is more difficult to ratify treaties in the United States than in other countries. The
requirements for ratification – presidential support and a two-thirds
vote of the Senate – are higher than almost any other country in the
world. These institutional rules magnify the power of domestic opposition to derail treaty ratification. At several points of time in the last
thirty years, CEDAW opponents have proven sufficiently powerful to
overcome opportunities that would otherwise bode well for ratification.
Changes in the geopolitical climate have created conditions that we
might expect would be propitious for CEDAW ratification – but domestic opposition has steadfastly prevented it from moving forward.

To illustrate partisan disagreements about the nature of the costs
that the Convention would entail, I analyze the transcripts of four
hearings that the Senate Committee on Foreign Relations has held on
CEDAW in 1988, 1990, 1994, and 2002.[1] I also examine a 2011 hearing on Women in the Arab Spring, during which the question of U.S.
ratification of CEDAW featured prominently. I focus on the transcripts
of Senate hearings because they are one of the few available sources
of information on what groups in civil society think about CEDAW.
There is little open public discourse on CEDAW because it has not
been a major issue in the national media. Members of Congress carefully manage hearings to highlight their preferred views and discredit
their opponents, but hearings nonetheless provide valuable information about the views that members of Congress hold.

CEDAW IN THE LEGISLATIVE WILDERNESS, 1980–1988

On November 12, 1980, President Carter transmitted CEDAW to the
Senate Committee on Foreign Relations for its advice and consent,
along with a memorandum of law explaining the rationale behind
Carter's support for the treaty. Carter's efforts to get the Senate to
move on CEDAW were the actions of a severely wounded lame-duck
president. Ronald Reagan had defeated Carter in the presidential election held a week earlier. Nonetheless, the Democrats still held a majority of seats in the lame duck congress and could have easily ratified
CEDAW with the support of moderate Republicans. Why did they not

---

[1] I discussed a fifth hearing, held in 2010, in Chapter 1.

do so? The main reason is that the Senate was already suffering treaty exhaustion. In 1978, Jimmy Carter, who had campaigned on a policy of putting human rights at the center of U.S. foreign policy, transmitted four treaties to the Senate at once: CERD, ICCPR, ICESCR, and the American Convention on Human Rights.[2] In 1979, the Senate Foreign Relations Committee held four days of hearings on all four treaties simultaneously. The administration sought to stress that none of the treaties would "have any impact on domestic constitutional or statutory law," but the treaties differed so much from one another and witnesses raised so many issues that the Senate declined to take action on any of them (Parry 2008, 1036). Moreover, a series of global crises in 1979, the last year of Carter's presidency, undermined his clout – the Nicaraguan revolution in July, the Iranian hostage crisis that began in November and ended the day of Reagan's inauguration in 1981, and the Soviet invasion of Afghanistan in December. CEDAW was so new that few feminist activists knew about it. The ERA to the U.S. Constitution was a more pressing priority. The country was in the middle of a campaign to ratify the ERA, which stated, "Equality of rights under the law shall not be denied or abridged by the United States or by any state on account of sex." In 1978, thirty-five of the required thirty-eight states had voted in favor of the amendment. Congress extended the deadline for ratification to June 30, 1982, which redoubled the efforts of the pro- and anti-ERA campaigns.

Another explanation for Senate inaction on CEDAW points to legal concerns. Carter's Secretary of State Edmund Muskie sent CEDAW to the Senate along with a letter reporting the findings of a State Department study of the treaty. Muskie's letter maintained that CEDAW was essentially compatible with U.S. law but contained a few issues that would need to be addressed with reservations. First on his list of concerns was the private jurisdiction issue, the "broad definition of 'discrimination against women' [that] applied throughout the Convention and has the effect of applying the Convention to private organizations and areas of personal conduct not covered by U.S. law" (U.S. Senate 1980, VIII). As Muskie put it: "The effect of this definition ... is to reach into areas that are not regulated by

---

[2] The American Convention on Human Rights is overseen by the Organization of American States. As of September 15, 2013, the United States has signed but not ratified it (Organization of American States n.d.).

the federal government either due to Constitutional restraint or as a matter of public policy" (U.S. Senate 1980, 1). Muskie's report reiterates the concern about private jurisdiction in a discussion of Article 5 of CEDAW: "The United States federal government does not regulate family education or interpersonal relationships ... therefore a statement of understanding may be appropriate" (U.S. Senate 1980, 4). The letter affirms that article 2(a) of CEDAW is adequately addressed by the 14th and 15th Amendments to the Constitution, which "provide a basis to invalidate any federal or state classification of distinction based on sex if it is not substantially related to an important government objective." Muskie's letter also maintains that existing constitutional guarantees would be strengthened by passage of the ERA. There are three interesting things to note here. First, the Carter administration acknowledged a disjuncture between CEDAW and existing U.S. law in terms of private jurisdiction. Second, the administration expressed confidence that the 14th Amendment provided adequate protection of women's rights. Third, the government expressed the hope that the ERA would address any remaining concerns about the degree to which U.S. law protects women's rights – a hope that was dashed by the failure of the ERA campaign in 1982. I will revisit these issues in Chapter 7 in an analysis of the degree to which existing law protects women's rights in the United States.

The Senate took no action on CEDAW during the Reagan era. From 1981 to 1987, Republicans controlled the presidency and the Senate. The lack of attention to human rights treaties during this period is consistent with the institutional story I tell in Chapter 1. Republican control of the Senate and the socially conservative politics of the Reagan administration kept CEDAW, as well as most other women's rights legislation, off the political agenda. CEDAW remained a low-salience issue in the international arena for most of this period for the reasons I discuss in Chapter 4: women's rights groups did not begin to pay attention to CEDAW until after the Nairobi World Conference on Women in July 1985. Even in contexts where we might expect support for CEDAW to be prominent, the Convention was conspicuously absent from debate.[3] Both houses of Congress held hearings on

---

[3] One exception is that the American Bar Association's House of Delegates adopted a resolution supporting ratification of CEDAW in August 1984, an action cited in the 1994 hearing (U.S. Senate 1994).

the ERA in 1983, the year after it was defeated. CEDAW was not mentioned once in hundreds of pages of testimony (U.S. House of Representatives 1990).

On June 7, 1984, the Senate Foreign Relations Committee held a hearing to review the U.S. Agency for International Development's Women in Development program, which was then celebrating its tenth anniversary. The hearing also served to brief the U.S. delegation to the Nairobi Conference. This was not a hearing about CEDAW, but given the focus of the hearing – women and international development and a UN conference on women – it is not unreasonable to expect that the subject of CEDAW would have come up. Witnesses speaking at the hearing focused a great deal of attention on the activities of the UN CSW, the IWY Conference held in Mexico City in 1975, and the upcoming Nairobi Conference. Yet CEDAW merits only 1 mention in 155 pages of hearing transcripts. This lacuna is even more surprising when we consider that two of the thirty-three witnesses who testified were intimately familiar with the Convention: Pat Hutar and Arvonne Fraser. Hutar had helped draft CEDAW in Geneva, and Fraser would create IWRAW to promote implementation of CEDAW the following year. Neither Hutar nor Fraser mentioned the Convention in their testimony during the 1984 hearing. Many of the other witnesses worked in countries that had already ratified CEDAW, yet none of them mentioned the Convention either. The one witness who mentioned CEDAW was Mildred Robbins Leet, co-director of Trickle Up, an antipoverty organization, who briefly referred to CEDAW as a "ray of hope" that put the United States "ahead of the times" (U.S. Senate 1984). Her comments make little sense given that the United States had not ratified CEDAW, but further establish that the Convention was not a priority issue at the time.

The House of Representatives also held a hearing on international women's issues in 1984. On Tuesday, September 18, 1984, Congressman Gus Yatron (D-PA), chair of the Subcommittee on Human Rights and International Organizations of the House Committee on Foreign Affairs, convened a hearing to discuss U.S. contributions to the UN Decade for Women and prepare for the Nairobi Conference (U.S. House of Representatives 1984). Of the eighteen statements made by representatives of nongovernmental organizations, only four mention CEDAW. The National Women's Conference Committee, a group created after the 1977 IWY meeting in Houston, noted that the United States had not ratified CEDAW but did not call for ratification (U.S. House of Representatives 1984, 208). CEDAW figured more prominently in the testimony offered by Valerie Levitan, the executive director of Zonta International, a global women's organization. Although "Zontians in all countries are urged to continue to press their governments for ratification of the Convention and implementation of its standards," Zontians in the United States were instructed to focus their energies on the ERA (U.S. House of Representatives 1984, 228). Finally, in a letter inserted into the record, Arvonne Fraser mentioned that CEDAW "was the result of years of work by U.S. and international women's organizations" – but even she did not call upon the United States to ratify it (U.S. House of Representatives 1984, 188). Ratification of the ERA was the "highest priority" for the AAUW, but "to help ensure that rights sought by women in the U.S. are attainable by women the world over, AAUW has advocated U.S. Senate ratification" of CEDAW (U.S. House of Representatives 1984, 184). After the hearing, Representative Yatron wrote a series of follow-up letters to government officials inquiring about their commitment to women's issues. Yatron mentioned CEDAW in one of these letters, written to Nancy Clark Reynolds, the U.S. delegate to the UN CSW. His first question to Clark addressed CEDAW: "Do you and does the Department of State plan to encourage the Senate to ratify the Convention prior to the 1985 Nairobi conference?" to which the State Department responded, "There is no specific action planned at this time to encourage the Senate to ratify the Convention prior to the [Nairobi] Conference" (U.S. House of Representatives 1984, 139, 142).

Given how important CEDAW would later become, and given the substantive focus of these two hearings, it is not unreasonable to expect that CEDAW would have been discussed at greater length. The virtual absence of the question of U.S. ratification of CEDAW during the 1980s indicates that advocates of women's rights did not yet see it as relevant to either domestic or foreign policy. Activists in the international development community did not yet realize how CEDAW could be relevant to their work.

With Republicans controlling both the presidency and the Senate during the Reagan era, women's rights advocates might not have considered it to be worth their while to promote CEDAW even if it was on their minds. What's surprising is that the Senate voted to approve another human rights treaty, the Genocide Convention, even though Republicans held the majority. The history of the Genocide Convention has been covered exhaustively elsewhere, so I will reprise it only briefly here. President Truman transmitted the treaty to the Senate in June 1949, with the expectation that it would be approved as a "routine matter" (LeBlanc 1991, 5). The prospects for ratification evaporated in the face of strident opposition from the American Bar Association and Senate Republicans, who framed the treaty as a Trojan horse that would empower communists and civil rights activists to control domestic policy. The Genocide Convention remained on the Senate agenda for decades thanks to lobbying by Jewish organizations and persistent support from Democratic Senator William Proxmire of Wisconsin, who gave more than 3,000 speeches in support of the treaty on the Senate floor. Sustained opposition from anticommunist groups with strong grassroots support made sure it never came to a vote. What ultimately changed the odds for the Genocide Convention was support from President Reagan, which "undermined the long-standing Republican opposition on the Senate Foreign Relations Committee" and paved the way for ratification (Power 2002, 163). Reagan kept the ball rolling by signing a third treaty, the UN Convention Against Torture, on April 18, 1988, and transmitting it to the Senate on May 20, 1988. The Senate voted to approve the Genocide Convention on November 25, 1988 – thirty-nine years after the United States signed it. It is significant that the Senate voted on the Genocide treaty during a lame-duck session, when the electoral costs of taking positions on controversial issues are relatively low.

A NEW ERA FOR HUMAN RIGHTS TREATIES IN THE UNITED STATES, 1988–1994

On December 8, 1988, one month after the presidential election in which George H. W. Bush defeated Massachusetts Governor Michael Dukakis, Senator John Kerry (D-MA) held a field hearing on CEDAW in Boston.[4] The Democrats had lost the presidency but maintained their majority in the Senate, with fifty-five seats to the Republicans'

---

[4] A field hearing is one that takes place in a location outside the Congress itself.

forty-five. Kerry held the hearing in response to requests from women who had attended the Nairobi Conference in 1985. When Elaine Binder, executive director of B'nai B'rith, the Jewish women's organization headquartered in Washington, DC, returned from Nairobi, she organized a coalition of nineteen women's rights organizations to lobby members of the Senate Committee on Foreign Relations to support CEDAW (U.S. Senate 1988).[5] The coalition could not persuade Senators to hold a hearing in Washington, but they got Senator Kerry to convene a local hearing in Boston. Kerry's rationale for holding the hearing was to gather information and jumpstart support for CEDAW in the Senate. As he affirmed at the start of the hearings:

Field hearings are not mere political exercises; they are really helpful, in that they provide a foundation of testimony of practitioners and people involved in these issues which can then be provided committee members, this hearing record will provide us with a record, which is the beginning of the larger process of convincing my colleagues and others of the importance of this kind of convention. (U.S. Senate 1988, 1)

With the exception of Binder, all of the witnesses worked in state-level politics in Massachusetts. They included government officials, leaders of local women's groups, a lawyer from the Massachusetts Attorney General's office, and members of the State Assembly. Kerry engaged them in a detailed discussion of the degree to which CEDAW was compatible with existing U.S. law and whether they thought it could get through the Senate. The witnesses responded by reflecting on the CEDAW articles most relevant to their work: child care, domestic violence, healthcare, and so forth. Paula Rayman, a scholar from Wellesley College, remarked that "reading Article 11 was a bittersweet experience for me, bitter because it is deeply discouraging to realize that in this year of 1988" American women do not have the rights that CEDAW guarantees (U.S. Senate 1988, 7). A comment by Laurie Sheridan, a community organizer on child care issues, reflects deep dissatisfaction about the status of women in the United States and outrage that the United States was behind standards articulated in

---

[5] At the 1994 CEDAW hearing, a representative of B'nai B'rith recalled that after the Nairobi Conference, the organization "held and appeared at countless meetings on the convention, made repeated visits to Capitol Hill and contacted dozens of grassroots organizations who, in turn, have held meetings and forums and produced materials to educate their constituents" (U.S. Senate 1994).

CEDAW, sentiments that other witnesses expressed as well: "It makes me ashamed for my country, to realize that we do not yet comply with articles that so many other poorer countries already take for granted; and angry that my country would be among the last" (U.S. Senate 1988, 71). Witnesses discussed abortion from a pro-choice perspective, as a right that was not sufficiently well protected because access for poor women was limited. They spoke passionately about the problems American women faced and the ways in which CEDAW would address those problems.

Two conservative organizations submitted written testimony but did not appear in person: the Massachusetts chapter of Concerned Women for America, the Christian women's organization, and Massachusetts Citizens for Life, a state-level anti-abortion group. The Massachusetts chapter of Concerned Women for America opposed CEDAW explicitly, but its statement reveals little of the sophistication or rhetorical flair that this organization would demonstrate in later years: CEDAW "leaves women at the mercy of those who would define the roll [sic] of women differently from the majority traditional view," and "finds greatest support among Communist countries" (U.S. Senate 1988, 85). The fact that the testimony came from the local chapter rather than from national headquarters suggests that CEDAW was not yet on the national radar. Massachusetts Citizens for Life argued that sex-selective abortion is a form of discrimination against women, and men too: "Abortion is discriminating not only against females, in denying them, literally, the right to be born, but it also deprives men of marriage partners in the long run" (U.S. Senate 1988, 88). This is a strange argument in that it ostensibly supports CEDAW as a way to prevent sex discrimination as applied to abortion. Two years later, anti-abortion groups would line up firmly against CEDAW.

The message that emerges most clearly from this hearing is that the biggest cost of CEDAW lies in *not* ratifying it. American women face harm because they lack the protections and guarantees that CEDAW provides, rights that women in even the poorest countries already have, at least on paper, because they have ratified CEDAW. Witnesses at the 1988 hearing testified about the problems that American women confront and spoke competently about the ways that specific articles of CEDAW might address those problems. Their testimony revealed that they had read CEDAW closely and understood how it could be relevant

to their work. Looking back at the 1988 hearing, what is most striking is that the substance of the discussion focused entirely on domestic
issues within the United States. Even when witnesses mentioned other
countries, they did so to emphasize that other countries had adopted
policies that the United States lacked. Twenty years later, the Senate
would still be debating CEDAW, but the primary focus would shift to
how U.S. ratification would help women in *other* countries.

Kerry's 1988 hearing did not lead to a vote, but it seems to have persuaded him that the Senate should move forward with CEDAW. When
President H. W. Bush took office in 1989, the Democrats remained in
control of the Senate, again with fifty-five seats to the GOP's forty-five.
The State Department initiated simultaneous review of four human
rights treaties: CAT, ICCPR, CERD, and CEDAW, thus linking the fate
of these treaties together. Bush's support for CEDAW indicated a rever-
sal of conservative social policy within the Republican Party. Putting
CEDAW under "active review" sent a strong signal to CEDAW supporters – including women leaders in the Republican Party. On June
11, 1990, a group of Republican members of congress sent a letter to
President Bush supporting ratification and urging the administration
to make CEDAW a priority. The congresswomen framed their concerns in terms of the domestic status of American women:

Although the United States is a leader among nations in advancing the role of
women, we feel that there is still much to be done in this county to eliminate
discrimination against women. For example, the *Washington Post* recently
reported a case in which a judge would not allow a married woman to assume
her maiden name without her husband's written permission. (U.S. Senate
1990, 98)

The one-page letter also highlighted the importance of ratification for
the international standing of the United States: "United States ratification of this Convention is equally important for the role of this
country as a leading advocate for international human rights. Our
diplomatic representatives well know the difficulty of representing
the U.S. in international fora when we ourselves have not ratified the
basic international human rights conventions" (U.S. Senate 1990, 99).
Twelve Republican congresswomen signed the letter: Helen Delich
Bentley (MD), Nancy L. Johnson (CT), Lynn Martin (IL), Jan Meyers
(KS), Susan Molinari (NY), Constance A. Morella (MD), Patricia F.

Saiki (HI), Claudine Schneider (RI), Ileana Ros-Lehtinen (FL), Marge Roukema (NJ), Virginia Smith (NE), and Barbara F. Vucanovich (NV). Republican Senator Rudy Boschwitz (MN) also signed it.

A State Department official responded to the congresswomen to report that the Bush administration "has urged approval" of CEDAW and the other human rights treaties. The letter stated, "We hope the Senate will provide its advice and consent to ratification of this important instrument in the near future," but indicated that the Bush administration had not yet decided which of the four treaties it would prioritize and needed to determine whether CEDAW should be ratified with RUDs or would require implementing legislation (U.S. Senate 1990). By the time the SFRC convened hearings two months later, on August 2, 1990, three of the congresswomen who initially supported CEDAW had reversed their positions: Vucanovich, Bentley, and Ros-Lehtinen. They said they changed their minds after reading the memorandum of law that President Carter had sent to the Senate in 1980. Carter's letter made them realize that CEDAW was "extremely vague." As Vucanovich testified during the hearing:

The interpretation [of CEDAW] can be so varied that its ratification could lead to several problems. The most objectionable provision is Article 16, section 1(e), which requires us to allow women "to decide freely and responsibly on the number and spacing of their children." What does this mean? It certainly can be read to require that an abortion be legal throughout 9 months of pregnancy in order that women can fulfill the equality objectives of the treaty. (U.S. Senate 1990, 96)

The issue for Vucanovich was not really vagueness – it was abortion. Meanwhile, progressive organizations insisted that the treaty was abortion neutral. Catherine Bocksor, representative from the American Bar Association, maintained that CEDAW "does not mention abortion" (U.S. Senate 1990, 72).

The CAT seemed to be the easiest of the four treaties to ratify, so it moved to the top of Bush's agenda. Recall that President Reagan had signed it in 1988, signaling his intent to ratify. The SFRC held hearings on CAT on January 30, 1990, and voted it out of committee on July 19, 1990. It was then ready for a vote on the Senate floor. The imminent vote on CAT and the loss of support among Republican women sharpened the intensity of lobbying for and against U.S. ratification of CEDAW. Democratic Senator Claiborne Pell (RI), Chair of the Foreign Relations Committee, convened a hearing for August 2, 1990. Democratic senators tried, but failed, to leverage the upcoming vote on CAT into administration support for CEDAW. Alan J. Kreczko, deputy legal adviser for the State Department, testified on behalf of the Bush administration. Kreczko reiterated the argument that the Bush administration had not yet decided which of the remaining unratified treaties it wanted to prioritize. Democratic senators interrogated Kreczko to explain administration thinking about CEDAW. Senator Paul Sarbanes, a Democrat from Maryland, exerted considerable if not unrelenting pressure on him. Sarbanes urged the administration to review all four pending treaties simultaneously and pointedly criticized the State Department for taking such a long time to review CEDAW. Kreczko responded that the administration wanted to consider each treaty separately in order to avoid the problems that President Carter encountered when he requested the Senate to consider four treaties simultaneously, that "any flaw identified in any convention then became associated with each of the conventions" (U.S. Senate 1990, 52).

In the 1990 hearings, attention to the domestic impact of CEDAW remained present in the comments of some advocates, but the rhetoric of CEDAW supporters shifted clearly toward the impact of the convention on women abroad, and on the foreign policy implications of the United States' failure to ratify. Senator Paul Simon (D-IL) inserted into the hearing record academic reports on the status of women in China, the EU, Nordic countries, Japan, and several African countries (Uganda, Zambia, Zimbabwe, Kenya, Namibia, and Senegal). Senator Barbara Mikulski (D-MD) also talked about women in other countries and said that U.S. failure to ratify CEDAW made her "an embarrassed American and a very embarrassed U.S. Senator." She contrasted her embarrassment to the "buoyancy" she felt at the Copenhagen Conference in 1980 when the United States signed CEDAW. Kerry's statement in 1990 also highlights both the foreign and domestic implications of CEDAW:

I think that for us in this country to deny what is at stake here loses us the moral high ground and sets us back in advocacy on a host of other issues and efforts around the world. It is extraordinary that we should be struggling, really, to pass it at this point in time ... this convention calls on us to be honest about the situation in our country, that we have enormous amounts of discrimination here, and that there is still a significant and absolutely unexplainable gap between men and women and what each can enjoy in terms of rights in our country. (U.S. Senate 1990, 41)

Harriet Horwitz, president of B'nai B'rith Women, said that the tenth anniversary of the United States signing "spawned a wave of activities and heightened interest in moving this human rights document forward" (U.S. Senate 1990, 65). In her testimony, Arvonne Fraser stressed the "international embarrassment" factor: "I have to explain every time I go overseas why, when we conform [to the treaty], when we have been a leader on women's rights, when we were very influential in writing this, why we have not ratified" (U.S. Senate 1990, 72).

By contrast, CEDAW's opponents invested heavily in arguments about CEDAW's potential domestic impact. Conservative Republicans attacked CEDAW article by article. Ellen Smith, a lobbyist for Concerned Women for America, asserted, "The convention assumes a definition of 'discrimination' that is of astonishing breadth and goes far beyond the understanding as it has been addressed in American law." It applies to "private associations and organizations, and even to private individuals in the scope of their thoughts, customs and interpersonal relations." She insisted that CEDAW reads "like a laundry list of radically feminist, antifamily policy objectives that have failed to gain acceptance as domestic policy initiatives" (U.S. Senate 1990, 82). Conservative activist Phyllis Schlafly challenged the view that ratification would have no domestic effect: "It would overturn or change many of our current laws. It would subject our society to attempted regulation by an international committee made up of persons who have no understanding of, or respect for, the inalienable rights enjoyed by American women" (U.S. Senate 1990, 85). Several witnesses claimed that Article 16, section 1(e), which guarantees women's right "to decide freely and responsibly on the number and spacing of their children," actually protects "abortion on demand." "We certainly don't want some international body to legislate in the area of abortion," Schlafly asserted (U.S. Senate 1990, 86).

Moderate Republicans in Congress continued to urge the Bush administration to support CEDAW after the hearing, but their numbers were dropping. Eight of the Republican congresswomen who had put the process in motion with their letter to the State Department followed up with a second letter to the president on September

20, 1990, criticizing the administration's inaction on CEDAW and demanding Bush make a clear recommendation.[6] Two more of the original twelve congresswomen did not sign the letter: Molinari and Smith joined Vucanovich, Bentley, and Ros-Lehtinen in reversing their position.

Discussion about CEDAW on Capitol Hill continued after the 1990 hearing. On September 25, 1990, Congressman Yatron sponsored a bill "expressing the sense of the House that the President should seek advice and consent of the Senate" on CEDAW.[7] On October 22, 1991, the House overwhelmingly approved a bill urging the president to complete its study of CEDAW, by a roll-call vote of 374–48.[8] The yays included 259 Democrats and 114 Republicans, plus one Independent; all the opposing votes came from Republicans. This vote means that a solid majority of Republican members of congress voted to support U.S. ratification. Two days later, on October 24, Congressman Christopher H. Smith, a Republican from New Jersey, introduced another version of the bill with slightly different language urging the president to "submit to the Senate reservations, understandings, and declarations necessary for the Senate to give its advice and consent to ratification."[9]

Rather than responding directly to the push from the House on CEDAW, however, the Bush administration turned its attention to CAT and the ICCPR. Senate Democrats failed in their efforts to leverage the upcoming vote on the CAT into administration support for CEDAW. The Senate voted to approve CAT on October 27, 1990. A year later, the SCFR held a hearing on the ICCPR, on November 21, 1991, just over a year after the 1990 hearing on CEDAW. Senator Helms, who

---

[6] Representatives Johnson, Martin, Meyers, Morella, Roukema, Saiki, and Schneider and Senator Boschwitz signed the second letter.

[7] H.Res.476, 101st Congress.

[8] H.Res.116, 102nd Congress.

[9] H.Res.261, 102nd Congress. I note that these last two bills were introduced less than two weeks after the Judiciary Committee's notorious confirmation hearings for Supreme Court Justice nominee Clarence Thomas. Anita Hill, a former employee of Thomas's at the Equal Employment Opportunity Commission, testified that Thomas had sexually harassed her. The hearings, which were televised, incited a huge national controversy. The members of the Judiciary Committee's misunderstanding of the issue of sexual harassment and mistreatment of Hill during the hearings generated a firestorm of public anger against both parties. The pro-CEDAW bills may have been introduced to address concerns about Congress' support for women's rights in the wake of the Thomas hearings.

led the hearing, turned out to be one of only three people in attendance who opposed the ICCPR. He opened the hearings with his characteristic prose: "Now to be frank, ladies and gentlemen, I cannot comprehend why the sudden rush to approve a convention that has been lying around this place for a quarter of a century ... this is a seriously flawed convention (U.S. Senate 1991, 1).

Harold W. Andersen, chairman of the World Press Freedom Committee, a network of news media organizations, also opposed ratification of ICCPR. Andersen maintained that ICCPR threatened freedom of the press and expression. The other opposing witness was Ronald D. Rotunda, a law professor from the University of Illinois, who spoke against ICCPR on legal grounds. No grassroots organizations spoke against it.

ICCPR advocates addressed how the collapse of the Soviet Union and the end of the Cold War eliminated worries about ceding too much power to the UN Human Rights Committee. Richard Schifter, assistant secretary of state for Human Rights and Humanitarian Affairs of the State Department, attested that "the changes that have occurred world-wide as a result of the collapse of communism make it much more likely that the Human Rights Committee of the United Nations can work much more effectively than it did in the past" (U.S. Senate 1991, 21). Senator Paul Sarbanes (D-MD) highlighted the role that human rights agreements played in precipitating the collapse of the communist world. He said that human rights "became the mechanism by which the United States, at these international conferences, was able, in effect, to help crack totalitarian regimes" (U.S. Senate 1991, 51). During the Cold War, many feared human rights treaties would strengthen the Soviet Union and contribute to the spread of communism. After the Cold War, people portrayed human rights as the weapon that crushed the hammer and sickle. The Foreign Relations Committee reported the bill ratifying the ICCPR out on March 24, 1992, and the full Senate voted to approve it on April 2, 1992, with five reservations, five understandings, and four declarations. Despite clear expressions of support for CEDAW from a majority of Republican members of the House of Representatives and a geopolitical climate that gave the United States a clear foreign policy interest in ratifying all human rights treaties, the Bush administration chose to prioritize CAT and the ICCPR over CEDAW.

Olympia Snowe, who at that time was a Republican congress-woman from Maine, tried a slightly different tactic to keep CEDAW on the congressional agenda and increase public awareness about it. On May 20, 1993, she introduced a bill that called for the creation of a position within the State Department to advocate on behalf of international women's human rights. Snowe's bill linked CEDAW ratification to this new position:

If the United Nations Convention on the Elimination of All Forms of Discrimination against Women (CEDAW) has not been submitted to the Senate for ratification, not more than 90 days after the date of enactment of this Act, the Secretary of State shall submit a report to the Congress on the administration's position on the ratification of CEDAW and timetable for submission of CEDAW for congressional consideration and approval.[10]

The bill was referred to committee and saw no further action, but it is worth noting that a Republican initiated it. Nonetheless, the Bush administration remained silent on CEDAW.

1994: RACIAL DISCRIMINATION, 1, GENDER DISCRIMINATION 0

When President Clinton took office in 1993, CEDAW appeared resurgent. President Clinton supported ratification and the Democrats controlled sixty-one seats in the Senate, the party's largest majority since the Carter administration; they needed only six Republicans to cross the aisle in order to ratify the Convention. Getting the required two-thirds of the Senate seemed imminent because sixty-eight senators had signed a letter asking President Clinton to ratify it. On September 27, 1994, the Senate Committee on Foreign Relations again held hearings on U.S. ratification of CEDAW. Only two senators attended – Chairman Claiborne Pell and Senator Paul Simon (D-IL). Senator Simon opened his remarks by referring to the UN International Conference on Population and Development that had taken place in Cairo, Egypt, two weeks earlier (from September 5 to 13, 1994), which he and several of the witnesses had attended. Abortion had been at the center of significant conflict at the Cairo conference. Fred Sai, the president of International Planned Parenthood and chair of

[10] Women's Human Rights Protection Act of 1993, H.R.2231, 103rd Congress.

the conference, had attempted to use the forum to define an international right to abortion. The measure failed and prompted both the UN and the United States to assert their rejection explicitly. Senator Simon said that the Cairo conference made him realize that "nothing can do more to resolve population problems than to give educational opportunity and equal opportunity generally to women," emphasizing the importance of international venues for protecting women's rights (U.S. Senate 1994b, 5).

The first witness called to testify was Jamison S. Borek, deputy legal adviser to the State Department. Borek framed his testimony in terms of the importance of ratifying CEDAW "to underscore our commitment to women's rights and to enhance our ability to protect and promote these rights internationally," to "work collectively with other nations," and "to promote the rule of law and respect for human rights throughout the world." He asserted that "by excluding ourselves from the process and dialog which is centered on this treaty, we hamper our own effects to work effectively with other countries in promoting women's rights around the globe" (U.S. Senate 1994b, 6).

Borek presented the Clinton administration's plan to ratify CEDAW with four reservations, three understandings, and two declarations to address the concerns raised by the opposition and minimize the impact of the Convention on U.S. law. Borek assured the Senate that CEDAW with the proposed RUDs would essentially have no effect on U.S. law and policy and emphasized that the RUDs were similar to the ones applied to other treaties, especially the Convention on the Elimination of Racial Discrimination. The first reservation addressed the sphere of private conduct. The second reservation asserted the primacy of the combat exclusion for women in the U.S. military that the Pentagon had recently put into effect: "We do not accept an obligation to assign women to all military units and positions which may require engagement in direct combat."[11] Borek explained the rationale this way: "There is room for continued debate domestically over the role of women in combat, but we do not believe that the ratification of this Convention should be the vehicle to preempt or settle the question" (U.S. Senate 1994b, 5). The third reservation addressed the issue

---

[11] The Department of Defense lifted the combat exclusion on January 24, 2013. Retrieved from http://www.defense.gov/Releases/Release.aspx?ReleaseID=15784.

of equal pay in Article 11. The administration felt that a reservation on Article 11 was warranted in light of the tendency of the CEDAW Committee to interpret it broadly in its recommendations to states parties. "While the Convention does not actually speak of 'comparable worth,' there is some negotiating history which could be viewed as taking it further than U.S. law" (U.S. Senate 1994b, 5). A fourth reservation prohibited paid maternity leave. The State Department proposed three understandings to clarify that the U.S. government (1) would not "federalize matters which are currently under state and local jurisdiction"; (2) violate free speech; or (3) require free health care services (U.S. Senate 1994b, 5). Finally, Borek recommended two declarations: first, that CEDAW would be non–self-executing and "will not create a new or independently enforceable private cause of action in U.S. courts," and second, the United States would be exempt from Article 29 (1), which permits the International Court of Justice to mediate interstate disputes regarding CEDAW.

Opposing witnesses forcefully argued about the danger that CEDAW posed on the issue of abortion. Cecelia Acevedo Royals, president of the National Institute of Womanhood, framed her remarks in terms of the Cairo Conference.[12] She quoted Fred Sai as having said that "women are crippled by unbridled fertility" and criticized the "demeaning concept of women" that his view represented. She insisted that CEDAW "takes on a very different meaning in light of this backdrop" of the Cairo conference (U.S. Senate 1994b, 22). What is important to note here is that the anti-CEDAW witnesses discussed abortion in the context of the Cairo Conference. Anti-CEDAW forces were very concerned that U.S. ratification of CEDAW would strengthen the status of abortion rights in international law.

On October 3, 1994, the Senate Committee on Foreign Relations approved the treaty by a vote of thirteen to five. Two Republican Senators, Frank Murkowski from Alaska and Jim Jeffords from Alaska, voted in favor of ratification, and one Democrat, Sherrod

---

[12] The National Institute of Womanhood is affiliated with the conservative Catholic organization Opus Dei, and runs Centro Tepeyac, a crisis pregnancy center in Silver Spring, Maryland. The Web site for Centro Tepeyac affirms, "We dedicate ourselves to saving unborn children and their mothers and fathers from abortion by reaching out to women one-on-one and recognizing their emotional, spiritual and physical needs" (Centro Tepeyac n.d.).

Brown from Ohio, voted against. The committee adopted an understanding proposed by Senator Helms "clarifying the U.S. view that nothing in the Convention creates a right to abortion and that abortion should not be promoted as a method of family planning." Under normal circumstances, the treaty would have proceeded to a vote on the Senate floor, but the GOP senators put a hold on it, which meant that the Convention would revert back to the SFRC when the new Senate reconvened in the next session.

The Clinton strategy of offering extensive RUDs did not placate CEDAW opponents, but it proved to be an effective strategy with the racial discrimination treaty, which the Senate approved on October 21, 1994, less than a month after the CEDAW hearing. The Senate Committee on Foreign Relations held a hearing on CERD on May 11, 1994. The CERD hearing is remarkable for its brevity: the Committee convened at 10:06 AM and ended promptly at 11:15 AM. During that one hour and nine minute period, seven witnesses testified, all of them in favor of ratification. They made three main arguments about CERD: it was compatible with existing U.S. law, it would demonstrate support for the rights of African Americans, and it would affirm U.S. commitment to global human rights, which was appropriate and important in the post–Cold War era. As Wade Henderson, a lobbyist for the NAACP, stated, "I believe for the most part that Federal and State laws are fully consistent with the requirements of the Convention, and we believe that if the United States were to adopt the Convention in its present form it would be in virtual full compliance" (U.S. Senate 1994a, 59). Henderson would later become chair of the Leadership Conference on Civil and Human Rights, the lead organization of the pro-CEDAW created in 2010. John Shattuck, Assistant Secretary of State for Democracy, Human Rights and Labor, focused his remarks on the changed climate for human rights in the post–Cold War era. "During the cold war," he said, "as we all know, much of the human rights agenda, including the fight against racial discrimination, became a political football. That is no longer the case. We are now seeing real material progress in combating racial and ethnic discrimination in some very important parts of the world" (U.S. Senate 1994a, 8). Shattuck's comments attest to the increased power of the UN and international human rights organizations since the collapse of the Soviet Union.

The Senate passed the advice and consent resolution on CERD on June 24, 1994, by a division vote, rather than a roll call vote. It approved CERD with three reservations, one understanding, one declaration, and one "proviso." The first reservation asserts that the United States does not accept any aspect of the treaty that contravenes freedom of speech, expression, or assembly. The second reservation affirms, "The United States does not accept any obligation under this Convention [to enact measures] with respect to private conduct except as mandated by the Constitution and laws of the United States." In other words, the "private conduct" provision of CERD, which provides protection from discrimination committed by private individuals, does not apply to the United States. The third reservation requires U.S. consent before any disputes involving the United States are sent to the International Court of Justice for adjudication. The declaration clarifies that the Convention applies to the federal government, but not necessarily to state and local governments. Finally, according to the proviso, unprecedented in previous human rights treaties, "Nothing in this Convention requires or authorizes legislation, or other action, by the United States of America prohibited by the Constitution of the United States as interpreted by the United States." The proviso has no status in international law; it is merely an affirmation of policy intended for an American audience (University of Minnesota Human Rights Library 1994). In the years since 1994, the United States has faithfully complied with its obligations to CERD, submitting periodic reports and attending regular sessions of the treaty committee. U.S. compliance with CERD has not prompted anyone to raise any alarms about the erosion of U.S. sovereignty or dramatic threats to the American way of life.

Racial discrimination is, arguably, the most persistently divisive issue in U.S. political history. The lack of mobilization against CERD is remarkable given the fears that Republican senators stoked in the 1940s and 1950s, about how African Americans might use the Commission on Human Rights to condemn racial discrimination in the United States. Why would the Senate find an international convention banning racial discrimination less problematic than a convention banning discrimination against women? Moreover, CERD raises many of the same legal issues that CEDAW does. Like CEDAW, CERD enjoins governments to take positive action to eliminate discrimination. Both treaties define discrimination in similar terms. Like CEDAW, CERD seeks to regulate private conduct and protect the rights of those discriminated against by private individuals or organizations, as well as by public ones. Thus, several of the aspects of CEDAW that opponents find objectionable are also part of CERD. The similarities between the two treaties are not surprising when we recall that the women who drafted CEDAW relied on CERD as a model (Brewer 2013). Unlike CEDAW, however, ratification of CERD raised barely a ripple of concern within the policy arena and generated little attention in the media.

THE HELMS YEARS 1995–2000

From 1995 to 2000, the GOP held a majority of Senate seats, and Republican Jesse Helms chaired the SFRC. Prospects for CEDAW ratification diminished considerably during this period, but pressure to ratify remained intense in 1995 because of the Fourth World Conference on Women scheduled to take place in Beijing that fall. CEDAW had grown in prominence and importance over the years, and U.S. failure to ratify would make things awkward for the United States at the Conference itself. Within the United States, however, the GOP majority continued to oppose ratification. On July 18, 1995, the House of Representatives held a hearing prior to the Beijing Conference, hoping to score points against the Clinton administration by arguing that widespread human rights violations in China made attending the Beijing Conference inappropriate. Several years earlier, the Bush administration had agreed to participate in the Beijing Conference, but members of the Republican-controlled House of Representatives now wanted to revisit the issue. The tenor of comments made during the hearing was often hostile. "I think it is very, very appropriate for us to suggest that going to Beijing in 1995 is analogous to going to Hitler's Germany in 1939 for a human rights conference," remarked Representative Christopher Smith (R-NJ) (U.S. House of Representatives 1995, 7). Congressman Matt Salmon (R-AZ) commented: "Press reports indicate that the First Lady [Hillary Clinton] has her bags packed for Beijing, ready as she is to push for an international fundamental right to terminate one's own child on demand and without apology. Let us not be part of this travesty" (U.S. House of Representatives 1995, 80). Congressman David Funderburk, a one-term Republican member from North Carolina, started his statement by asserting, "I am ashamed that the United States of America is sending a delegation to the United Nation's Conference on Women." Funderburk refers to CEDAW as "a treaty in which fathers and husbands are described as the primary abusers of women and children" (U.S. House of Representatives 1995, 78). A comment from Laurel Heiskel, legislative coordinator for Concerned Women for America, laid bare the stakes involved in the global arena: "Is the exportation of abortion on demand to every nation of the world truly the No. 1 priority of our State Department?" (U.S. House of Representatives 1995). The United States' delegation did attend the Beijing Conference, and the speech that Hillary Clinton gave, in which she declared that "women's rights are human rights, and human rights are women's rights," won accolades worldwide. Nevertheless, the U.S. Senate – and the treaty itself – were unmoved.

Members of the House of Representatives continued to raise public awareness and build popular support for CEDAW by introducing bills supporting ratification. Congresswoman Lynn Woolsey, a Democrat from California, introduced resolutions supporting CEDAW ratification at the start of every Congress in which she served – in 1993, 1995, 1997, 1999, 2001, 2003, 2005, 2007, 2009, and 2011. When Congresswoman Woolsey retired, Representative Carolyn Maloney, a Democrat from New York, took up this role, introducing a CEDAW resolution on January 4, 2013.[13] In the fall of 1999, Congresswoman Woolsey sought to arrange a meeting with Senator Helms, then chair of the Senate Committee on Foreign Relations, to ask him to hold hearings on CEDAW. Helms had offered to have his senior staffers meet with Woolsey, but she was holding out to meet with the senator himself. After months of unsuccessful efforts, Woolsey adopted a more dramatic approach. On October 27, she marched a group of Democratic congresswomen across the Capitol to Helms' office on the Senate side. Nine women accompanied her: Tammy Baldwin (D-WI), Rosa De Lauro (D-CT), Eddie Bernice Johnson (D-TX), Nita Lowey (D-NY), Carolyn Maloney (D-NY), Patsy Mink (D-HI), Delegate Eleanor Holmes Norton (DC), Nancy Pelosi (D-CA), and Jan Schakowsky (D-IL) They carried poster-sized copies of a letter urging the Senate to act on CEDAW, which 111 members of Congress had

[13] H.Res.19, 113th Congress.

signed. Woolsey described the move as a spur of the moment idea, but her actions suggest a more carefully planned publicity stunt. In a press conference, Woolsey reported "When [Helms'] staff told us on Wednesday, after we had called and said we were coming, that he was not available and they didn't know his whereabouts, we learned he was in fact chairing a hearing just down the hall from his office. So we went there" (FDCH Political Transcripts 1999).[14]

The women entered the hearing room and interrupted the proceedings by demanding to meet with Senator Helms. The Senator responded: "This is a hearing on China and we have some guests who are not interested in that; they want to demonstrate another issue and I hope the security people will escort them out in the corridor and let them wait there." Woolsey again addressed Helms from the back of the room, which prompted Helms to bang his gavel and tell her, "You are out of order. You cannot demonstrate in this hearing." When Woolsey spoke up a third time, Helms famously replied, "You're out of order. You know you are out of order and I would not be discourteous to you where you work. Now you please be a lady." He banged his gavel again. Woolsey tried again but Helms banged his gavel to drown her out. Security guards then escorted the women out of the chamber. In a press conference held after the incident, Woolsey stated, "Today the women of the House met with Senator Boxer to review our strategy to stop one man, Senator Jesse Helms, from blocking democracy ... he will not stonewall the women of the House and the women of the Congress in our efforts to promote and ratify CEDAW" (all quotes from FDCH Political Transcripts 1999).

A few weeks after the incident, on November 19, 1999, Senator Barbara Boxer (D-CA) introduced a resolution calling on the Senate Committee on Foreign Relations to ratify CEDAW before March 8, 2000, International Women's Day.[15] All but one of the nine women serving in the Senate cosponsored the bill; Kay Bailey Hutchison, a Republican from Texas, was the one holdout. When March 8 came

---

[14] Both claims about being unable to locate Senator Helms were disingenuous. The hearing that he chaired that day – confirmation of Clinton's nominee for ambassador to China – was open to the public. The times and locations of Senate hearings are public information and would have been accessible to any reader of the *Washington Post*. Both Helms's staff and Woolsey and her cohort would have known where Helms would be.

[15] S. Res. 237, 106th Congress, 1st Session.

around and the Senate had not taken any action, Boxer gave a speech in support of the bill in which she explicitly addressed Helms's reasons for opposing ratification. She identified more than 100 organizations that supported CEDAW to counter Senator Helms's claim that only "radical groups" backed it. She reminded the Senate that the SFRC approved ratification of the treaty in 1994 with the understanding that "nothing in the convention reflects or creates a right to abortion" and that "in no case should abortion be promoted as a method of family planning." On March 30, 2000, with the March 8 deadline having passed, Boxer reintroduced the bill, this time with thirty-two cosponsors, including Republicans Olympia Snowe and Susan Collins, both from Maine. This bill called for ratification of CEDAW by July 19, 2000, the twentieth anniversary of the U.S. signing of the Convention.[16]

Two months later, Helms checkmated Boxer by introducing a bill opposing U.S. ratification of CEDAW. He introduced the bill on Thursday, May 11, 2000, just before Mother's Day that Sunday. He framed the legislation as a defense of motherhood. The Senate should oppose CEDAW on the grounds that it is "incompatible with the tradition and policy of the United States to uphold motherhood and to regard motherhood with the highest degree of honor and respect" and that the "Convention would create negative perceptions toward motherhood."[17] In a statement introducing the bill, Helms quipped, in his famous Southern drawl, CEDAW "rhymes with hee-haw."[18] Helms described the treaty as "clearly negotiated by radical feminists with the intent of enshrining their radical anti-family agenda into international law" and "so obviously bad that the Democrats never brought it up for a vote" even when they controlled the Senate. He affirmed that "if I have anything to do with [CEDAW] – and I think I do – it will never see the light of day on my watch." He concluded by listing more than 100 organizations that opposed ratification.

During the next CEDAW hearing, in 2002, Senator Biden made a comment that sums up the status of CEDAW during the Helms era:

Because of the strong opposition of the then-chairman of the committee, there was no likelihood we [Democrats] were going to get a hearing on the treaty,

---

[16] S. Res. 279, 106th Congress, 2nd Session.
[17] S. Res. 306, 106th Congress, 2nd Session.
[18] You can watch video footage of this session at C-SPAN May 11, 2000.

and so we had planned a half-a-dozen different ways to try to bring the treaty up on the floor even without a hearing, and we found that we ran into road-blocks that would make it virtually impossible to get it done. (U.S. Senate 2002, 4)

2002 SENATE HEARINGS

By 2002, the Democrats had regained a majority in the Senate and control of the Foreign Relations Committee. Biden, a longtime sup-porter of women's rights, had replaced Jesse Helms as chair of the SFRC on June 6, 2001. One of his first actions as chair was to ini-tiate action on CEDAW by writing to Secretary of State Colin Powell. Nearly a year later, Powell responded by announcing that it had placed CEDAW in the category of treaties that are "generally desirable and should be approved" (U.S. Senate 2002, 3). Biden responded by con-vening a hearing, even though the State Department said it was not ready and declined to appear at the hearing. Perhaps to compensate for the administration's absence, the hearings included an ample list of witnesses both for CEDAW and against.

The geopolitical context in which this hearing took place was par-ticularly significant for the status of women abroad. The United States had invaded Afghanistan on March 1. The pretext for war was to destroy the Taliban regime, which had supported the Al-Qaeda mili-tants that carried out the terrorist attacks on September 11, 2001. President George W. Bush also framed the war as an effort to stop the Taliban war on Afghan women. In this context, the rhetorical strategy of CEDAW proponents shifted even more decidedly toward emphasiz-ing how the convention would strengthen the rights of women in other countries. With the Bush administration still enjoying broad support for its policies toward the region, hitching support for CEDAW to the Afghan invasion appeared to be a promising strategy for defusing opposition among Republicans.

Democrats framed support for the Convention in terms of the status of women in Taliban-controlled Afghanistan. They sought to highlight the inconsistency between the U.S. government's willing-ness to go to war to protect Afghan women from the Taliban and its unwillingness to ratify CEDAW. Biden ended his opening statement by affirming,

If we need any more graphic illustration of why this treaty is needed for women of the world, I just invite you to come back to Afghanistan with me ... stand there with the Minister for Women's Affairs, and observe that even after the liberation, the majority of women are still wearing burkas. Even after this, they are still worried about their future. (U.S. Senate 2002, 6)

Biden then handed the gavel over to Senator Barbara Boxer, who inserted into the record a letter supporting U.S. ratification written by Dr. Sema Samar, the Afghan Minister of Women's Affairs. Samar's letter asserted that U.S. ratification of CEDAW would strengthen both CEDAW and the status of women in Afghanistan:

We will then be able to tell our countrymen that the United States, where women already have full legal rights, has just seen the need to ratify this treaty. This treaty will then truly be the international measure of the rights that any country should guarantee to its women. We will be able to refer to its terms and guidelines in public debates over what our laws should say. (U.S. Senate 2002, 10)

Senator Boxer began her remarks by asserting, "I think there is no better time than right now to show our commitment to women by approving this treaty" because of the status of women in Afghanistan (U.S. Senate 2002, 7). Congresswoman Woolsey's statement also focused on Afghanistan: "As the U.S. works to help Afghanistan rebuild, we are presented with a shameful irony: while we are trying to teach the Afghan people that women must be an equal part of a post-Taliban democracy, we contradict ourselves by refusing to ratify the one international treaty that ensures the rights of all women" (U.S. Senate 2002, 13). Congresswoman Maloney commented that "it is tremendously embarrassing as a Member of Congress to face these questions, especially when President and Mrs. Bush have spoken so forcefully about the need to help women in Afghanistan" (U.S. Senate 2002, 26). The Committee's final report stated that "the treatment of women in Afghanistan under Taliban rule serves as a reminder that the struggle for women's rights is far from complete. Although women in the United States enjoy equal opportunity and equal protection of the law, these rights are not universally guaranteed elsewhere. The Convention provides an important means to advance these rights" (U.S. Senate 2002, 5).

Given the administration's focus on the status of women under the Taliban regime, one might expect this to have proven a persuasive argument, but it did not. Opponents of CEDAW also framed their arguments in terms of Afghanistan. In a letter to Senator Biden dated July 8, 2002, Secretary of State Colin Powell affirmed support for Afghan women even as he demurred on the CEDAW question: "Our recent actions in Afghanistan underscore this commitment to promote the rights of girls and women who suffered under the draconian Taliban rule, including in education, employment, healthcare, and other areas. It is for these and other reasons that the Administration supports CEDAW's general goal of eradicating invidious discrimination against women across the globe" (U.S. Senate 2002, 16).

Powell went on to say that "the vagueness of the treaty and the reach of the official U.N. body" that oversees CEDAW warrant careful consideration, consideration that the Bush administration did not ultimately provide. Opposition senators pointed out that an authoritarian government signed CEDAW in Afghanistan: "It is through their personal heroism and sacrifice, not a multilateral treaty, that Afghan women have been relieved of the burden of an oppressive, antiwoman government whose equally lawless predecessor signed CEDAW in 1980" (U.S. Senate 2002, 21).

Senator Boxer briefly mentioned abortion, to ensure CEDAW opponents that "we are using as a starting point the recommendations made by the Clinton administration and the understanding added by Senator Helms that says that nothing in the treaty shall be construed to reflect or create any right to abortion" (U.S. Senate 2002, 8).

After the hearing, Secretary of State Powell asked Senator Biden to postpone the Committee vote until the Department of Justice completed its review of the Convention, but Biden held the vote anyway. The Committee split along party lines, with the twelve Democratic senators for (Biden, Sarbanes, Dodd, Kerry, Feingold, Wellstone, Boxer, Torricelli, Nelson, Rockefeller, Smith, and Chafee) and the seven Republican senators against (Helms, Lugar, Hagel, Frist, Allen, Brownback, and Enzi). In contrast to previous years, the vote on the treaty broke cleanly on party lines.

Biden's maneuver prompted the Republican senators on the Foreign Relations Committee to file a minority report explaining their vote against CEDAW. The report contended that their concerns about the impact of the treaty had not been definitively resolved. The report lists a series of domestic policies that were not discussed during the hearing:

The Convention has also generated vigorous debate about the implications of U.S. compliance with regard to important social issues such as abortion on demand (including restrictions on Federal funding), comparable worth salary laws, women in the military, same-sex marriage, health care, single-sex education and potential government intrusion into areas traditionally within the scope of family privacy. That debate perforce must continue, given that these issues have not, unfortunately, been laid to rest by Committee action on the Convention. (U.S. Senate 2002, 15)

Second, the vote was not legitimate because the Bush administration did not participate in the CEDAW hearing. Biden had tried to maneuver around the administration's delaying tactics, but his Republican colleagues maneuvered right back at him. Finally, "ratification of CEDAW will help lawyers and other pro-abortion advocates reach the goal of enshrining unrestricted access to abortion in the United States" (U.S. Senate 2002, 22). The 2002 hearings took place in a brief window in which Democrats narrowly controlled the Senate after Vermont Senator Jim Jeffords defected from the Republican Party, became an Independent, and voted with the Democrats. The Republicans took back control in the next election, shutting the window on the prospects for action until the election of Barack Obama as president.

WOMEN AND THE ARAB SPRING

Chapter 1 opens with a description of the hearings that took place in the Senate in 2010. Since then, Democrats have held one more event to raise awareness for CEDAW. On November 2, 2011, the Senate held a hearing, Women and the Arab Spring, to discuss the ways in which the United States could support women in the midst of the wave of civil uprisings taking place in the Middle East and North Africa. This was not a hearing on U.S. ratification of CEDAW, but many of the witnesses focused their comments on the treaty's importance. Senator Barbara Boxer opened the hearings by posing the following questions: "How can the United States provide meaningful support to help ensure that women have a seat at the table? How can international tools be used to encourage governments to afford women full and equal rights?" (U.S. Senate 2011). Several of the witnesses answered this question by affirming that U.S. ratification of CEDAW would benefit women in other countries. Melanne Verveer, ambassador-at-large for Global Women's Issues in the State Department, reiterated the point she had made in the 2010 hearings:

As I travel around the world, there is one question I get consistently, particularly from women who have been on the front lines of their own struggle in their countries, and that question is why has the United States not ratified the Convention for the Elimination of Discrimination against Women and why do we stand with a few pariah countries like Somalia and Iran in not having done that. And it is not that we are lousy on these issues when it comes to women's rights. We have a phenomenal record to stand on. (U.S. Senate 2011)

The Leadership Conference on Civil and Human Rights, the organization behind the CEDAW coalition, affirmed that U.S. ratification would strengthen CEDAW abroad: "The United States is rightfully known as a global leader in standing up for women and girls. Yet our failure to ratify CEDAW enables opponents of women's rights in the Middle East and elsewhere to decide that U.S. arguments on behalf of women's rights need not be taken seriously" (U.S. Senate 2011).

Mahnaz Afkhami, CEO of Women's Learning Partnership, a coalition of women's rights activists and NGOs from twenty countries in the Middle East and North Africa, reaffirmed this point: "U.S. ratification would strengthen the efforts of activists for democracy and women's equality throughout the Middle East. Our partners in the region have made clear to us that U.S. ratification of CEDAW would reinforce their own efforts to fully institutionalize and implement the treaty provisions for gender equality within their national legislation and constitutional reforms" (U.S. Senate 2011).

CONCLUSION

This chapter begins with President Carter's submission of CEDAW to the Senate Committee on Foreign Relations in November 1980. CEDAW remained a low priority throughout the 1980s, in part because of the conservative political climate that predominated during the Reagan era, and in part because activists did not yet appreciate how an international treaty could strengthen women's rights within the United States. The years between 1988 and 1994 witnessed a flurry of treaty activity in the Senate, which held hearings on five human rights treaties: the Genocide Convention, CAT, ICCPR, CERD, and CEDAW. The Senate held three hearings on CEDAW alone during this period, in 1988, 1990, and 1994. By 1994, the Senate had ratified all four of the other treaties – but the defection of moderate Republicans prevented ratification of CEDAW. From 1995 to 2002, socially conservative Republican Senator Jesse Helms kept CEDAW off the agenda during his tenure as Chair of the Foreign Relations Committee. His opposition to the Convention prompted Democrats to press harder for ratification. When the Democratic Party regained majority control of the Senate in 2002, Senators Joe Biden and Barbara Boxer reintroduced CEDAW. They framed it in terms of the U.S. war in Afghanistan to capitalize on then-popular arguments that the United States went to war in order to free Afghan women from the authoritarian rule of the Taliban regime. Although their control over the committee agenda allowed the Democrats to hold a hearing, they could not get the sixty-seven votes needed for ratification, and then they quickly lost control of the agenda when the Republicans took back the majority. Democrats held a fifth hearing in 2010 in the hopes of translating the Obama administration's explicit support for CEDAW into ratification, still to no avail, as increasing party polarization on the treaty diminished the prospects for picking up the necessary Republican votes to achieve a two-thirds vote. The theme that emerges here is the Republican Party's abandonment of women's rights and the Democratic Party's insufficient efforts to build a broader consensus of support.

Intensifying differences between Republicans and Democrats on CEDAW reflect a partisan realignment on women's issues that occurred in the late 1970s. Prior to 1980, both parties held the same views on a range of women's rights policies. Both parties supported CEDAW, and both President Ford and then Carter sent delegates to participate in the committee that drafted CEDAW in the late 1970s. By the time CEDAW opened for signature in 1980, as I showed in Chapter 3, partisan conflicts over women's rights had erupted and seized center stage in domestic politics. Social conservatives gained control of the Republican Party and reversed the party's support for women's equality. Opposition to the ERA and abortion became central pillars of the Republican platform. Social conservatives have organized successfully against CEDAW by equating U.S. ratification with the imposition of

UN mandates on women's issues that remain unresolved domestically, such as abortion, state-funded child care, and comparable worth (Wolbrecht 2000).

The CEDAW debate goes well beyond domestic politics. With the end of the Cold War, the status of women's issues in the international arena changed dramatically. In the past, ideological conflicts between the Americans and Soviets and grandstanding by the non-aligned countries dominated discussions about women's rights within the UN. The change in geopolitical context that occurred with the dissolution of the communist bloc threw the international arena into a period of flux. In the 1990s, human rights treaties, and the international conferences in which they were discussed, suddenly mattered more than they had in the past. Struggles over interpretation of what human rights norms meant in the new world order took place at UN conferences. The participation of hundreds, if not thousands, of NGOs at conferences such as Beijing and Cairo increased the stakes of those discussions.

This chapter highlights the political reversals that lie behind the failure to ratify CEDAW. The party largely responsible for championing CEDAW in the 1970s – the Republican Party – has become the main obstacle to ratifying CEDAW in the United States. The Democratic Party, which ostensibly took up the banner of support for the Convention, has framed that support in terms of arguments that de-emphasize its impact on the constituents who would be most likely to support it. The Democrats now argue that CEDAW's greatest benefit is that it will strengthen the rights of women in other countries, while having virtually no impact at home. They have done so largely in response to opponents' colorful arguments about the dire consequences that CEDAW could have at home. The Senate has treated CEDAW differently from any of the other UN human rights treaties. Comparing the legislative history of CEDAW to that of the other human rights treaties unmasks the politics at stake and reveals that the Senate has subjected CEDAW to far greater scrutiny. The stakes are political, not legal or constitutional, and they pertain to control over the agenda for women's issues both domestically and internationally.

7

CEDAW and Domestic Violence Law
in the United States

Conflicts between those who support U.S. ratification of CEDAW and those who oppose it have grown sharper over time. As this book has shown, advocates maintain that the Convention will strengthen U.S. foreign policy but will have relatively little impact in the United States. CEDAW opponents, on the other hand, predict that dire domestic policy consequences will ensue if the United States ratifies CEDAW. The intense conflicts between the two sides have obscured the fact that there are two points that the pro and con sides agree upon. First, American women already enjoy all the rights that CEDAW guarantees. The rhetoric of both sides rests on a claim that the status quo with regard to women's rights policy in the United States is fine. Second, both sides concur that the private jurisdiction clause of CEDAW, which obligates states "to take all appropriate measures to eliminate discrimination against women by any person, organization or enterprise," is a problem. CEDAW proponents consider the private jurisdiction issue as either moot because human rights treaties are non–self-executing, or easily circumvented through appropriate legislation or reservations.[1] For CEDAW opponents, the private jurisdiction clause of CEDAW is its bête noir. Conservatives acknowledge the expanded scope of rights guaranteed by CEDAW – and fear it as a vehicle for unwanted state

---

[1] The arguments I make in Chapter 5 bolster this perspective by showing that that ratification of CEDAW would not impose a set of policies on the United States; it would not require the United States to do anything except participate in a regular process of reporting.

intervention into the private sphere.[2] The con side sees the private jurisdiction clause as a problem that can only be avoided by not ratifying CEDAW in the first place. Neither side sees the private jurisdiction clause as a potential asset for women's rights.

In this chapter, I examine the validity of these claims. Does U.S. law already guarantee the rights that CEDAW promises? Is the private jurisdiction clause of CEDAW a problem for women's rights? I consider these questions with regard to domestic violence. If existing U.S. law is sufficient to protect women's rights, then women should enjoy equal protection under the law with regard to domestic violence as well as other instances of discrimination against women. In cases of domestic violence, however, the private sphere provides little protection for women. Current strategies for protecting women hinge on redefining the boundaries between public and private life in order to permit law enforcement to intervene when intimate partners threaten women with violence. The private jurisdiction clause of CEDAW is thus potentially very relevant to anti–domestic violence policy.

I establish two central claims with regard to existing constitutional protections of women's rights. First, although women in the United States enjoy an impressive array of statutory rights in every arena of their lives, the U.S. Constitution may not provide sufficient guarantees of those rights. The Supreme Court has interpreted the 14th Amendment of the Constitution as providing a guarantee against sex discrimination, but that interpretation has been applied unevenly and inconsistently. Moreover, the Supreme Court's interpretation of the 14th Amendment is subject to change depending on the views of seated justices. Second, the U.S. Constitution does not protect individuals from harms done to them by private individuals and thus cannot provide women with a source of legal relief in cases in which they are subject to discrimination by non-state actors. This is a basic premise of the doctrine of state action: the U.S. Constitution protects citizens from discrimination at the hands of state actors, but provides no relief from private acts of discrimination.

---

[2] In a 1990 Senate hearing on CEDAW, Ellen Smith, legislative counsel for Concerned Women for America, argued that the Convention goes far beyond constitutional and legal rights already guaranteed in the United States: "The convention assumes a definition of 'discrimination' that is of astonishing breadth" and it applies to "private associations and organizations, and even to private individuals in the scope of their thoughts, customs, and interpersonal interactions" (U.S. Senate 1990, 82).

The limitations of constitutional protections of women's rights are most relevant to the issue of domestic violence. Domestic violence, which CEDAW defines as a central form of discrimination against women, involves private acts of discrimination. One of the main forms of protection that women have against intimate partner violence is a restraining order against an abusive or potentially abusive partner. According to existing interpretations of domestic law, police retain discretion about when to enforce a restraining order. The Supreme Court has rejected claims that the 14th Amendment guarantees women a right to protection in cases of domestic violence. Thus both of the limitations of the 14th Amendment are in play here: American women do not enjoy sufficiently strong protection from domestic violence because discrimination on the basis of sex is not a constitutionally guaranteed right and the doctrine of state action precludes protecting individuals from private discrimination.

Faced with these limitations, I turn to possible solutions. How might we provide a more muscular basis for legal protection of women from sex-based discrimination? In this chapter I examine three possible remedies: first, appeal to international human rights standards; second, pass the ERA; and third, ratify CEDAW. I will argue that CEDAW provides the most viable solution.

DOES THE U.S. CONSTITUTION PROTECT WOMEN'S RIGHTS?

The concept of a separation between the public and private spheres has long been a hallmark of liberal conceptions of the law. According to this view, the purpose of government in this view is to guarantee equality among citizens within the public sphere and allow freedom from government intervention in the private sphere. The concept of a separation between public and private spheres has also long been subject to criticism by feminists on the grounds that liberal conceptions of the law relegate women to the private sphere and thus deny them full citizenship and protection from violence in the home. Critical race scholars have also critiqued the conception of a private sphere as a privilege unavailable to people of color.

In determining the constitutionality of laws that discriminate on the basis of sex, the Supreme Court has for the past forty years invoked the 14th Amendment of the Constitution. The 14th Amendment is one of the three amendments adopted to guarantee freedom and citizen-ship rights for African Americans in the Reconstruction Era after the Civil War.[3] Section 1 of the 14th Amendment reads as follows:

All persons born or naturalized in the United States, and subject to the juris-diction thereof, are citizens of the United States and of the state wherein they reside. No state shall make or enforce any law which shall abridge the privi-leges or immunities of citizens of the United States; nor shall any state deprive any person of life, liberty, or property, without due process of law; nor deny to any person within its jurisdiction the equal protection of the laws.

The precise meanings of the three main clauses of the 14th Amendment – the privileges and immunities clause, due process clause, and equal protection clause – have emerged over time in the context of Supreme Court decisions. The 14th Amendment does not address discrimina-tion on the basis of sex explicitly, despite the efforts of women's rights groups to include it.[4] Nonetheless, shortly after the 14th Amendment was adopted, litigants began to bring cases that invoked the amendment to defend a woman's right to freedom from discrimination on the basis of sex. In 1871, five years after the adoption of the 14th Amendment, Myra Bradwell, a lawyer, sued the state of Illinois after the state bar denied her admission on the basis of her sex. In *Bradwell v. Illinois* (83 U.S. 130 1873), the Supreme Court upheld the decision of the state of Illinois to deny Bradwell's claim for admission to the bar.

It would be 100 years before the Supreme Court interpreted the 14th Amendment as barring discrimination on the basis of sex. In the late 1960s, women's rights advocates mounted a series of challenges to existing jurisprudence on sex discrimination. Ruth Bader Ginsburg and her colleagues at the Women's Rights Project of the American Civil Liberties Union sought to persuade the Supreme Court to interpret sex discrimination cases in the same way that it interpreted cases of racial discrimination. This meant two things: first, applying strict scrutiny to laws that discriminate on the basis of sex, and second, defining sex as a suspect class.

---

[3] This section draws upon a paper by Kate Thorstad (2013) that provides an exception-ally clear explanation of the way the Supreme Court has used the 14th Amendment to adjudicate sex discrimination cases.

[4] The issue of whether to demand the inclusion of rights for women in the 14th Amendment split the suffrage movement into two factions, those who wanted to keep women's rights off the agenda because they believed it was "the Negro's hour" versus those who opposed the 14th Amendment because it did not include women.

Supreme Court decisions vary in terms of the standard of evidence that justices apply in determining the constitutionality of a law. According to the *rational basis test*, the most lenient and commonly applied standard, a law must be rationally related to a legitimate government interest. The court presumes the law is valid and the burden of proof is on the plaintiff to show that the law is irrational. To pass the *strict scrutiny test*, a higher standard of evidence, a law must further a *compelling* government interest, be narrowly tailored to meet that interest, and be the least restrictive means of accomplishing that interest. The Court generally applies the strict scrutiny standard in cases where a fundamental right has been violated or the law involves a *suspect class*. The Court has defined race, skin color, ethnicity, and national origin as suspect classes. Laws that discriminate on the basis of one of these characteristics are almost always determined to be unconstitutional.[5]

In the 1970s, the Supreme Court rendered a series of decisions that heeded Ruth Bader Ginsburg's arguments, in part. The Court struck down a series of laws that discriminated on the basis of sex on the grounds that they violated women's right to equal protection under the law as established by the 14th Amendment. With *Craig v. Boren* (429 U.S. 190, 1976), the Court established what has become known as an *intermediate* level of scrutiny. According to this standard, a law can be upheld as constitutional if it meets an important (not compelling) government standard and is substantially related (rather than narrowly tailored) to that interest. The Craig standard has improved the odds that sex discriminatory laws will be struck down, but the application of that standard has been inconsistent and has led to less predictable results than either rational basis or strict scrutiny (Baldez, Epstein, and Martin 2006). Moreover, some conservative judges, most notably Supreme Court Justice Antonin Scalia, have suggested that the 14th Amendment does not and should not provide a constitutional guarantee of sex equality (*New York Times*, January 9, 2011, p. WK1).

DOMESTIC VIOLENCE LAW IN THE UNITED STATES

The history of the movement against domestic violence in the United States reveals a series of efforts to assert the existence of a constitutional right to protect women from inaction on the part of state

---

[5] This discussion draws from Baldez, Epstein, and Martin 2006.

officials. This approach met with some initial success in the 1980s, but recent Court decisions have weakened this legal strategy. I demonstrate through a review of legislation and litigation that existing U.S. law, at the statutory and constitutional levels, does not sufficiently protect women from domestic violence.

Prior to the twentieth century, it was not considered a crime for a man to beat his wife. The state generally viewed "chastisement" as one of the privileges that a man enjoyed as a husband. In 1824, the Supreme Court of Mississippi decided that men had a right to beat their wives (see *Bradley v. State 1 Miss. 157*). Courts often blamed women for provoking their husbands' violent response. Governments generally upheld the view that a man's home is his castle and that state actors should stay outside the gates when it came to protecting women from abusive husbands (Rambo 2008).

Norms about intimate partner violence began to change in the late 1800s in response to social reform movements that burned across the country, the abolition and temperance movements in particular. Communities sometimes took it upon themselves to punish batterers "with acts ranging from expulsion of batterers from church congregations to public flogging of batterers" (Rambo 2008, 2/34).[6] Laws criminalizing domestic violence began to appear in the late nineteenth century and "by 1910, 35 of the 46 states had passed laws classifying wife beating as assault" (Rambo 2008, 2/81).

The movement against wife battering picked up steam with the emergence of the feminist movement in the late 1960s. Reframing domestic violence as a public issue was central to feminist claims that "the personal is political." At that time, the movement focused primarily on raising awareness, providing shelters for victims and mobilizing people to demand legislative change. At the Houston Conference for International Women's Year in 1977, a group of advocates for battered women came together to form the National Coalition against Domestic Violence. This group succeeded in getting conference delegates to support a measure that "called for federal government attention to domestic violence, state funding for battered women's shelters, and awareness of the bilingual and multicultural needs of ethnic and

---

[6] Rambo (2008) is an electronic book and does not have page numbers per se. The numbers in the citation refer to the chapter and paragraph in which quoted text appears.

minority women" (Rambo 2008, 3/27). Activists did not yet rely on the courts as a vehicle of legal change. They sought legal relief only in private cases, in which individual women brought suits against abusive partners.

The prospects for a judicial remedy in domestic violence cases changed in 1978, when the Supreme Court decided in *Monell v. Department of Social Services of the City of New York*, 436 U.S. 658 (1978) that municipal governments had legal personhood and could be sued in civil court. This was not a case about domestic violence, but lawyers in the battered women's movement capitalized on the identification of municipal employees as legal persons to file a series of suits accusing police of negligence in failing to enforce restraining orders. This constituted a strategic change from the earlier focus on private cases. Lawyers brought these cases under Section 1983 of the Civil Rights Act of 1871, which allows individuals to file suit against state actors who violate their right to due process or equal protection (Rambo 2008). The plaintiffs in these cases argued that "when police systematically refused to arrest abusive partners, they failed to protect battered women to the same extent that they protected men or victims of nondomestic (i.e., 'stranger') violence" (Rambo 2008, 4/2). In other words, victims of "regular" crimes enjoyed more effective protection than did victims of domestic violence. Patterns of police inaction prompted lawyers to file a series of "failure to protect" cases in civil courts in the 1980s. Most of these cases rested on the claim that state actors had denied the defendants' rights to equal protection under the 14th Amendment. For a brief window of time in the 1980s, courts found these claims persuasive. Toward the end of the 1980s, however, these suits no longer brought the relief that battered women sought. In the later cases, courts increasingly found in favor of state actors, deciding that police enjoyed "discretionary freedom [that] superseded the physical protection of battered women" (Rambo 2008, 4/60).

What changed the prospects for victims in these cases was the Supreme Court's decision in *DeShaney* v. *Winnebago County Department of Social Services*, 489 U.S. 189 (1989). The Court took the case in the hopes of resolving the conditions under which "the failure of a state or local government entity or its agents to provide an individual with adequate protective services constitutes a violation of the individual's due process rights" (i.e., right to fair treatment under the law) (Rambo 2008, 4/66). In *De Shaney*, the Court defined the scope of the state's obligation to protect citizens from private conduct in narrow terms. The majority averred that the state had a responsibility to protect an alleged victim only if the victim had been taken into state custody and held against her will. *De Shaney* was not about restraining orders, but it limited the conditions under which any state actor, including police, could be held liable for failing to prevent private discrimination. As a result of *De Shaney*, activists in the movement against domestic violence cautioned against bringing "due process cases" forward, and sure enough, in domestic violence cases following *De Shaney*, judges found that restraining orders did not require the police to intervene. The *DeShaney* decision put an end to the "failure to protect" or due process strategy for pursuing legal relief in cases of domestic violence.

U.S. law defines domestic violence as physical violence or the threat of physical violence, and treats domestic violence as a crime. Domestic violence is primarily addressed by state and local-level laws but the 1994 Violence Against Women Act (VAWA) expands the definition of domestic violence as a federal crime. Under VAWA, domestic violence is a federal crime if the perpetrator crosses state lines or Indian country to physically injure, stalk, or harass an "intimate partner" or violate a protective order. VAWA also prohibits individuals subject to a protective order and those convicted of domestic violence from possessing firearms and/or ammunition.

The Constitution does not establish a right to be free from violence committed by private actors and thus does not establish a right for women to be free from domestic violence committed against them by intimate partners. One might think that women who have a court-issued protective order barring contact with an intimate partner have the right to protection from the police when their intimate partner threatens them, but a series of Supreme Court decisions have asserted that the Constitution does not guarantee this right. Loads of current legislation can and does protect people – including women – against discrimination by private entities. Prohibitions of this kind are particularly strong in the area of employment, such as Title VII of the Civil Rights Act, the Pregnancy Discrimination Act, and the Lily Ledbetter Act. Such a right's application to nonstate actors is not a fundamental or basic feature of the U.S. Constitution, however. As legal scholar Sonu Bedi affirms, "Because nothing in the equal protection clause constrains private employers, the value of non-discrimination as applied to such entities is simply at the level of lower law" (Bedi 2012, 13). In other words, the Supreme Court will have no occasion to invoke higher law in deciding cases where there is discrimination by private actors.

Castle Rock v. Gonzales, (04-278) 545 U.S. 748 (2005) illustrates this logic. In this case, litigants adopted a new legal strategy for addressing domestic violence. In this case, Jessica Gonzales argued that a protection order against her husband gave her a legitimate right to state protection and enforcement of the order. The Supreme Court struck down Gonzales' claim, deciding that she had no constitutional right to protection form the police or enforcement of a restraining order. As this decision constitutes a centerpiece of current constitutional jurisprudence on domestic violence, I will describe the case in detail.

The incident that precipitated the case took place in Castle Rock, Colorado, on June 22, 1999. Jessica Gonzales's estranged husband abducted their three daughters despite a restraining order she had placed against him. She called the police to report that her husband had violated the restraining order, but police did not respond to her calls. Ten hours later, the husband arrived at the police station and opened fire. Police shot and killed him and then discovered the bodies of the three girls in his truck. Jessica Gonzales filed a USC § 1983 lawsuit against the police department, alleging violation of due process according to the 14th Amendment. She argued that police failure to enforce the temporary restraining order violated her fundamental right to substantive due process. She also made a procedural due process claim that "the state had deprived her of a property right without due process of law" (Rambo 2008, 4/88). She claimed that the protective order against her husband constituted a property interest, a "legitimate claim of entitlement" to state protection (Rambo 2008, 4/88). The circuit court judge ruled that the police did not have infinite discretion whether to act. When there was probable cause, "the restraining order and its enforcement statute took away the officers' discretion to do nothing and instead mandated that they use every reasonable means, up to and including arrest, to enforce the order's terms" (quoted in Rambo 2008, 4/91).

The case was dismissed but eventually ended up in the Supreme Court. The Supreme Court decided that Jessica Gonzales did not have a right to claim violation of due process because the state reserved discretion regarding the enforcement of restraining orders. In the words of the opinion, "A benefit is not a protected entitlement if officials have discretion to grant or deny it."[7] Furthermore, "Colorado law has not created a personal entitlement to enforcement of restraining orders. It does not appear that state law truly made such enforcement *mandatory*. A well-established tradition of police discretion has long coexisted with apparently mandatory arrest statutes." In other words, the Court decided that the state does not have an obligation to enforce a restraining order and thus to protect women from domestic violence. The bottom line of this case is that if a woman has a restraining order against an abusive spouse, she does not have a constitutional right to have police enforce that restraining order. Even with laws that criminalize domestic violence, police have been unwilling to intervene in domestic disputes. The horrific details of the Gonzales case provide jarring evidence of this point.

Given the limitations of existing legal strategies, what other avenues might prove more fruitful to protect the rights of women in cases of domestic violence? In the sections that follow, I explore three different possibilities. The first one, an appeal to international human rights standards, has already been tried. After the Supreme Court rejected her claim to equal protection in the case of domestic violence, Jessica Gonzales (now Lenahan) brought her case to the Inter-American Commission on Human Rights of the Organization of American States. The second strategy involves ratification of the ERA and the third rests on U.S. ratification of CEDAW.

A RIGHT TO PROTECTION FROM PRIVATE DISCRIMINATION: *Lenahan vs. United States*

Having been denied relief by the Supreme Court in *Castle Rock v. Gonzales*, Jessica Gonzales, who by then had obtained a divorce and went by her maiden name of Lenahan, then took her case to the Inter-American Commission on Human Rights(IACHR), the judicial body of the Organization of American States, claiming that the IACHR has

---

[7] *Castle Rock v. Gonzales* (04–278) 545 U.S. 748 (2005).

jurisdiction because the United States is a signatory of the American Declaration of the Rights and Duties of Man, an agreement overseen by the Organization of American States (OAS). The crux of Jessica Lenahan's claim in the case was that the "U.S. has an affirmative obligation to act with 'due diligence' to protect the rights guaranteed in the American Declaration from violations not only by the state or its agents, but also by private actors" (Bettinger-Lopez 2008, 187). According to this logic, "Where a State fails to effectively prevent domestic violence, protect women and children whom it knows are at risk, and provide a remedy when the government fails to fulfill these guarantees … the State incurs international liability for the acts of private individuals who committed the violent acts" (Bettinger-Lopez 2008, 187). In other words, the federal government assumes responsibility to protect individual citizens from violence at the hands of private individuals, either to prevent the harm, respond to it, or compensate the victim.

On August 17, 2011, the IACHR decided in Lenahan's favor, affirming her claim that her rights as a U.S. citizen were violated by failure to enforce the restraining order and her human rights were violated by the Supreme Court decision. Although this case constitutes an interesting innovation in domestic violence strategy, it sets only a weak precedent within international law because the American Declaration merely affirms principles of human rights.

Lawyer Caroline Bettinger-Lopez took this case in the hopes of challenging the way Americans think about human rights, by reframing human rights in terms of the government's failure to protect citizens from violence rather than as "grave and widespread abuses [of government power] 'out there' in other parts of the world" (Bettinger-Lopez 2008, 188). This is an ambitious venture. Nonetheless, the case is weak from the standpoint of international law. The American Declaration is merely a statement affirming human rights. It is not an instrument of international law and does not obligate states to take action to comply with it. Not that Bettinger-Lopez had many options. She might have been better off claiming that the Supreme Court decision violated the American Convention on Human Rights, which is an actual treaty and does have standing within international law. Nonetheless, this option was not available to her because the United States has not ratified the American Convention.

STRENGTHENING A CONSTITUTIONAL RIGHT TO EQUALITY:
THE EQUAL RIGHTS AMENDMENT

Some advocates of women's rights believe that passing an ERA to the U.S. Constitution will strengthen women's claims to protection from discrimination. The ERA would amend the constitution by adding this text: "Equality of rights under the law shall not be denied or abridged by the United States or by any state on account of sex." According to this view, the ERA would provide an explicit guarantee of gender equality in the Constitution, which would force the Supreme Court to take charges of sex discrimination as seriously as it does charges of race-based discrimination. With an ERA, the Constitution would explicitly prohibit discrimination on the basis of sex, and Supreme Court justices would have to apply strict scrutiny to sex discrimination cases. There are two questions relevant to domestic violence here. First, how likely is it that an ERA would strengthen the prospect for legal relief in cases of sex discrimination, and domestic violence in particular? Second, would the ERA address the private jurisdiction issue so central to cases of domestic violence?

It is possible that Supreme Court judges could interpret the Constitution to provide stronger protection for women's rights without an ERA. As Jane Mansbridge points out, the Supreme Court does not need the ERA to interpret a broad scope of state action (Mansbridge 1986, 42). The ERA campaign in the 1970s prompted the Supreme Court to strike down as unconstitutional laws that distinguished between men's and women's "rights and responsibilities in the family," even before it was clear whether the amendment would pass (Mansbridge 1986, 91).[8]

Yet while the Supreme Court could decide to interpret the Constitution this way, it has not – leading some to believe that we need a constitutional amendment explicitly guaranteeing sex equality. Some advocates of women's rights see stronger constitutional guarantees as critical in the current political climate in which statutory protections of women's rights have been eroded. As an amendment to the U.S. Constitution, the ERA would be interpreted in terms of

---

[8] The same argument could be made for CEDAW; the Supreme Court would not necessarily interpret it as guaranteeing gender equality, nor does the Court require CEDAW to guarantee gender equality.

the doctrine of state action and would not apply to discrimination by private individual organizations and individuals. Even if the ERA were to succeed, any impact it has would be limited to cases involving public actors. The doctrine of state action would limit jurisdiction of the ERA so that it would not establish a constitutional right to being free from violence committed by private individuals or institutions.

Would an ERA strengthen the court's proclivity to apply a higher standard of scrutiny to sex discrimination cases? In an analysis of constitutional sex discrimination litigation in the fifty states, Baldez, Epstein, and Martin (2006) find that the presence of an ERA in a state constitution (over a third of U.S. states have them) does not have direct effect on sex discrimination cases. Having a state-level ERA in and of itself does not lead judges to apply a higher standard of law (i.e., strict scrutiny) and does not make them more likely find in favor of those charging discrimination. This research on state-level sex discrimination cases offers suggestive, but far from conclusive, evidence that an ERA at the federal level would not achieve the desired effect of raising the level of scrutiny applied to cases of sex discrimination in the Supreme Court.

Although the ERA ratification campaign ended in 1982, some argue that it remains a live issue. Congress passed the ERA in 1972 with the stipulation that states ratify it within seven years. By 1978, thirty-five of the required thirty-eight states had ratified the ERA. With only three states to go and the 1979 deadline for ratification looming, ERA proponents persuaded Congress to extend the deadline until June 30, 1982. No additional state ratified ERA before the new deadline passed, however, and the ERA ostensibly died. More recently, some have argued that the time limit that Congress placed on ratification is unconstitutional. The basis for this view is that the 27th amendment to the Constitution passed in 1992, 202 years after Congress passed it. Proponents of this view argue that the number of approvals that existed at the deadline (thirty-five) should stand today, and effort should be made to get three additional states to ratify. In December 1993, a coalition of women's organizations announced the "three state strategy" that focused on passing the ERA by getting three of the remaining fifteen states to ratify it. At its 2012 national conference, NOW passed a resolution calling for "removing the time limit from the Equal Rights Amendment" on the basis of the claim that time limits imposed on constitutional amendments are not constitutional (National Organization for Women 2012).

Even if it were to pass, the ERA is unlikely to have a significant impact on domestic violence law in the United States. An ERA might persuade judges to apply strict rather than intermediate scrutiny to laws that discriminate on the basis of sex. Nonetheless, judges would likely interpret the ERA in light of the state action doctrine. The ERA would do little to protect women from harm done to them by private individuals, which is the crux of the problem in cases of domestic violence.

WHAT WOULD CEDAW DO?

Few studies have examined the status of U.S. domestic violence policy in the context of CEDAW. Many articles assessing the impact of CEDAW in the United States do not mention domestic violence (see, for example, Anderson 2003; Gregg 1993; Hoff Somers 2011). Domestic violence has been largely absent from debates about CEDAW ratification and those who do mention it address it superficially as an issue that would be improved with ratification. *CEDAW: The Treaty for the Rights of Women*, a book written by a coalition of pro-CEDAW advocates, focuses on how other countries have used the Convention to eliminate violence against women and how U.S. ratification would enhance the United States' position as a global leader on this issue (Milani, Albert, and Purushotma 2004). These claims tend to be asserted rather than shown.

I argue that CEDAW could be used to strengthen women's claims to constitutional protection in the instance of domestic violence. Advocates could use CEDAW to make two arguments relevant to domestic violence in the United States. First, CEDAW stipulates that the state has an obligation to respond in cases in which private individuals have harmed women's rights. CEDAW explicitly addresses the constitutional lacuna regarding women's rights. Article 2(e) states, "States Parties condemn discrimination against women in all its forms, agree to pursue by all appropriate means and without delay a policy of eliminating discrimination against women and, to this end, undertake: to take all appropriate measures to eliminate discrimination against women by any person, organization or enterprise." Second, women could invoke CEDAW to demand that state actors, namely police, respond to violations of protection orders in cases of intimate violence or threats of such violence. Appealing to Article 2(e) could reduce the discretion that police have in deciding whether or not to respond to restraining orders by requiring them to act when women are threatened. CEDAW, by establishing a right to freedom from all forms of discrimination, would raise the priority of violence against women and require that police respond to incidents in which a restraining order has been violated. CEDAW could be used to elevate the legal status of failure to protect women from violence at the hands of private individuals. CEDAW could have a dramatic impact on strengthening the rights that American women enjoy by guaranteeing women protection from discrimination regardless of whether public or private actors cause the harm. By expanding the scope of discrimination to cover acts committed by private individuals and organizations, CEDAW would give American women the right to make legal claims of discrimination that they do not currently possess.

This argument, that CEDAW could address limitations in existing legislation on domestic violence in the United States, rests on the resolution of two thorny issues. First, the United States would have to ratify CEDAW. Second, the articles of CEDAW would have to be domesticated, by writing implementing legislation that would translate CEDAW into U.S. law. Ratification of CEDAW would by no means be sufficient to change the legal terrain of violence against women in the ways I describe in this article. Given the non–self-executing nature of the human rights treaties that the United States has ratified, ratification would need to be accompanied by implementing legislation that spelled out the relationship between international law and the U.S. Constitution on that count. Seated Supreme Court justices are deeply divided when it comes to incorporating international standards into U.S. law. There are some precedents that bode well for CEDAW. For example, "U.S. Supreme Court Justices Stephen Breyer and Ruth Bader Ginsburg have spoken widely of the positive benefits of applying international standards to the pursuit of equality under U.S. law" (Chavkin and Chesler 2005, 14). The majority opinion in *Grutter v. Bollinger*, 539 U.S. 306 (2003) cited both CEDAW and the UN Convention on the Elimination of Racial Discrimination, for example, and in her concurring opinion Justice Ruth Bader Ginsburg quoted from Article 2(2) of CERD and Article 4(1) of CEDAW to "underscor[e] the temporary nature of affirmative action measures" (Facio and Morgan 2009, 1168). In *Lawrence vs. Texas*, 539 U.S. 558 (2003), Justice Kennedy's majority opinion against a state statute prohibiting sodomy cited a ruling by the European Court of Human Rights (Chavkin and Chesler 2005, 15). The opinions in *Lawrence v. Texas* and *Roper v. Simmons*, 543 U.S. 551 (2005) made explicit reference to international law – but Justice Scalia wrote forcefully against it in dissenting opinions. Predictions that consideration of international law has put us at "the beginning of a 'revolution' in U.S. constitutional law" (Facio and Morgan 2009, 1167) are no doubt premature, but the battle lines have been drawn.

CONCLUSION

A key question about the impact of CEDAW in the United States, and one that has not generally been asked, centers on the degree to which existing U.S. law guarantees against discrimination by public *and* private individuals and organizations. This is the area in which CEDAW is perhaps the furthest out of step with the U.S. legal system. Or, to put it differently, this is the area in which the United States is the furthest out of step with international law. The issue of public/private jurisdiction goes to the core of the constitutional guarantees that are at the heart of the U.S. political system. In this regard, CEDAW could be used to justify an expansion of the scope of legal protections for women that are currently available in the U.S. Constitution and statutory law.

From the perspective of women's human rights, women enjoy the right to physical integrity and freedom from violence. The Supreme Court's decision in *Castle Rock v. Gonzales* reveals that American women do not enjoy full protection of the right to be free from discrimination on the basis of sex. Even with the strongest legislation, the Constitution does not protect women from violence committed by private individuals – which constitutes the core of the problem of violence against women. Statutory relief is subject to repeal by Congress, as debates about the reauthorization of the VAWA have shown. This analysis of domestic violence law raises important questions for those who maintain that existing constitutional protections of women's rights are sufficient. Violence against women constitutes a glaring area of vulnerability for American women who believe that they already enjoy all the rights that women need. The international law "lite" approach represented by *Lenahan vs. United States* may go far in changing public opinion about the legal status of domestic violence claims; in fact, a documentary about the case is already in the works.[9] The case sets a weak precedent in terms of international law, however. An ERA to the U.S. Constitution would be unlikely to provide the necessary protections to victims of violence against women. CEDAW contains a broader scope of action that is instructive regarding the limitations of existing constitutional law in guaranteeing women's human rights.

This chapter departs from the primarily historical account of CEDAW presented in the rest of this book in order to offer some theoretical speculations about the way that CEDAW might reshape U.S. policy toward domestic violence. I start from two points of agreement between the pro and anti sides of the CEDAW debate. The two sides maintain that existing women's rights law in the United States is sufficient and that the "private jurisdiction" clause of CEDAW is problematic. Often, identifying shared views between adversaries can present a platform on which to build greater consensus. In this case, however, I contend that these shared assumptions are inaccurate when it comes to domestic violence. If we think about domestic violence, existing U.S. law does not sufficiently protect a woman's right to be free from discrimination or enjoy equal protection under the law. Further, when viewed from the perspective of domestic violence, the state action clause of the U.S. Constitution limits women's right to be free from violence.

---

[9]   Retrieved from http://www.jessicagonzalesvsunitedstates.com/Jessicas_Story.html.

8

Conclusion

The question that motivates this book is why the United States has not ratified CEDAW, the most important guarantee of rights for women in international law. In order to understand this puzzle, I examine three sets of issues. First, I evaluate non-ratification by the United States in a broader historical context of the role that the U.S. government played in shaping the global women's rights agenda and ultimately in making CEDAW possible. Second, I illuminate U.S. debates about ratification of CEDAW by explaining what the treaty entails. Finally, I examine why the United States remained immune to the process of diffusion that has led all but six other countries to ratify CEDAW. These three themes make up the three parts of the book.

THE UNITED STATES, UN, AND EVOLUTION OF WOMEN'S RIGHTS AS A GLOBAL NORM

The first part of the book (Chapters 2 and 3) presents a historical account of how women's rights emerged as a global norm. The history of global feminism is often presented as a story of ever-advancing efforts to secure women's rights within the UN and beyond. Scholars trace a progressive arc from the text of the UN Charter, which guarantees the equal rights of men and women, to CEDAW as a treaty that legally obligates countries to take positive action to eliminate discrimination. A focus on the role of the United States in this process, as well as conflicting views among women themselves, challenges this progressive account.

The United States' contribution to the emergence of a global women's rights norm is mixed. During the UN's first few decades, the United States sought to limit the ability of UN agencies to influence domestic policy. To a certain extent, the Commission on the Status of Women overcame the obstacles that U.S. opposition set before it, succeeding in establishing a series of international agreements that provided the framework for future progress. The prospects for real progress changed in the 1970s when U.S. political leaders perceived a benefit to be had from supporting women's rights issues on the world stage. Support from the United States proved pivotal in two relatively minor decisions that had major consequences: holding the Mexico City Conference to celebrate IWY in 1975, and initiating the process of drafting an international women's rights treaty. The Mexico City Conference provided a venue in which governments hammered out agreements about basic rights for women and activists pushed their governments to take action. This and the future World Conferences on Women (in Copenhagen in 1980, in Nairobi in 1985, and Beijing in 1995) set the international women's movement in motion. CEDAW constituted the institutional infrastructure by which governments would be held accountable to their promises over the long term.

Geopolitical factors have shaped the opportunities for the acceptance or rejection of demands for women's rights, making it more or less likely that politicians at the domestic level will respond to those demands. Attention to the broader political environment – both domestic and international – provides a more nuanced explanation of the gains and limitations of global efforts to promote women's rights. The spirit of international cooperation that characterized the founding of the UN during the period immediately following World War II, plus the need to court support for the new institution at home, made the U.S. government willing to support incorporation of women's rights into the UN. As relations between the United States and Soviet Union deteriorated into the mutual distrust that characterized the Cold War, the United States sought to limit UN power over domestic politics. Divisions among advocates of women's rights and a deep suspicion of the Soviet Union during the Cold War era steered the United States to ensure that UN institutions could exert little influence over women's rights policy in any UN member countries. The geopolitical context changed again in the early 1970s, as Third World countries formed a

restive majority within the UN. The United States sought to reestab-
lish its status in the UN by embracing women's rights and throwing
its support to policies that made CEDAW possible. These initiatives
enjoyed bipartisan support within the United States. Leaders from the
Republican took the lead in the process of drafting CEDAW. Leaders
from the Democratic Party joined them later.

National interests and geopolitical context are not the only factors that complicate the question of CEDAW ratification. The history
of women's rights movements in the United States firmly establishes
that women do not agree on how best to go about improving the status of women. Even when they share the goal of equality, reasonable
people may disagree about strategies for how to achieve it. Strategic
considerations caused deep rifts within the suffrage movement in the
nineteenth century, for example. With the creation of the UN, divisions
among women within countries as well as across national boundaries
challenged efforts to procure global women's rights. U.S. delegates who
helped draft the UN Charter in 1945 supported equal rights, but did
not want to separate women's rights from the more general category
of human rights because they believed doing so would marginalize
women. A different coalition of women's organizations in the United
States worked with women in foreign delegations to ensure explicit
guarantees for women's rights in the UN Charter and supported the
creation of a separate CSW. By the 1970s, these divisions dissipated
and the United States enjoyed a brief era of bipartisan consensus on
women's issues. When the U.S. government began to devote resources
toward achieving feminist goals, particularly in the wake of celebrations of IWY in the late 1970s, a conservative backlash emerged. The
cleavages that materialized at the end of that decade remain with us
today. Similarly, as CEDAW became more powerful in the international arena, the debate over U.S. ratification sharpened.

Over time, CEDAW has become the center of increasingly polar-
ized views within the U.S. The diminution of conflict over racial discrimination and human rights is striking by contrast. There is little
evidence that U.S. ratification of CERD is controversial, or that it has
even been noticed. This differs not only from global women's issues
but also from the conflictual status of race and human rights in the
United States in the middle of the twentieth century. In the period after
World War II, white southern politicians opposed the UN because they

feared that African Americans would use it to challenge racial discrimination in the United States. This fear, along with concerns that the Soviet Union would use the UN to expand its power and challenge the United States, led American policymakers to ensure that the UN had no jurisdiction over domestic affairs. By 1994, however, these fears appear to have been forgotten. Without fanfare or controversy, the Senate ratified CERD. Since then, the United States has presented six periodic reports to the CERD Committee, the first three in 2001 and the second three in 2008. News about U.S. compliance with CERD is scarce, with the exception of an occasional piece by conservative bloggers (see, for example, The Foundry September 23, 2013).

The comparisons between CEDAW and CERD raise a number of questions. How should we interpret the lack of media attention to CERD? It is unlikely that the United States is in full compliance with the provisions of the treaty, and we have not succeeded in eliminating all forms of racial discrimination in this country. A quick read of the shadow reports provided by civil rights NGOs during the CERD sessions suggests that this is not at all the case, but it is worth examining further. To what extent has CERD proven to be an effective tool for addressing racial discrimination in the United States? To what extent is it possible to use the CERD process as a proxy for CEDAW, to press for improving the status of women in racial minority groups? These questions warrant investigation and may help us draw inferences about the likely impact of CEDAW were it to be ratified.

A POWERFUL AND UNENFORCEABLE TREATY

The second part of the book (Chapters 4 and 5) shifts the focus to questions about the substance and implementation of CEDAW. What are the measures that CEDAW obligates states to take and how does it work? A solid grasp of the logistics of CEDAW is particularly important given that few Americans know that CEDAW exists and are not aware of the decades-long efforts that have been exerted both to ratify and oppose it. Debate about CEDAW has remained limited to members of Congress and a relatively small constellation of non-governmental organizations. The vast majority of the American public knows little about it, and those who do know are likely to have learned about it from sources that have a political interest in highlighting some issues and obfuscating others. This book represents an attempt, albeit surely a limited and imperfect one, to explain what ratification would and would not entail for the United States.

A growing body of research maintains that the effectiveness of human rights treaties rests on their ability to empower domestic political actors. This study adds to this literature by highlighting two factors that both reflect and facilitate the participation of domestic actors and may account for the positive effect that CEDAW exerts on women's rights worldwide: evolution in the treaty itself and the interactions between government officials and treaty experts that take place during the reporting sessions, the meetings where governments present their reports on compliance with the treaty.

The CEDAW Committee has interpreted the articles of the Convention in an increasingly expansive way over time that has allowed it to keep pace with changes in conceptions of women's rights worldwide. The definition of women's rights that CEDAW articulates continues to evolve as CEDAW Committee experts interact with government officials and NGOs during the CEDAW sessions. The autonomy of the CEDAW Committee from the states parties of the Convention has given it significant leeway in expanding definitions of discrimination against women over time. The CEDAW experts do not represent countries and do not serve on the official diplomatic delegations of their home countries. The independence of the Committee experts, an issue that was the object of considerable debate during the drafting process, has proven critical to developing an understanding of CEDAW that reflects both an international consensus and a set of goals to which all countries can aspire regardless of their national traditions.

My focus on CEDAW's evolving jurisprudence will, no doubt, provide fodder for conservative rhetoric that fans fears about the expanding scope of the UN. I emphasize a couple of points to respond to this concern. First, the general recommendations are intended to guide states parties in their preparation of periodic reports. Their aim is to standardize the nature of information about women's rights that countries provide. Second, CEDAW articulates a clear agenda – but it does not impose that agenda upon the countries that have ratified the treaty. Finally, the formal text of CEDAW is sufficiently flexible to allow countries to adapt its requirements to conform to what is appropriate for that particular context. The CEDAW Committee's most significant power is to make recommendations to countries; the power of those recommendations depends on the ability and willingness of government officials and non-governmental organizations to publicize and act upon those recommendations. The impact of CEDAW on women's lives depends on the ability of grassroots activists to use the process to achieve their goals, mobilize public support for their positions, and use the media effectively to highlight lack of compliance with the treaty.

An apparent ambiguity about the impact of the treaty runs through the analysis in this book. On the one hand, I argue that that CEDAW does not require states parties to do anything other than participate in the periodic review process. The CEDAW Committee cannot force states to take action and does not have the power to impose certain policies upon them. CEDAW provides countries with a blueprint for change and the CEDAW experts guide states in their implementation of the treaty. On the other hand, what distinguishes CEDAW from the scores of other international agreements about women's issues that countries have signed is that CEDAW is an instrument of international law that requires countries to take action to eliminate discrimination against women. By ratifying CEDAW, states assume a legal obligation to comply.

Debates about CEDAW ratification in the United States have portrayed CEDAW as requiring states to adopt policies that they otherwise would not adopt. During the many hearings on CEDAW that have taken place in the Senate, policymakers on both sides of the issue have emphasized the substantive impact it will have on women's rights policy, whether in other countries, in U.S. foreign policy, or on domestic reform within the United States itself. This portrayal misapprehends how CEDAW works. Literature that describes socialization as a dynamic process provides a more accurate way to think about it. Scholars have invoked a series of vivid metaphors to convey the interactive nature of communication between activists, international institutions, and government officials, such as the boomerang effect (Keck and Sikkink 1998), the spiral model (Risse and Sikkink 1999), and the ping-pong and pincer effects (Friedman 2009). Former CEDAW expert

Aurora Javate de Dios, from the Philippines, describes the dynamic nature of the CEDAW process as a "circle of empowerment":

The relevance and efficacy of human rights for women lies in the extent to which women actually claim and reclaim, as well as assert and reassert, these rights by pursuing a number of strategies, such as monitoring States Parties' compliance with respect to their obligations in protecting, respecting, and fulfilling human rights; sharpening and specifying the general human rights discourse by integrating a gender perspective; documenting violations of women's human rights; and sustaining public awareness of women's human rights. Without this proactive process, international laws such as the CEDAW Convention would be a dead instrument. (Javate de Dios 2007, 312)

These metaphors capture the dynamics of the CEDAW reporting process. The iterative, in-person, back-and-forth deliberation between government officials and CEDAW experts – in full view and with the participation of activists from civil society – is where and how socialization occurs.

CEDAW MATTERS

The third part of the book (Chapters 6 and 7) focuses on the history of efforts to ratify CEDAW and provides a critical examination of some of the issues that ratification would present for the United States. My analysis of the U.S. case suggests that the high institutional barrier for treaty ratification magnifies the relevance of domestic conflict where it exists. The decision to ratify a treaty is decided on the basis of conflicts over anticipated compliance costs *within* a particular country. Existing research on treaty ratification would predict that the United States would have ratified CEDAW long ago. Many factors point in this direction. Presidents, members of Congress, and, most importantly, scores of senators support ratification. Large networks involving more than 100 organizations have mobilized to keep ratification. Despite the U.S.'s inaction, CEDAW has become a powerful institution that has produced remarkable effects worldwide. It is these precise factors that make the stakes of ratification higher today than they were in the past and have prompted conservative organizations to mobilize against it.

Many Americans think of the struggle for women's rights as a battle that was waged – and won – in the 1970s. The status of women in the United States is better than it is in many other countries on most measures of rights and equality. The United States comes out near the top on many cross-national measures of the status of women – but certainly not all. Women in the United States enjoy a level of rights and overall quality of life that women in other countries envy. Perhaps because of these gains, CEDAW advocates have had trouble expanding concern for the treaty beyond a relatively small community of policy-makers and advocates. There are so many other pressing issues facing American women and so many debates to be had. My discussion of domestic violence in Chapter 7 highlights just one of the ways in which CEDAW allows us to rethink the contours of women's rights in the United States.

The analysis I offer throughout this book challenges arguments that ratification of CEDAW will exert a direct effect on domestic policy on the status of women. CEDAW obligates the governments that ratify it to "take all appropriate measures" to eliminate all forms of discrimination against women. The CEDAW Committee provides ample guidance about what kinds of measures are appropriate, but ultimately it puts the onus for determining what measures will be taken on the state itself. In the United States, the current interpretation of human rights treaties as non–self-executing should remove any concerns that ratification of CEDAW would either *require* the United States to adopt certain policies or *impose* any policies. During the reporting process, the Committee experts exert as much pressure as they can reasonably exert on government officials to bring their policies and practices into line with the articles of CEDAW. This process, as the description of the Russian Federation's experiences reveal, can be extremely uncomfortable. In a country where the media decide to cover the reporting sessions, the results are likely to prove embarrassing to the government. In that regard, the CEDAW process is likely to expand the opportunities for discussion of women's rights policies and may heighten awareness of limitations not only in U.S. policy but raise the priority of women's issues on the political agenda.

The insistence that existing policies in the United States are sufficient to guarantee the rights of American women, arguments shared by those who support CEDAW as well as those who oppose it, prevents us from asking questions about how things could be better. CEDAW provides the United States with some ways of thinking differently about the protection of individual rights. In the case of domestic violence, the incorporation of concepts of rights from CEDAW could strengthen claims about the responsibility that state actors have to address private discrimination. Appeals to CEDAW could bolster claims to constitutional rights to protection by reducing the discretion that state actors have in cases where women face discrimination.

Those who support CEDAW have focused their arguments on effects outside the United States. They maintain that the treaty has benefitted women in other countries and that U.S. ratification would strengthen CEDAW by enhancing its legitimacy in the eyes of foreign governments. Both of these goals would consolidate the U.S.'s role as a global leader in women's rights and enhance U.S. foreign policy objectives. These claims raise two sets of questions that warrant further research. First, to what extent are they accurate? To what extent would U.S. ratification serve the interests of women abroad? Would U.S. participation in CEDAW strengthen what is already an effective institution? Second, to what extent are they right that CEDAW's effect would be felt far more abroad than at home?

Although CEDAW opponents have remained largely silent about CEDAW's impact abroad, the awareness and participation of conservative women's organizations in international forums such as the international conferences on population and the World Conferences on Women suggests that many of them care very deeply about the direction of U.S. foreign policy with regard to women's issues. U.S. ratification would impede the efforts of social conservatives in the United States to pursue their own agenda abroad, an agenda that centers largely, but not entirely, on abortion restrictions. By linking CEDAW with controversial and unresolved policy issues at home, opponents of the treaty may have raised just enough doubts among members of the Senate to prevent getting the necessary two-thirds vote. As this book has shown, these arguments have little bearing in fact.

Throughout this book I have emphasized how geopolitics – conflicts among states and the national interests of states – shape the contours of global women's rights policy. What I mean by this is that the interests of states and relations between them determine the opportunities that exist to advance the status of women. During the Cold War, the opportunities to press for change at the global level were limited; opportunities expanded for a brief period during the 1970s. *Détente*, the temporary thaw in relations between the United States and USSR, explains part of the changed climate, but the rise of the non-aligned countries within the UN and U.S. responses to that rise led more directly to changes in UN women's rights policy within the UN. After the Cold War, the opportunities changed again as nations and groups within nations battled to reshape the human rights agenda. Treaty bodies such as the CEDAW Committee ceased to be platforms for ideological grandstanding. The human rights treaties that many nations had signed in an era when they may not have expected them to have much effect became more important as human rights became a real indicator of commitment to democracy and a huge new population of NGOs began to hold countries accountable to their promises.

Ultimately, CEDAW has mitigated the power that geopolitical context and national interests exert on the evolution of women's rights in the international arena today. The analysis offered in this book provides suggestive evidence that geopolitical conflicts may have less power to derail the pursuit of women's rights at the international level than they did in the days before CEDAW. The autonomy of CEDAW experts fosters their ability to engage in critical dialogue with the countries that have ratified the treaty and challenge all countries to do better. As an institution, CEDAW represents *the world's* women – it represents no particular country. CEDAW experts come from particular countries but do not represent their countries; instead, they represent CEDAW, a set of rights by which nearly every country in the world has agreed to abide. What those rights entail and the way they are defined is subject to continuous negotiation, debate, and evolution. This is true for CEDAW as it is for most countries in the world. U.S. ratification will not settle discussions about the rights of women, either in the United States or the international arena, but it would allow American women to participate in that conversation in a more direct way. I am reminded of the famous quote from Virginia Woolf's *Three Guineas*: "As a woman I have no country. As a woman I want no country. As a woman, my country is the whole world." CEDAW is the world that Woolf envisions. It is a world that all the countries in the world came together to create, a world that puts rights for women first.

Works Cited

Achmad, Sjamsiah. 2007. "A Source of Inspiration." In *The Circle of Empowerment*, eds. Hanna Beate Schöpp-Schilling and Cees Flinterman. New York: The Feminist Press. 333–335.

Afsharipour, Afra. 1999. "Empowering Ourselves: The Role of Women's NGOs in the Enforcement of the Women's Convention." *Columbia Law Review* 99 (1): 129–172.

Anderson, Carol. 2003. *Eyes Off the Prize: The United Nations and the African American Struggle for Human Rights, 1944–1955*. Cambridge, UK; New York: Cambridge University Press.

2009. "A "Hollow Mockery": African Americans, White Supremacy, and the Development of Human Rights in the United States." In *Bringing Human Rights Home*, eds. Cynthia Soohoo, Catherine Albisa, and Martha F. Davis. Philadelphia: University of Pennsylvania Press. 68–99.

ANNA National Centre for the Prevention of Violence. 2010. "Violence against Women in the Russian Federation." Retrieved from http://www2. ohchr.org/english/bodies/cedaw/cedaws46.htm.

Aouij, Emna. 2007. "Personal Reflections: In the Muslim World." In *The Circle of Empowerment*, eds. Hanna Beate Schöpp-Schilling and Cees Flinterman. New York: Feminist Press. 86–87.

Athanasakos, Betty. 2011. Telephone interview with the author. May 25.

Avdeyeva, Olga. 2007. "When Do States Comply with International Treaties? Policies on Violence against Women in Post-Communist Countries." *International Studies Quarterly* 51: 877–900.

Baldez, Lisa. 2002. *Why Women Protest: Women's Movements in Chile*. New York: Cambridge University Press.

Baldez, Lisa, Lee Epstein, and Andrew D. Martin. 2006. "Does the U.S. Constitution Need an Equal Rights Amendment?" *Journal of Legal Studies* 35: 243.

Bedi, Sonu. 2012. "Higher Lawmaking and the Horizontal Effect of Rights: Religious Employers and the Right to Non-Discrimination." Presented at Dartmouth College, Department of Government, Hanover, NH.

Bernard, Désirée Patricia. 2007. "The First Twelve Years." In *The Circle of Empowerment*, eds. Hanna Beate Schöpp-Schilling and Cees Flinterman. New York: The Feminist Press. 266–267.

Bettinger-Lopez, Caroline. 2008. "*Jessica Gonzales v. United States:* An Emerging Model for Domestic Violence & Human Rights Advocacy in the United States." *Harvard Human Rights Journal* 21: 183–195.

Bradley, Curtis A. 2010. "The United States and Human Rights Treaties: Race Relations, the Cold War, and Constitutionalism." *Chinese Journal of International Law* 9(2): 321–344.

Brewer, Lindsay. 2013. "CEDAW Ratification: Lessons from CERD." Unpublished paper, Dartmouth College.

Byrnes, Andrew C. 2010. "The Convention on the Elimination of All Forms of Discrimination against Women and the Committee on the Elimination of Discrimination against Women: Reflections on Their Role in the Development of International Human Rights Law and as a Catalyst for National Legislative and Policy Reform." *UNSW Law Research Paper No. 2010-2017.*

Byrnes, Andrew, and Marsha Freeman. 2012. "The Impact of the CEDAW Convention: Paths to Equality," *University of New South Wales Faculty of Law Research Series.* Retrieved from http://papers.ssrn.com/sol3/papers.cfm?abstract_id=2011655 (accessed July 25, 2013).

C-SPAN. May 11, 2000. "Senate Footage: Senator Jesse Helms." Retrieved from http://www.c-spanvideo.org/clip/4334420 (accessed July 25, 2013).

Cartwright, Silvia. 1997. "Rights and Remedies: The Drafting of an Optional Protocol to the Convention on the Elimination of All Forms of Discrimination against Women." *Otago Law Review* 9 (2): 239–254.

Cartwright, Silvia Rose. 2007. "Personal Reflection: Interpreting the Convention." In *The Circle of Empowerment*, eds. Hanna Beate Schöpp-Schilling and Cees Flinterman. New York: Feminist Press. 30–35.

Center for Health and Gender Equity. 2014. "Helms Amendment." http://www.genderhealth.org/the_issues/us_foreign_policy/helms/ (accessed March 2, 2014).

Centro Tepeyac. n.d. "About Us and Our Services." http://www.centrotepeyac.org/pregnant/services.php (accessed February 11, 2014).

Chavkin, Wendy, and Ellen Chesler, eds. 2005. *Where Human Rights Begin: Health, Sexuality, and Women in the New Millennium.* New Brunswick, NJ: Rutgers University Press.

Chayes, Abram, and Antonia Handler Chayes. 1993. "On Compliance." *International Organization* 47 (2): 175–205.

Cho, Seo-Young. 2010. "International Human Rights Treaty to Change Social Patterns: The Convention on the Elimination of All Forms of Discrimination against Women," *CEGE (Centre for European Governance and Economic Development Research) Discussion Paper No. 93*. Retrieved from http://ssrn. com/abstract=1553083 (accessed February 11, 2012).

Clark, Belinda. 1991. "The Vienna Convention Reservations Regime and the Convention on Discrimination Against Women." *American Journal of International Law* 85 (2): 281–321.

Committee on the Elimination of Discrimination against Women. 2000. "Third Periodic Report: Belarus." Retrieved from http://www2.ohchr.org/ english/bodies/cedaw/cedaws22.htm (accessed February 11, 2012).

————. 2009. "List of Issues and Questions with Regard to the Consideration of Periodic Reports: Russian Federation." Retrieved from http://www2.ohchr. org/english/bodies/cedaw/cedaws46.htm (accessed October 8, 2013).

————. 2010a. "Concluding Observations of the Committee on the Elimination of Discrimination against Women: Russian Federation." Retrieved from http://www2.ohchr.org/english/bodies/cedaw/cedaws46.htm (accessed October 1, 2013).

————. 2010b. "Provisional Agenda, 46th Session (12–30 July) New York." Retrieved from http://www2.ohchr.org/english/bodies/cedaw/cedaws46. htm (accessed October 8, 2013).

————. 2010c. "Responses to the List of Issues and Questions with Regard to the Consideration of the Combined Sixth and Seventh Periodic Report: Russian Federation." Retrieved from http://www2.ohchr.org/english/bodies/cedaw/cedaws46.htm (accessed October 8, 2013).

————. 2010d. "Summary Record of the 930th Meeting, Forty-Sixth Session." Retrieved from http://www2.ohchr.org/english/bodies/cedaw/cedaws46. htm.

————. 2013. "Follow Up Procedure." Retrieved from http://www2.ohchr.org/english/bodies/cedaw/followup.htm (accessed September 8, 2013).

Concerned Women for America. 2010. "Save Mothers' Day: A Campaign to Educate America about the Dangers of CEDAW." Retrieved from http:// www.savemothersday.com/ (accessed August 25, 2011).

————. 2013. "Concerned Women for America." Retrieved from http://www.cwfa. org/about/ (accessed October 1, 2013).

Connelly, Matthew. 2008. *Fatal Misconception: The Struggle to Control World Population*. Cambridge, MA: Belknap Press of Harvard University Press.

Connors, Jane. 2007. "On Twenty Years of Involvement." In *The Circle of Empowerment*, eds. Hanna Beate Schöpp-Schilling and Cees Flinterman. New York: The Feminist Press. 282–285.

Consortium of Women's Non-Governmental Associations. 2010. "Implementation by the Russian Federation of UN Convention on Elimination of All Forms of Discrimination against Women." Retrieved from http://www2. ohchr.org/english/bodies/cedaw/cedaws46.htm (accessed September 8, 2013).

Cortell, Andrew P., and James W. Davis, Jr. 1996. "How Do International Institutions Matter? The Domestic Impact of International Rules and Norms." *International Studies Quarterly* 40 (4): 451–478.

Corti, Ivanka. 2007. "Relationships with UN Conferences, Specialized Agencies, Programs and Funds." In *The Circle of Empowerment*, eds. Hanna Beate Schöpp-Schilling and Cees Flinterman. New York: Feminist Press. 36–51.

Costain, Anne N. 1992. *Inviting Women's Rebellion: A Political Process Interpretation of the Women's Movement.* Baltimore: Johns Hopkins University Press.

Dairam, Shanti. 2007. "From Global to Local: The Involvement of NGOs." In *The Circle of Empowerment*, eds. Hanna Beate Schöpp-Schilling and Cees Flinterman. New York: The Feminist Press. 313–325.

2011. Interview with the author. Kuala Lumpur, Malaysia, April 29.

2012. "International Norms and the Realization of Women's Human Rights: The Role of Civil Society Organizations." Presented at the 30th Anniversary of the Committee on the Elimination of Discrimination against Women, New York.

den Boer, Andrea. 2008. "Evaluating CEDAW's Impact on Women's Empowerment." Presented at the International Studies Association 49th Annual Convention, San Francisco, CA.

Downs, George W., David M. Rocke, and Peter N. Barsoom. 1996. "Is the Good News about Compliance Good News about Cooperation?" *International Organization* 50 (3): 379–406.

DuBois, Ellen, and Lauren Derby. 2009. "The Strange Case of Minerva Bernardino: Pan American and United Nations Women's Right Activist." *Women's Studies International Forum* 32: 43–50.

East, Catherine. 1983. "Newer Commissions." In *Women in Washington*, ed. Irene Tinker. Beverly Hills, CA: SAGE. 35–44.

Eleanor Roosevelt et al. February 12, 1946. "An Open Letter to the World." Retrieved from http://www.unspecial.org/2012/03/an-open-letter-to-the-women-of-the-world/ (accessed July 18, 2013).

Englehart, Neil A., and Melissa K. Miller. 2012. "The CEDAW Effect: Women's Rights, International Law and Domestic Politics." Unpublished paper, Bowling Green State University.

Evatt, Elizabeth. 2007. "Private Global Enterprise, International Trade, and Finance." In *The Circle of Empowerment*, eds. Hanna Beate Schöpp-Schilling and Cees Flinterman. New York: The Feminist Press. 106–121.

Facio, Alda, and Martha I. Morgan. 2009. "Equity or Equality for Women? Understanding CEDAW's Equality Principles." *IWRAW Asia Pacific Occasional Papers Series* No. 14: 1–38.

Farrior, Stephanie. 1997. "The International Law on Trafficking in Women and Children for Prostitution: Making It Live Up to Its Potential." *Harvard Human Rights Journal* (10): 213–255.

FDCH Political Transcripts. November 3, 1999. "U.S. Representative Lynn Woolsey (D-CA) Holds News Conference on Senator Helm's Hold on the CEDAW." Accessed through Dartmouth College Library.

Flinterman, Cees. 2007. "Strengthening Women's Human Rights Through Individual Complaints." In *The Circle of Empowerment*, eds. Hanna Beate Schöpp-Schilling and Cees Flinterman. New York: The Feminist Press. 286–297.

Fraser, Arvonne. 2007. *She's No Lady: Politics, Family and International Feminism*. Minneapolis, MN: Nodin Press.

Fraser, Arvonne S. 1995. "The Convention on the Elimination of All Forms of Discrimination against Women (The Women's Convention)." In *Women, Politics and the United Nations*, ed. Anne Winslow. Westport, CT: Greenwood Press. 77–94.

Fraser, Arvonne S., and Irene Tinker, eds. 2004. *Developing Power: How Women Transformed International Development*. New York: The Feminist Press.

Freeman, Jo. 2000. *The Politics of the Women's Liberation Movement*. Lincoln, NE: iUniverse.com.

Freeman, Marsha. 2008. Interview with the author. Minneapolis, MN, March 4.

Freeman, Marsha A. 2008. "Women's Human Rights in the 21st Century: Crisis, Challenge, and Opportunity." In *Human Rights in Crisis*, ed. Alice Bullard. Burlington, VT: Ashgate Publishing Company. 67–86.

Friedman, Elisabeth J. 2009. "Re(gion)alizing Women's Human Rights in Latin America." *Politics & Gender* 5: 349–375.

Front Line & International Commission of Jurists. 2010. "Consideration of the 6th and 7th Periodic Reports of the Russian Federation." Retrieved from http://www2.ohchr.org/english/bodies/cedaw/cedaws46.htm (accessed October 8, 2013).

Galey, Margaret E. 1979. "Promoting Nondiscrimination against Women: The UN Commission on the Status of Women." *International Studies Quarterly* 23 (2): 273–302.

1984. "International Enforcement of Women's Rights." *Human Rights Quarterly* 6 (4): 463–490.

1998. "The Significance of the UN World Women's Conferences." In *To Beijing and Beyond: Pittsburgh and the United Nations Fourth World Conference on Women*, ed. Janice Auth. Pittsburgh, PA: University of Pittsburgh Press. 11–32.

Garner, Kimberly. 2010. *Shaping a Global Women's Agenda: Women's NGOs and Global Governance, 1925–85*. Manchester, UK: Manchester University Press.

Ghodsee, Kristen. 2010. "Revisiting the United Nations Decade for Women: Brief Reflections on Feminism, Capitalism and Cold War Politics in the Early Years of the International Women's Movement." *Women's Studies International Forum* 33: 3–12.

Gildersleeve, Virginia Crocheron. 1954. *Many A Good Crusade*. New York: The Macmillan Company.

Global Justice Center. "CEDAW Case Bank." Retrieved from http://www. wunrn.com/news/2007/10_07/10_15_07/101507_cedaw.htm (accessed September 18, 2011).

Goodliffe, Jay, and Darren G. Hawkins. 2006. "Explaining Commitment: States and the Convention Against Torture." *Journal of Politics* 68 (2): 358–371.

Goonesekere, Savitri. 2007. "Universalizing Women's Human Rights Through CEDAW." In *The Circle of Empowerment*, eds. Hannah Beate Schöpp-Schilling and Cees Flinterman. New York: The Feminist Press. 52–67.

Gray, Mark M., Miki Caul Kittilson, and Wayne Sandholtz. 2006. "Women and Globalization: A Study of 180 Countries, 1975–2000." *International Organization* 60 (2): 293–333.

Gregg, Robert W. 1993. *About Face? The United States and the United Nations*. Boulder and London: Lynne Rienner.

Group of 77. 1967. "Charter of Algiers." Retrieved from http://g77.org/doc/algier~1.htm (accessed February 10, 2012).

Gubbins, Joan, et al. 1978. "To Establish Justice...': Minority Report." In *The Spirit of Houston: The First National Women's Conference*, Washington, DC: Government Printing Office. In Kathryn Kish Shklar and Thomas Dublin, *Women and Social Movements in the United States, 1600–2000*. Accessed through Dartmouth College Library.

Hafner-Burton, Emilie M., and Kiyoteru Tsutsui. 2005. "Human Rights in a Globalizing World: The Paradox of Empty Promises." *American Journal of Sociology* 110 (5): 1373–1411.

Hathaway, Oona A. 2003. "The Cost of Commitment." *Stanford Law Review* 55 (5): 1821–1862.

     2007. "Why Do Countries Commit to Human Rights Treaties?" *Journal of Conflict Resolution* 51 (4): 588–621.

     2008. "Treaties' End: The Past, Present, and Future of International Lawmaking in the United States." *The Yale Law Journal* 117 (7): 1236–1372.

Hayes, Ceri. 2011. *CEDAW: The 30-Year Struggle for Equality*. London: WOMANKIND Worldwide.

Henkin, Louis. 1995. "U.S. Ratification of Human Rights Conventions: The Ghost of Senator Bricker." *American Journal of International Law* 89 (2): 341–350.

Heyns, Christof H., and Frans Viljoen. 2002. *The Impact of the United Nations Human Rights Treaties on the Domestic Level*. The Hague, London, New York: Kluwer Law International.

Hoff Somers, Christina. 2011. "Feminism by Treaty," *Policy Review* (167). Retrieved from http://www.hoover.org/publications/policy-review/article/80191 (accessed April 9, 2012).

Humphrey, John P. 1984. *Human Rights & the United Nations: A Great Adventure*. Dobbs Ferry, NY: Transnational Publishers, Inc.

Inglehart, Ronald, and Pippa Norris. 2003. *Rising Tide: Gender Equality and Cultural Change around the World*. New York: Cambridge University Press.

IWRAW-Asia Pacific. 2013. "IWRAW-Asia Pacific." Retrieved from http://www.iwraw-ap.org/ (accessed October 1, 2013).

Jackson, Richard L. 1983. *The Non-Aligned, the UN, and the Superpowers*. New York: Praeger.

Jacobson, Roberta. 1992. "The Committee on the Elimination of Discrimination against Women." In *The United Nations and Human Rights*, ed. Philip Alston. Oxford: Clarendon Press. 444–472.

Javate de Dios, Aurora. 2007. "Personal Reflection: The Circle of Empowerment." In *The Circle of Empowerment*, eds. Hanna Beate Schöpp-Schilling and Cees Flinterman. New York: The Feminist Press. 309–312.

Joachim, Jutta. 2003. "Framing Issues and Seizing Opportunities: The UN, NGOs, and Women's Rights." *International Studies Quarterly* 47: 247–274.

Josiah, Ivy. 2011. Interview with the author. Kuala Lumpur, Malaysia, April 25.

Keck, Margaret E., and Kathryn Sikkink. 1998. *Activists Beyond Borders: Advocacy Networks in International Politics*. Ithaca, NY: Cornell University Press.

Kenyon, Dorothy. September 12, 1945. "The Response of the United States to the Brazilian Declaration Recommending the Establishment of a Commission of Women in the United Nations Organization, from Report to the President on the Results of the San Francisco Conference: Charter Hearings Revised." Sophia Smith Collection, Smith College, Northampton, MA.

September 19, 1945. "Report of Conference on the United Nations and the Special Interests of Women." Sophia Smith Collection, Smith College, Northampton, MA.

March 29, 1946. "Report on Conference between Representatives of National Women's Organizations and Members of Staff of Department of State." Sophia Smith Collection, Smith College, Northampton, MA.

November 27, 1946. "Memorandum of Conversation." Sophia Smith Collection, Smith College, Northampton, MA.

Koh, Harold Hongju. 1997. "Why Do Nations Obey International Law?" *The Yale Law Journal* 106 (8): 2599–2659.

Lauren, P. G. 1998. *The Evolution of International Human Rights: Visions Seen*. Philadelphia: University of Pennsylvania Press.

Laville, Helen. 2008. "A New Era in International Women's Rights? American Women's Associations and the Establishment of the UN Commission on the Status of Women." *Journal of Women's History* 20 (4): 34–56.

LeBlanc, Lawrence J. 1991. *The United States and the Genocide Convention.* Durham and London: Duke University Press.

Manalo, Rosario G. 2007. "The Female Face of Migration." In *The Circle of Empowerment*, eds. Hanna Beate Schöpp-Schilling and Cees Flinterman. New York: The Feminist Press. 183–195.

Mansbridge, Jane J. 1986. *Why We Lost the ERA.* Chicago: University of Chicago Press.

McPhedran, Marilou, Susan Bazilli, Moana Erickson, and Andrew Byrnes. 2000. *The First CEDAW Impact Study: Final Report.* Toronto, Ontario: Centre for Feminist Research, York University and the International Women's Right Project.

Melander, Göran. 2007. "Important Changes and Further Reforms Needed." In *The Circle of Empowerment*, eds. Hanna Beate Schöpp-Schilling and Cees Flinterman. New York: The Feminist Press. 346.

Melich, Tanya. 1998. *The Republican War against Women: An Insider's Reports from Behind the Lines.* New York: Bantam.

Melish, Tara J. 2009. "From Paradox to Subsidiarity: The United States and Human Rights Treaty Bodies." *Yale Journal of International Law* 34: 389–462.

Milani, Leila Rassekh, Sarah C. Albert, and Karina Purushotma. 2004. *CEDAW: The Treaty for the Rights of Women.* Washington, DC: Working Group on Ratification of the UN.

Moravcsik, Andrew. 2000. "The Origins of Human Rights Regimes: Democratic Delegation in Postwar Europe." *International Organization* 54 (2): 217–252.

Morvai, Krisztina. 2007. "Personal Reflection: Rethinking Prostitution and Trafficking." In *The Circle of Empowerment*, eds. Hanna Beate Schöpp-Schilling and Cees Flinterman. New York: The Feminist Press. 141–144.

Moynihan, Daniel Patrick, and Suzanne Weaver. 1978. *A Dangerous Place.* Boston: Little, Brown and Company.

Musawah. 2011. *CEDAW and Muslim Family Laws: In Search of Common Ground.* Petaling Jaya, Malaysia: Sisters in Islam.

National Commission on the Observance of International Women's Year. 1978a. "Biographies of National Commissioners." In *The Spirit of Houston: The First National Women's Conference.* Washington, DC: Government Printing Office. In Kathryn Kish Shklar and Thomas Dublin, Women and Social Movements in the United States, 1600–2000. Accessed through Dartmouth College Library.

1978b. "The Torch Relay." In *The Spirit of Houston: The First National Women's Conference*, Washington, DC: U.S. Government Printing Office. In Kathryn Kish Sklar and Thomas Dublin, Women and Social Movements in the United States, 1600–2000. Accessed through Dartmouth College Library.

National Organization for Women. 2012. "Removing the Time Limit from the Equal Rights Amendment." Retrieved from http://www.now.org/organization/conference/resolutions/2012.html#I (accessed October 8, 2013).

Non-Aligned Movement. 2001. "The Non-Aligned Movement: Description and History." Retrieved from http://www.nam.gov.za/background/history.htm (accessed August 18, 2011).

Nussbaum, Martha C. 2001. "India: Implementing Sex Equality Through Law." *Chicago Journal of International Law* 2: 35–58.

Office of the Special Adviser on Gender. 2000. "Landmark resolution on Women, Peace and Security." Retrieved from http://www.un.org/womenwatch/osagi/wps/ (accessed October 1, 2013).

Office of the United Nations High Commissioner for Human Rights. 2012. "Report of the Committee on the Elimination of Discrimination against Women – Forty-ninth session (11–29 July 2011) – Fiftieth session (3–21 October 2011) – Fifty-first session (13 February–2 March 2012)." Retrieved from http://tb.ohchr.org/default.aspx?ConvType=15&docType=36 (accessed September 8, 2013).

2013a. "Committee on the Elimination of Discrimination against Women – General recommendations." Retrieved from http://www2.ohchr.org/english/bodies/cedaw/comments.htm (accessed September 8, 2013).

2013b. "Committee on the Elimination of Discrimination against Women, 55th session (8–26 July 2013)." Retrieved from http://www2.ohchr.org/english/bodies/cedaw/cedaws55.htm (accessed September 8, 2013).

n.d.a. "The United Nations Human Rights Treaty System: An Introduction to the Core Human Rights Treaties and the Treaty Bodies, Fact Sheet No. 30." Retrieved from http://www.ohchr.org/EN/AboutUs/Pages/Handbook_ReferencelinksfromChapter4.aspx (accessed March 2, 2014).

n.d.b. "The Core International Human Rights Instruments and their monitoring bodies." Retrieved from http://www.ohchr.org/EN/ProfessionalInterest/Pages/CoreInstruments.aspx (accessed July 31, 2013).

Olcott, Jocelyn 2010. "Globalizing Sisterhood: International Women's Year and the Politics of Representation." In *The Shock of the Global: The 1970s in Perspective*, ed. Charles S. Maier, Niall Ferguson, Erez Manela, and Daniel J. Sargent. Cambridge, MA: Belknap Press of Harvard University Press. 281–293.

Organization of American States. n.d. "American Convention on Human Rights." Retrieved from http://www.oas.org/dil/treaties_B-32_American_Convention_on_Human_Rights.htm (accessed August 5, 2013).

Ostrower, Gary B. 1998. *The United Nations and the United States*. New York: Twayne Publishers.

Otto, Diane. 2002. "'Gender Comment': Why Does the UN Committee on Economic, Social and Cultural Rights Need a General Comment on Women?" *Canadian Journal of Women and Law* 14: 1–52.

Parry, John T. 2008. "Torture Nation, Torture Law." *Georgetown Law Journal* 97: 1001–1056.

Powell, Catherine. 2002. "Comment: United States Human Rights Policy in the 21st Century in an Age of Multilateralism." *St. Louis University Law Journal* 46: 421–430.

Power, Samantha. 2002. *A Problem From Hell: America and the Age of Genocide.* New York: Perennial.

Ramaseshan, Geeta. 2007. *Addressing Rape as a Human Rights Violation: The Role of International Human Rights Norms and Instruments.* Kuala Lumpur, Malaysia: International Women's Rights Action Watch Asia Pacific (IWRAW-AP).

Rambo, Kirsten S. 2008. "Trivial Complaints: The Role of Privacy in Domestic Violence Law and Activism." Retrieved from http://www.gutenberg-e.org/ rambo/index.html (accessed July 9, 2013).

Rawalt, Marguerite. 1983. "The Equal Rights Amendment." In *Women in Washington*, ed. Irene Tinker. Beverly Hills, CA: SAGE. 49–78.

Reanda, Laura. 1992. "The Commission on the Status of Women." In *The United Nations and Human Rights*, ed. Philip Alston. Oxford: Clarendon Press. 265–303.

Risse, Thomas, and Kathryn Sikkink. 1999. "The Socialization of International Human Rights Norms into Domestic Practices: Introduction." In *The Power of Human Rights*, eds. Thomas Risse, Stephen C. Ropp, and Kathryn Sikkink. New York: Cambridge University Press. 1–39.

Robb, Janet. October 20, 1951. "The Work of the Commission on the Status of Women." *Dorothy Kenyon Papers.* Sophia Smith Collection, Smith College, Northampton, MA.

Robins, Dorothy B. 1971. *Experiment in Democracy: The Story of U.S. Citizen Organizations in Forging the Charter of the United Nations.* New York: The Parkside Press.

Rudolf, Beate, Marsha A. Freeman, and C. M. Chinkin. 2012. *The UN Convention on the Elimination of all Forms of Discrimination against Women: A Commentary* Oxford; New York: Oxford University Press.

Russian LGBT Network. 2010. "Shadow Report: Discrimination and Violence against Lesbian and Bisexual Women and Transgender People in Russia." Retrieved from http://www2.ohchr.org/english/bodies/cedaw/cedaws46. htm (accessed October 9, 2013).

Rymph, Catherine E. 2006. *Republican Women: Feminism and Conservatism from Suffrage Through the Rise of the New Right.* Chapel Hill: University of North Carolina Press.

Schlafly, Phyllis. 2012. Skype Conversation. Hanover, NH, May 15.

Schneider, Elizabeth M. 2008. "Domestic Violence Law Reform in the Twenty-First Century: Looking Back and Looking Forward." *Family Law Quarterly* 42 (8): 353–363.

Schöpp-Schilling, Hanna Beate. 2007. "The Nature and Mandate of the Committee." In *The Circle of Empowerment*, eds. Hanna Beate Schöpp-Schilling and Cees Flinterman. New York: The Feminist Press. 248–261.

Schöpp-Schilling, Hanna Beate, and Cees Flinterman, eds. 2007. *The Circle of Empowerment: Twenty-Five Years of the UN Committee on the Elimination of Discrimination against Women*. New York: The Feminist Press.

Schwelb, Egon. 1966. "The International Convention on the Elimination of All Forms of Racial Discrimination." *The International and Comparative Law Quarterly* 15 (4): 996–1068.

Scoop News. July 13, 2012. "Minister to present gender equality report to UN." Retrieved from http://www.scoop.co.nz/stories/PA1207/S00165/minister-to-present-gender-equality-report-to-un.htm.

Shahani, Leticia Ramos. 2004. "The UN, Women, and Development: The World Conferences on Women." In *Developing Power*, eds. Arvonne Fraser and Irene Tinker. New York: The Feminist Press. 26–36.

Shalev, Carmel. 2007. "Women's Health: Accommodating Difference." In *The Circle of Empowerment*, eds. Hanna Beate Schöpp-Schilling and Cees Flinterman. New York: The Feminist Press. 196–211.

Simmons, Beth A. 2009. "Women and International Institutions: The Effects of the Women's Convention on Female Education." In *Power, Interdependence, and Nonstate Actors in World Politics*, eds. Helen Milner and Andrew Moravcsik. Princeton: Princeton University Press. 108–125.

    2010. *Mobilizing for Human Rights: International Law in Domestic Politics.* New York: Cambridge University Press.

Skard, Torild. 2008. "Getting Our History Right: How Were the Equal Rights of Women and Men Included in the Charter of the United Nations?" *Forum for Development Studies* 1: 37–60.

Snider, Christy Jo. 2007. "Planning for Peace: Virginia Gildersleeve at the United Nations Conference on International Organizations and Institutions." *Peace & Change* 32 (2): 168–185.

Spruill, Marjorie. 2008. "The Conservative Challenge to Feminist Influence on State Commissions on the Status of Women." In Kathryn Kish Sklar and Thomas Dublin, Women and Social Movements of the United States, 1600–2000. Accessed through Dartmouth College Library.

Stephenson, Carolyn M. 1982. "Feminism, Pacifism, Nationalism and the United Nations Decade for Women." *Women's Studies International Forum* 5 (3/4): 287–300.

Tallaway, Mervat. 2007. "Dual Perspectives." In *The Circle of Empowerment*, eds. Hanna Beate Schöpp-Schilling and Cees Flinterman. New York: The Feminist Press. 272–273.

Tan Beng Hui. 2007. *Exploring the Potential of the UN Treaty Body System in Addressing Sexuality Rights*. Kuala Lumpur, Malaysia: International Women's Rights Action Watch Asia Pacific (IWRAW-AP).

The Foundry. September 23, 2013. "The Latest Priorities of the U.N. Treaty Enforcers." Retrieved from http://blog.heritage.org/2013/09/23/the-latest-priorities-of-the-u-n-treaty-enforcers/ (accessed October 1, 2013).

Thorstad, Katherine M. 2013. "To What Extent Does the Fourteenth Amendment Guarantee Equality on the Basis of Gender?" Unpublished paper. Dartmouth College.

Tripon, Olivia H., ed. 2007. *Shaping the Global Women's Agenda: Filipino Women in the United Nations*. Manila: National Commission on the Role of Filipino Women.

UN Commission on the Status of Women. 1964. "Draft Declaration on the Elimination of Discrimination against Women." October 30 (E/CN.6/426). Accessed through Harvard College Library.

     1965. "Summary Records of the 18th Session". Accessed through Harvard College Library.

     1974. "Summary Records of the 25th Session, January 14–22". Accessed through Harvard College Library.

     1976. "International Instruments Relating to the Status of Women: Draft Convention on the Elimination of All Forms of Discrimination against Women" (E/CN.6/591). Accessed through Harvard College Library.

UN General Assembly. 1946. "Political Rights of Women A/RES/56(I)." Retrieved from http://www.un.org/depts/dhl/resguide/r1.htm (accessed July 18, 2013).

     1962. "United Nations Assistance for the Advancement of Women in Developing Countries (A/RES/1777(XVII))." Retrieved from http://www.un.org/depts/dhl/resguide/r17.htm (accessed July 18, 2013).

     1967. "Declaration on the Elimination of Discrimination against Women (A/RES/2263(XXII))." Retrieved from http://www.un.org/documents/ga/res/22/ares22.htm (accessed October 4, 2013).

     1979. Report of the Working Group of the Whole on the Drafting of the Convention on the Elimination of Discrimination Against Women (A/C.3/34/14).

     1997. "Convention on the Elimination of All Forms of Discrimination against Women, A/RES/51/68." Retrieved from http://www.un.org/depts/dhl/resguide/r51_en.shtml (accessed October 8, 2013).

     1998. "Follow-Up to the World Conference on Human Rights, A/53/372". Retrieved from http://www.unhchr.ch/Huridocda/Huridoca.nsf/TestFrame/1c977d5ec7198374802566c00058c60d?Opendocument (accessed October 13, 2013).

UN Third Committee of the General Assembly. 1979. "Records of Meetings Nos. 70 and 71 Held on 6 and 7 of December 1979." Retrieved from http://untreaty.un.org/cod/avl/ha/cedaw/cedaw.html (accessed June 28, 2013).

UN Women. 1995. "Platform for Action." Retrieved from http://www.un.org/womenwatch/daw/beijing/platform/plat1.htm (accessed October 1, 2013).

     2000. "Reservations to CEDAW." Retrieved from http://www.un.org/womenwatch/daw/cedaw/reservations.htm (accessed October 1, 2013).

2011. "The World Conferences on Women." Retrieved from http://www. unwomen.org/en/how-we-work/intergovernmental-support/world-con- ferences-on-women (accessed October 1, 2013).

2013a. "About UN Women." Retrieved from http://www.unwomen.org/en/ about-us/about-un-women (accessed October 1, 2013).

2013b. "General Recommendations." Retrieved from http://www. un.org/womenwatch/daw/cedaw/recommendations/index.html (accessed October 1, 2013).

United Nations. 1945. "Charter of the United Nations." Retrieved from http:// www.un.org/en/documents/charter/index.shtml (accessed August 5, 2011).

October 30, 1964. "Draft Declaration on the Elimination of Discrimination against Women: Memorandum by the Secretary General (E/CN.6/426)".

1984. "Contributions of the [CEDAW] Committee to International Conferences; Report of the Committee on Progress Achieved in the Implementation of the Convention".

1986. "Report of the Committee on the Elimination of Discrimination against Women (fifth session)". Retrieved from http://tb.ohchr.org/default. aspx?ConvType=15&docType=36 (accessed October 1, 2013).

1993. "Declaration on the Elimination of Violence against Women, A/ RES/48/104." Retrieved from http://www.un.org/documents/ga/res/48/ a48r104.htm (accessed October 1, 2013).

1996. *The United Nations and the Advancement of Women 1945–1996.* New York: United Nations.

2007. "Short History of the Commission on the Status of Women." Division for the Advancement of Women. Department of Economic and Social Affairs, Retrieved from http://www.un.org/womenwatch/daw/CSW60YRS/ (accessed August 12, 2011).

2013a. "UN System Organizational Chart." Retrieved from http://www. un.org/en/aboutun/structure/org_chart.shtml (accessed June 25, 2013).

2013b. "United Nations Treaty Collection." Retrieved from http://trea- ties.un.org/Pages/ViewDetails.aspx?src=TREATY&mtdsg_no=IV- 8&chapter=4&lang=en (accessed September 8, 2013).

2013c. "United Nations Treaty Collection." Retrieved from https://treaties. un.org (accessed October 1, 2013).

n.d. "Short History of the Commission on the Status of Women." Retrieved from http://www.un.org/womenwatch/daw/CSW60YRS/ (accessed August 12, 2011).

United States. 1973a. "Telegram 4973 From the Mission to the United Nations to the Department of State, November 21, 1973, 1600Z." Retrieved from http://history.state.gov/historicaldocuments/frus1969-76ve14p1/d9 (accessed July 12, 2011).

1973b. "Telegram 250151 From the Department of State to All Diplomatic Posts, December 26, 1973, 2137." Retrieved from http://history.state.gov/ historicaldocuments/frus1969-76ve14p1/d10 (accessed July 12, 2011).

1974a. "Abstract of a Research Study Prepared in the Bureau of Intelligence and Research, Washington, January 15, 1974." Retrieved from http://history.state.gov/historicaldocuments/frus1969-76ve14p1/d11 (accessed July 12, 2011).

1974b. "Memorandum from the Executive Secretary of the Department of State (Springsteen) to the President's Counselor in the White House Office for Women's Programs (Armstrong), Washington, May 14, 1974." Retrieved from http://history.state.gov/historicaldocuments/frus1969-76ve14p1/d171 (accessed July 12, 2011).

1974c. "Telegram 383 From the Mission to the United Nations to the Department of State, February 4, 1974, 1954Z." Retrieved from http://history.state.gov/historicaldocuments/frus1969-76ve14p1/d170 (accessed July 12, 2011).

1974d. "Telegram 104050 From the Department of State to All Diplomatic Posts, May 17, 1974, 2304Z." Retrieved from http://history.state.gov/historicaldocuments/frus1969-76ve14p1/d14 (accessed July 12, 2011).

1974e. "Telegram 184584 From the Department of State to All Diplomatic Posts, August 22, 1974, 2013Z." Retrieved from http://history.state.gov/historicaldocuments/frus1969-76ve14p1/d17 (accessed July 12, 2011).

1975a. "Action Memorandum From the Assistant Secretary of State for Management (Eagleburger) and the Director of the Policy Planning Staff (Lord) to Secretary of State Kissinger, Washington, September 24, 1975." Retrieved from http://history.state.gov/historicaldocuments/frus1969-76ve14p1/d30 (accessed July 12, 2011).

1975b. "Intelligence Memorandum Prepared in the Central Intelligence Agency, Washington, February 11, 1975." Retrieved from http://history.state.gov/historicaldocuments/frus1969-76ve14p1/d20 (accessed July 12, 2011).

1975c. "Letter From the Director of the United States Center for the International Women's Year (Bacon) to Secretary of State Kissinger, Washington, July 24, 1975." Retrieved from http://history.state.gov/historicaldocuments/frus1969-76ve14p1/d185 (accessed July 12, 2011).

1975d. "Memorandum of Conversation, White House, Washington, September 26, 1975, 11:30 a.m.–noon." Retrieved from http://history.state.gov/historicaldocuments/frus1969-76ve14p1/d31 (accessed July 12, 2011).

1975e. "Telegram 883 From the Mission to the United Nations to the Department of State, March 19, 1975, 1354Z." Retrieved from http://history.state.gov/historicaldocuments/frus1969-76ve14p1/d176 (accessed July 12, 2011).

1975f. "Telegram 303856 From the Department of State to All Diplomatic Posts, December 29, 1975, 2324Z." Retrieved from http://history.state.gov/historicaldocuments/frus1969-76ve14p1/d35 (accessed July 12, 2011).

1976a. "December 17 Cable: Draft Convention on the Elimination of Discrimination Against Women; Approval of Article 21 Concerning Procedures for Implementation of the Convention." Retrieved from http://aad.archives.gov/ (accessed July 12, 2011).

1976b. "December 20 Cable: 26th Resumed Session of the UN Commission on the Status of Women; Roundup." Retrieved from http://aad.archives.gov/ (accessed July 12, 2011).

1976c. "Diplomatic Cable, September 17: Twenty-Sixth Session of the UN Commission on the Status of Women, September 13-October 1." Retrieved from http://aad.archives.gov/ (accessed July 12, 2011).

[1976]. Department of State Background Paper: The Interrelationships of Population Matters to the Status of Women and to the Involvement of Women in Socio-Economic Development. Retrieved from http://history.state.gov/historicaldocuments/frus1969-76ve14p1/d189 (accessed July 12, 2011).

University of Minnesota Human Rights Library. 1994. "U.S. Reservations, Declarations, and Understandings, International Convention on the Elmination of All Forms of Racial Discrimination." Retrieved from http://www1.umn.edu/humanrts/usdocs/racialres.html (accessed September 22, 2013).

2008. "Ratification of International Human Rights Treaties, by country." Retrieved from http://www1.umn.edu/humanrts/research/ratification-index.html (accessed July 31, 2013).

U.S. Department of State. 1976. "Report of IWY Secretariat on International Women's Year." Retrieved from http://history.state.gov/historicaldocuments/frus1969-76ve14p1/d188 (accessed July 11, 2011).

1980. "Report of the United States Delegation to the World Conference of the United Nations Decade for Women: Equality, Development and Peace." Accessed through Dartmouth College Library.

U.S. House of Representatives. 1983. Hearing on H.J. Res. 1, July 13, September 14, October 20, 26, and November 3, 1983. *Equal Rights Amendment*. 98th Cong., 1st session. Accessed through Dartmouth College Library.

1984. Hearing before the Subcommittee on Human Rights and International Organizations of the House Committee on Foreign Affairs. *U.S. Contribution to the UN Decade for Women*. September 18. 98th Cong., 1st session. Accessed through Dartmouth College Library.

1986. Report of Congressional Staff Advisors to the Nairobi Conference to the Committee on Foreign Affairs. *U.N. Conference to Review and Appraise the U.N. Decade for Women*. January. 99th Cong., 2nd sess. Accessed through Dartmouth College Library.

1995. Subcommittee on International Operations and Human Rights of the Committee on International Relations. *United Nations Fourth World Conference on Women*. July 18 and August 2. 104th Cong., 1st sess. Accessed through Dartmouth College Library.

U.S. Senate. n.d. "Treaties." Retrieved from http://www.senate.gov/artandhistory/history/common/briefing/Treaties.htm (accessed July 26, 2013).

n.d. "Majority and Minority Leaders and Party Whips." Retrieved from http://www.senate.gov/artandhistory/history/common/briefing/Majority_Minority_Leaders.htm (accessed July 31, 2013).

1980. "Treaty Doc. 96-53: Convention on the Elimination of All Forms of Discrimination against Women." Retrieved from http://www.foreign.senate.gov/treaties/096-53 (accessed March 2, 2014).

1984. Hearing Before the Committee on Foreign Relations. *Women in Development: Looking to the Future.* June 7. 98th Cong., 2nd sess. Accessed through Dartmouth College Library.

1988. Hearing before the Subcommittee on Terrorism, Narcotics and International Operations. *Issues Relating to the United Nations Convention to End All Forms of Discrimination against Women.* December 5. 100th Cong. 2nd sess. Accessed through Dartmouth College Library.

1990. Hearing before the Committee on Foreign Relations. *Convention on the Elimination of All Forms of Discrimination against Women.* August 2. 101st Cong., 2nd sess. Accessed through Dartmouth College Library.

1991. Hearing before the Committee on Foreign Relations. *International Covenant on Civil and Political Rights.* November 21. 102nd Cong., 1st sess. Accessed through Dartmouth College Library.

1994a. Hearing before the Committee on Foreign Relations. *International Convention on the Elimination of All Forms of Racial Discrimination.* May 11. 103rd Cong., 2nd sess. Accessed through Dartmouth College Library.

1994b. Hearing before the Committee on Foreign Relations. *Convention on the Elimination of All Forms of Discrimination against Women.* September 27. 103rd Cong., 2nd sess. Accessed through Dartmouth College Library.

2002. Hearing Before the Committee on Foreign Relations. *Convention to End All Forms of Discrimination against Women: Report Together with Minority and Additional Views.* June 13. 107th Cong., 2nd sess. Accessed through Dartmouth College Library.

2010. Hearing Before the Committee on Foreign Relations. *Women's Rights are Human Rights: U.S. Ratification of the Convention on the Elimination of All Forms of Discrimination against Women (CEDAW).* Retrieved from http://judiciary.senate.gov/hearings/hearing.cfm?id=e655f9e2809e5476862f735da164da79 (accessed August 23, 2011).

2011. Hearing before the Subcommittee on International Operations and Organizations, Human Rights, Democracy and Global Women's Issues; Committee on Foreign Relations. Senate; Subcommittee on Near Eastern and South and Central Asian Affairs; Committee on Foreign Relations. *Women and the Arab Spring.* November 2. Retrieved from http://www.foreign.senate.gov/hearings/women-and-the-arab-spring (accessed March 2, 2014).

Vogelsgang, Sandra. 1978. "What Price Principle? U.S. Policy on Human Rights." *Foreign Affairs* 56 (4): 819–841.

Vreeland, James Raymond. 2008. "Political Institutions and Human Rights: Why Dictatorships Enter into the United Nations Convention Against Torture." *International Organization* 62 (Winter): 65–101.

Winslow, Anne, ed. 1995. *Women, Politics and the United Nations*. Westport, CT: Greenwood Press.

Wolbrecht, Christina. 2000. *The Politics of Women's Rights: Parties, Positions, and Change*. Princeton, NJ: Princeton University Press.

Women's Candidacy Initiative. 2009. "How Can CEDAW Help Us End Discrimination?" Retrieved from http://www.youtube.com/watch?v=bx4Xr_F6Z94 (accessed August 10, 2011).

Wright, Wendy. 2002. "CEDAW Committee Rulings." Retrieved from http://www.cwfa.org/content.asp?id=1870 (accessed August 24, 2011).

YouTube. 1995. "First Lady Hillary Rodham Clinton's Remarks to the Fourth Women's Conference in Beijing, China." Retrieved from http://www.youtube.com/watch?v=xXM4E23Efvk (accessed September 8, 2013).

2010. "President Obama Supports CEDAW." Retrieved from http://www.youtube.com/watch?v=qPubL3LORCQ (accessed September 22, 2013).

Zinsser, Judith P. 2002. "From Mexico to Copenhagen to Nairobi: The United Nations Decade for Women, 1975–1985." *Journal of World History* 13: 139–67.

Index